MEDIA AND LEARNING

MEDIA AND LEARNING

Shahzad Ahmed

ANMOL PUBLICATIONS PVT. LTD.
NEW DELHI - 110 002 (INDIA)

ANMOL PUBLICATIONS PVT. LTD.
4374/4B, Ansari Road, Daryaganj
New Delhi - 110 002
Ph.: 23261597, 23278000
Visit us at: www.anmolpublications.com

Media and Learning

First Published, 2006

ISBN 81-261-2562-4

PRINTED IN INDIA

Published by J.L. Kumar for Anmol Publications Pvt. Ltd., New Delhi - 110 002 and Printed at ARORA Offset Press, Delhi.

Contents

Preface ix

1. **Media Perceptions** 1
The Notion • The Methodology • The Vocabulary • Speedy Transfer • Working Characteristics • Presenting Art

2. **Art of Learning** 49
Definition and Scope • Communication in three Dimensions • Evaluation Exercise • The Improvement • Learning Operations • Dual Processes

3. **Media's Effect on Learning** 61
Masses and Technological Media • Educational Television (ETV) • Part Played by Teacher • Facilities of Physical Nature • Relevance of Films • Film Society for Children • Medium of Newspapers

4. **Media Issues** 83
The Idea • Practical Characteristics • Varied Formats • Streams of Different Nature • Affection Reality • Common Point of View • Political Viewpoint • Modern Viewpoint

5. Significance of Learning 107

Kid's Importance • Psychological Principles • General Principles • Conclusive Part

6. Magic of Media 125

Interest Creation for Journals • Happenings and Seminars • Editorial Challenges

7. Scheduled Learning 159

Technological Revolution • Scope and Definition • Major Aspects • Programmes based on Illustration • Evaluative Exercise • Linear Programming • Intrinsic Programming • Role of Teacher • Attitude in Classroom Teaching • Instruction-based Programme

8. Role of Media 183

The Status • Encountering all Odds • Honours of Professional Nature • Concerns in Entirety • Efforts in Collective Way • Liberty of Expression • Sense of Authority • Major Works • Future Challenges • The Ability

9. Computer Learning 197

Computer's Role • Most-modern Devices • Societal Characteristics

10. Medium for Learning 203

The Nomenclature • Scope and Definition • Importance and Benefits • Problems of Grave Nature • Categorising Teaching Aids • Explaining Various Aids • Museum's Importance • Employing Three-dimensional Aids

11. New Educational Pattern **239**
Introducing the New Method of Education
• Commission's Recommendations

12. Aims and Goals **245**
Objectives of Education and Productivity
• General View • Fresh Scheme for Education
• Comprised Form

13. Global Media **255**
Global Journalism • Medium's Significance
• Aspects of Technology • Promoting Science
• Information Power • Press in Germany

Bibliography 293

Index 297

Preface

Perhaps, stressing upon the importance of media in learning and the educational sphere, as a whole may sound off-repeated and much talked about. However, an analytical and in-depth study covering every dimension of the same will certainly have many takers. In modern times, it has emerged as a fact that media is an inextricable part of learning. The infatuation of the children, even at primary level, with high-tech learning and their experiments with computers and the related facilities are the reflection of media's effect on learning. Different forms of media, such as; educational T. V., film society for children and newspapers, help children enormously.

The teachers have a herculean task ahead for them to mould the character of the students and it is they, who should take initiative to direct the students to their areas of interest. The teachers play a vital role in exposing the students to the modern technology to enable them to take on the great challenges ahead.

In all respects this book, would prove to be the first of its kind, as a sincere attempt has been made to incorporate all the relevant aspects of modern media and learning.

—Editor

1

Media Perceptions

In a news organisation, editing plays a vital role. A news item or a news story, as it is called, is written by hurried reporters, and is rough-edged like, raw diamond. Hence, the copy is polished and honed by a team of editors, who form the Editorial Desk. The team, also called the desk persons, works under tremendous pressure and severe time constraint. The desk persons work well past midnight, and ensure that your newspaper reaches you on time in the morning.

A newspaper office or news agency receives a large assortment of news items. These originate from different sources, mainly local sources and wires (Teleprinter and telex). The news copy is written by experienced and inexperienced people, and, hence, lack readability.

The news reporters are the main news writers. They are in a hurry, especially in the evenings, when the news development gathers momentum. The copy written by them under pressure in bound to carry errors of all types. In any newspapers, there is always a shortage of space for all news items, which are received in the office. The newspaper's advertisement department is ever eager to grab the valuable but limited space. Moreover, newsprint and means of production cost a lot of money. Ultimately, a newspaper's success largely depends on the space and its most efficient, judicious and economic use. Hence, within the space set aside for news, as much news as possible need to be packed to serve a divergent readership. Considering these factors, editing of the news copy becomes essential.

The Notion

All incoming news items, collectively called copy, is sifted, before being processed, to achieve a balance of news between that originating within the organisation and that pouring in from outside. Sorting out and sifting also helps induce parity between the well-written articles and those written by the inexperienced reporters. In the process, the unwanted matter gets weeded out. Only the newsworthy stories are finally, selected. These are checked for grammar, syntax, facts, figures, and sense, and also clarified for betterment, and are condensed for economy of space.

News editing is tailoring news items or a news story to the required shape and size, using the right kind of expressions and symbols. A copy is edited to highlight the "news sense" in a story, and to bring uniformity of language and style in an issue of newspaper. The newsroom in a newspaper or a news agency office is the hub of the entire activity in a news organisation. The Editorial Desk (also known as the Editorial Department or Copy Desk or News Desk) is the nerve centre of a newsroom. It is here that everyday the newspaper issues are planned and made.

However, in a news agency, the news desk is the final stop before a story is sent to the transmission room or creed room for transmission on the wires. In news agencies, there news operations are computerised, such as the Press Trust of

India (PTI) or the united News of India (UNI), the edited copy is transmitted directly to the newspapers by the News Desk itself. The newsroom is headed by an editor or a chief editor or an editor-in-chief or a chief news editor. The designation varies according to the choice of the organization. He plans and directs the day's news operations. He is supported by a team consisting of the news editors, chief sub-editors (chief sub), senior sub-editors and sub-editors (sub).

The news desk-usually operates in three shifts: morning, afternoon and night (till late in the evening, even up to 2.30 a.m.). In between, there are two link shifts-morning and evening-which are headed by the news editors and or chief subs. They are also called 'slot' men. Ideally, in a newspaper, it is the news editor who plans and directs page-making, while the chief sub helps and implements it.

In a news agency, news editors and chief subs looks after the smooth functioning of the news desk. They plan and write "leads" (updated versions of developing stories). Here, there is an additional shift called "Extra Night" (from 2 a.m to 8 a.m.), which is managed by a senior sub-editor.

News has a number of characteristic elements. Five conventional determinants of the news values are:

Proximity: The nearer the origin of news, i.e., the closer it is to home, the more is its impact. For example, on a particular day, there may be 45 deaths in a boat tragedy in Bangladesh. But, on the same day, a local bomb blast that kills five people is sure to have more impact on the readers.

Timeliness: News grows old quickly. It decays and perishes fast. The more recent its occurrence, the more worthy it is. On the contrary, an event that happened six months back, but is discovered and reported now could grab the front page. For example, the bank securities' scan involving Harshad Mehta and others, or the Bofors gun deal.

Prominence: Names make news and the newspapers like to use as many local names as possible. For example, if the Vice-chancellor of a university gets hurt while playing cricket, few people will take note of the incident. But, if a public figure like a minister is injured in a game, we have a more interesting story. When the film celebrity, Satyajit Ray, and the Nobel Laureate, Mother Teresa, were hospitalised, most papers carried everyday reports on their health.

Consequence: A reader's interest is aroused in a large measure if an event or occurrence affects him, and more so, if he participates in the event. He is eager to know what will this mean to him in the long run. How will it affect him and his family. For example, weather stories attract consistently high readership. A brief storm that leaves behind some casualties, and causes heavy damage in, a town or city, will receive better coverage will be given a good display, and attract large readership. A steep hike in the prices of petrol, cooking gas, milk or an increase in water and electricity tariffs will have widespread consequences.

Human Interest: Any interesting story about people and their peculiarities, and their infinite variety, make for wider readership. The human interest stories are pure identification. These are the little things that have happened, or could happen to yourself or to your neighbours or friends. These stories are worth little or nothing as news in any strict sense. Yet these are worth telling. For example, a 30 year old women with a baby in her arms is trapped in a building on fire. Such a story interests the readers.

The five elements cited above, generally, have a direct bearing on a majority of news stories. In addition, there are various other elements that could come into play in judging the news:

(i) To be newsworthy, a story must interest a large number of the readers.

(ii) A story's worth is determined by its impact on the readers. That's why the functioning, of the government and the politicians receive a lot of coverage. On the contrary, lack of impact sometimes makes news; and also, the unusual, odd, provocative, intriguing, moving and educative make news.

Scientific discoveries, even the hints of some, find space in the newspapers. For example, any seeming step toward the cure of cancer or AIDS is sure to generate headlines, even though the scientists might not have discovered the drug or vaccine. But the hint will be newsworthy. Archaeological events relating the present to the past, could make headlines. The state and local news always rank as the major focal points in the newspapers. These are followed by (the order or selection depends on the Desk) accidents, accords, agreements or pacts, announcements, business, the common people's interest (rise in milk or sugar prices), crime, cultural events disasters, education, elections, environment, fashion, health, labour, obituaries, and tragedies.

Under the managing editor in most organizational lineups are two or three people with whom you will have most of your dealings. One is the news editor (or in some instances there are both an executive news editor and a news editor), who supervises the placement of your stories in the newspaper and dictates the typography or "layout" of the pages. However, the news editor often is a distant figure in your daily work concerns. Most of your dealings will be with the city editor (called metro editor on some newspapers). The city editor selects your daily assignments, determines to a large degree who does what, and controls any number of assistants who carry out directions. The city editor usually is the authority figure whom you, as a reporter, are most responsible to. However, his or her assistants generally carry much authority in editing your stories. Especially on big projects-series and such-the city editor usually assumes direct command in doing the planning and resolving confusions.

Organizational structures, of course, vary from one newspaper to the next. Some of the largest papers have national editors, in control of a national desk-a collection of reporters and assistant editors charged with covering the nation. Some newspapers also have a state desk responsible for state news coverage. Also, there are special feature sections with special editors-feature editors, life-style editors, people editors, fashion editors, women's editors (a position, of growing obsolescence in feminist times), special assignment editors, ad infinitum. In the sports department, the sports editor usually is very much like the editor in that he or she is charged primarily with opinion making. The overseer of the daily sports news flow is the executive sports editor, who is to the sports department what the city editor is to the news operation.

Unless you move into a specialized area, you usually will be assigned to the city desk and will be controlled by the city editor. "City editor" on most newspapers actually is a euphemism of sorts, since the person carrying that title often has responsibility for state and national coverage as well. Such papers may also have a national and state editor, but often as not their function is strictly that of reviewing wire copy, which comes from various national news agencies, for placement in the newspaper.

Once you have carried out an assignment, having conducted the interview, taken all the necessary notes and written the story, you encounter the classic editing process.

On smaller, less technologically advanced newspapers, editors may use the old pencil technique, drawing lines on your copy through stuff they do not like, and inserting by pencil stuff they want added.

More, likely, you will relate to your editor through some sort of computer network. At most dailies, you will have written your story by either of two means: (1) on scanner ready paper, or (2) directly into a Video Display Terminal (VDT), tied to a computer that remembers your story and holds it ready for transmission to the newspaper. The scanner ready copy is typed on an electric typewriter using various codes that can be read by an optical scanner that records the story on computer tape. Increasingly, the scanner is becoming an unnecessary step, with reporters being trained to write their stories directly into the computer via the VDT. What is on the VDT is what is being fed into the all-important computer. The computer is capable of setting the material in type ready to be pasted into a page that then can be photographed and transferred to a plate that can be put on the presses for printing.

Often as not, the editor who checks a story uses the same kind of VDT the reporter uses to write the story. However, ancient rules and techniques apply to editing, regardless of the method used. The editor basically looks for two things: (1) Does the story make sense? and (2) What mistakes has the reporter made? then, your version is either altered or accepted as it is.

More than likely, as a novice reporter, you will not have to concern yourself with the finer points of editing, but it does help to know what the editor is doing. In fact, it helps to be an editor of your own copy. The more problems you eliminate, the more impressed the editors are by your skills. Review everything you write, and insert or delete that which appears necessary to insert or delete. To help you be able to do that, let us offer a few hints as to what the editor is doing and looking for:

- Does the story really make sense? First, the editor reads through the whole story. If he or she is confused, the logical assumption is that the reader will be confused. Sometimes, the editor will try to fix the story; other times, you may get it back for repair.
- Is all the pertinent information high up in the story? If not, the editor may move buried-details toward the

top. More likely, it will be handed back to you with such put-downs as "lacks focus" or "get to the point" or "I think your lead is in the 13th graph."

- Do you have a working knowledge of English grammar? For every sentence you write, there are rules that some editor has memorized. Split modifiers, mixed metaphors, and just plain poor syntax are hazards of deadline pressure. A merciful editor will patch these up with merely a word. A wise teacher will draw them to your attention-if time permits- and tell you never to do that again.

- Can you spell? F. Scott Fitzgerald had a problem with spelling. Unless you have a novel such as The Great Gatsby to your credit, learn to spell. Newspaper editors expect you to know how to spell and are apt to ridicule your slightest lapse, especially if you misspell the name of somebody important. An otherwise excellent reporter we know once spelled a recent Georgia governor's last name "Busby." Unfortunately, his name was Busbee.

- Is the 'story too' long? Ever more frequently, newspapers are faced with space shortages-the so-called "shrinking news hole"-because of newsprint paper shortages and increasing cost. In addition, readership surveys tell editors that people really don't like to read long stories. If the story is, say, 18 inches long, and the editor thinks it would be fine if it were 12 inches long, he or she may cut it, which is the editor's prerogative. Hardly anyone is immune from being cut. Even Ralph McGill, the Pulitzer Prize-winning 'editor and publisher of the Atlanta Constitution, used to complain that his front-page columns were cut.

What can be eliminated? To cut a story, the editor may whack out (or blip off the VDT screen) whole paragraphs deemed superfluous. In the enthusiasm for detail, some reporters are inclined to repeat certain facts and ideas. To an editor, these repetitions are readily obvious and easily cut out. After that, the process becomes more tedious and arbitrary. After lopping off paragraphs, the editor may begin cutting sentences within paragraphs, with the constant question: "Do we really need that?" Then, the individual words are scrutinized. Could a shorter, perhaps simpler word to better? (Obfuscate might be changed to confuse.) is the wording as accurate as possible? (A "gutted" house may replace one the reporter has "burned to the ground except for the walls.") Is the reporter relying too heavily on the words of the interviewee? (Rules that have been "promulgated" may become merely "made public.") Some nonessential words often an be eliminated at first glance. ("The mayor related to the press that he is of the opinion that ice cream tastes quite good" can be written simply as, "The mayor says he likes ice cream.")

Editors, of course, have their quirks that can cause a reporter misery. Some editors, for instance, think that said is the very best word you can use when somebody had said something. Others like variety: "he declared" or "she commented" or "he related" or even "she opined." (However, do not confuse merely saying and commenting with words that lend slightly different meaning to the qualifier, such as "he guessed" or "he implied" or "she hinted" or "she gurgled.") Some editors like to draw fine lines of distinction. Slay or kill, they argue, is not the same as murder, which is a criminal act of homicide. (Homicide, in fact, may or may not be a murder.) But chances are pretty, good that a slain person who died under suspicious circumstances has been murdered as well. Some editors also insist that who rather than that should be the pronoun of choice in modifying a reference to a person. (The man who, rather than the man that.) Other editors prefer that for almost everything, arguing correctly that is a "neutral" pronoun. The safest way to walk across such deep waters is to find out what your editors like and try to, do it their way.

There are definite regional quirks that are not the editors' fault. In the South, particularly, there seems to be a grander tolerance of colloquialisms, slang, and, most definitely, dialect. Because of the South's rich and disparate dialects, you find editors letting pass such quotes as "I heard the shots, then I seen "running" or "How bout them dogs" or "I be sitting' here." And 'y' all" of course is almost as common in Southern newspapers as "you." But again, an editor's quirks can take precedence. Some editors forbid dialect, arguing that it can be viewed as an act of condescension. Others argue just as forcefully that newspapers are too stuffy already and that dialect often adds a touch of color and genuineness.

The Methodology

In the editing process, each newspaper has its set of rules that generally are strictly enforced. These are contained in something called a stylebook. At some smaller newspapers, this may be no more than a mimeographed sheet of paper. At larger newspapers, the stylebook may consist of up to two hundred pages and resembled a dictionary in format. Most commonly, newspapers rely on the stylebooks adopted by the associated Press and United Press International, which vary slightly. Top editors also add their personal idiosyncrasies. In Atlanta, for instance, Atlanta Hartsfied International Airport abruptly became just Hartsfield Airport. There was a brief move on one newspaper to use no middle initials in identifying people in stories. This presented a problem when, Robert E. Brown ran against Robert H. Brown in a municipal election. Middle initials quickly were reinstated.

The chief keepers of the stylebook rules are the newspaper's copy editors. The copy desk is something of a court of last resort in the newsroom, providing a final check to the balancing act of the city desk. In the modern newsroom, copy editing is done via the VDT. Once a city-desk editor has finished reviewing a story on the VDT, he or she presses a few magic buttons, and the story blips from the screen into the computer' memory bank, from which the copy editor can summon it onto his or her VDT screen by pushing another set of magic buttons. It is this last reading by the copy editor, with rare exceptions, that renders the story ready for putting on the presses in the form that readers will see in that day's newspaper.

By the time story reaches the copy desk at most dailies, the basic wording of the story is considered Approved and will be tampered with only sparingly. The copy editors function much as quality controllers in an auto plant. The reporter and the city desk have built the car. The copy editors make sure nobody has left a screwdriver stuck in the fan belt. They look primarily for errors that jump out at them: any glaring grammatical stupidity, misspelled words, or inaccurate street addresses. Copy-desk veterans often are old-timers who know the city and thus know that at a certain point Peachtree Street becomes Peachtree Road. Names are given particular scrutiny, since printing a misspelled name is a cardinal sin.

The copy editor handling a particular story also usually is the one to write a headline for it. That is not an easy job. Countless periodicals thrive on reprinting the worst faux pas of headline writers, and headline ridiculing is a favorite pastime of reporters. An example of an amusing and misleading headline was: Murderer sentenced to life in Washington, D.C.

Such misplaced modification occurs because it is very difficult to summarize an entire story in a few words, and occasionally headline writers goof. The Colombia journalism Review's editors contend that their most popular feature is the reprinting of hilarious clubs and bloopers. Gloria Cooper, the Review's managing editor, compiled some of the best examples in a book, Squad Helps Dog Bite Victim and other clubs from the nation's press. The reporters themselves often get criticized unfairly by readers for "that dumb title you put on the story." At major dailies, reporters have absolutely nothing to do with what headline appears over their stories. One reporter we know was chastised by a reader for a headline mentioning ham radio operators over a story about citizens-band-radio operators. The reporter had made no reference to ham operators, but the headline writer erroneously assumed that the terms were synonymous. (Ham operators, who must undergo a battery of tests before getting a Federal Communications commission license for long-range broadcasting, consider CB operators rank amateurs who merely toy with their short-range equipment.)

The headline writer is like the football lineman who gets attention only when he misses a tackle. However, filling the big hole above the story with something that will draw a reader's attention to it takes a special skill. Writing headlines is not simply a matter of attaching a "title" to the story. For one thing, the headline must fit. Only so many letters can be stuffed into the space reserved for the headline without having them fall off the page or extend past the column. The headline count, as it is called, varies according to the size of type and how many columns the headline is to cover. Newspapers also have various other rules that make headline writing even ore trying-such as requiring that a preposition and its object be on the same line. The headline is expected to capture in five or six words the essence of a story that may run thirty or forty inches long. This is another reason for the inverted pyramid mid in that it helps the copy editor who is pressed for time sum up the essence of the story.

Puns are fun for copy editors and sometimes catch the mood of a story. Over a sports story about the Atlanta Braves baseball team losing a third straight game to the Cincinnati Reds, one copy editor wrote: BRAVES BLUE AFTER REDS, 3-0. Sometimes, however, puns can be misleading. Over a story about the new popularity of row housing in the city, a feature section-copy editor wrote: A "ROW" OVER HOUSING. Actually, there was no "row" in the sense of an argument; the copy editor thought the pun could be used by putting the word in quotes, but he misled some readers into thinking there was something along the line of a zoning dispute. Double meanings and bad taste have to be guarded against.

Questions to Solve : The story and headline are parts of a puzzle the copy editor helps put together for the news editor and assistant news editors, who control the page layout. These editors call themselves line drawers, and they basically are that. They draw lines on a dummy-a blank, miniature page that serves as a guide for printers who will compose the plate for actual printing. What the news editors, or layout editors, do is measure the length of a story (by counting characters) and then draw in the appropriate space on the dummy along with the desired space for a headline. Space also is mapped out for photographs, charts, logos, and anything else that is to greet the reader in the first edition. (On some newspapers, the news editors decide only priority play for stories, with separate makeup editors designing the layout accordingly.) The space allotted for a particular headline usually includes a code to ell the copy editor what size type to specify and what the letter count will be. At this point, stories also are sometimes cut, usually from the bottom of the story (which is another argument for the old inverted pyramid), in order to fit the space.

Headline writing and type sizing are handled by computers at most large modem dailies. Into the VDT is sent the typed story and headline with all the necessary codes to help it pop out magically ready for paste-up in the composing room, or backshop, as it often is called in the trade. From typewriter-size letters on the VDT may come a two-inch-high banner headline.

Problems do not end in the backshop. Therefore, the news desk normally has a representative in the composing room to stomp on any news bugs. The makeup editor has to make hasty and sometimes arbitrary decisions. A story that was supposed to fit often doesn't. The bottom is sliced again. The headline comes out with a 72-point error: "Mr. Dinnan" has been made into "Mr. Drinnan." Editors scream. The makeup editor calls for hurried changes to save embarrassment before the presses roll.

A news story must play upon the event reported therein. Ideally, read every story, preferably thrice-once for familiarisation, once while you edit, and the third time to check your work. If the story has no glaring problems, and if you fully understand it, you would be ready to edit it. Now, you are concerned with spelling, punctuation, grammar, consciousness of expression, smoothness of writing, general accuracy and comprehensibility.

Format: A news story is divided in to two parts-the opening-para called the "intro" (introduction) or the "lead", and the body. The lead describes, simply and briefly, what happened. The body documents also elaborates the lead.

Adequate attention should be paid to the lead, the most vital part of the story. Written in a single sentence, it should grab the reader and compel him to read the body. Normally, the lead is in about 25 words, or may be less. At the maximum, it should be limited to 40 words. The intro should be concise and crisp. It the maximum, it should be limited to 40 words. The intro should be concise and crisp. It should not meander or puzzle the reader, but summarise the story. Details should be dispersed and blended in the subsequent paragraphs.

There is a famous example of any eye-catching intro.

"James Wilson lit a cigarette while bathing his feet in gasoline. He may live."

This is a masterpiece of economy of words in writing. It tells the whole story at once: the careless stupidity of the act, the swift of retribution and the grisly consequences, all conjured up in our minds in vivid detail.

In sense, we do not need to read on. But, we all would. We

would want to know more about James Wilson, why he was soaking his feet in gasoline, where he was performing this act, and so on. And, all this would be told in subsequent paragraphs, in a logical order.

This particular example is what is called a "teasing" intro, for it arouses our curiosity and makes us read on.

Opening Para: Conventionally, the news story has followed the "inverted pyramid" structure. The most significant information is placed at the top, the story's beginning and other details follow in their order of importance. Thus, the story tapers to smaller and smaller details, until it disappears. It may begin with the five Ws and one H, i.e., the who-what-why-when-where and low lead. Basically, a news story should answer what, when and where. The answers should find place in the opening para. The three other questions - who, why and how - do not necessarily arise in all the news copy. In case they do, the answers are accommodated in the subsequent paras. Each succeeding para should add an essential detail without being dependent in content or style on what follows.

The inverted pyramid style enables :

(i) a new story, to be self-contained, even if paras are deleted at the bottom due to space; shortage [consequently, a coherent story is left at each point where it could be cut];

(ii) a hurried reader to skip over many stories in a short time by just reading the opening paras [those with greater interest could read a story completely];

(iii) a sub-editor, to write the headline gets in the gist in the gist in the first few paras; and

(iv) a sub-editor, to change the order of paras or insert news material, even after the matter has been sent to the press for composing.

If the news is not in the opening para, trace out where it is buried. Bring it to the top, and also locate its supporting details. If there are two important news points or angles that vie for the top spot, assess and evaluate which one is better and more catchy. This could call for rewriting the entire news item.

Next, see if the second para supports the lead. It should deliver the promise made in the opening para. The third para should continue the development implicit in the lead and in the second para. The paras should preferably be of one sentence, and not more than two. This helps a lot while trimming the story, and makes for easy comprehension by the reader, if there are any direct quotes, ascertain if these should be retained. Find out if there are opinions, and if there are, make sure these are suitably attributed, i.e., given within quotes.

Rewriting: 'While editing a story, the sub-editor should, as far as possible, look for errors in spelling, grammar and syntax, and correct these and 'pass' the copy. But an instant second look might sometimes compel him/her to rewrite it. The opening para may lack the punch, or the copy may seem confusing, or the news may be hidden below. Hence, rewriting may become necessary for the sake of clarity. Highlight the news point, taking care to avoid distortion and respect the facts produced by the reporter. Sometimes, the reports obtain the information but fail to exploit it. This could happen particularly when some one is reporting the press conferences and disasters.

Art of Making Headline : Every morning, when a reader looks for something interesting in a newspaper, it is the heading which catches his eyes. After scanning the headings, he settles down to read the story in detail.

A story, howsoever well-edited, would no attract him unless it is given a heading or headline, the most vulnerable spot in a newspaper. The headline attracts the reader to go through the story. It tells him what the story is about. Thus, a headline sells the story. Besides, a headline serves the reader in several ways.

The size of the headline determines the importance of a story: the larger or bolder the headlines, the most important is the news story. Writing a headline is like applying the finishing polish on a well-crafted piece of furniture. While writing headlines, you should keep the following points in mind:

(i) A headline should speak. It should say something which educates and entertains the reader. Avoid headlines like, Lok Sabha, S.D. Sharma.

(ii) A headline should stimulate the readership, and lead you to reading the story under it. The news items with bad headline do not get read.

(iii) A headline should be sharp, and convey the essence of a story.

(iv) A headline should be active and positive.

(v) The best headline is written in the present tense, because it provides a sense of immediacy. The use of the present tense verbs lends an air of urgency and freshness to the news, making it up-to date. The past tense headlines make it seem that the publication is reporting history.

(vi) Use commonly-known abbreviations.

(vii) Never split names between lines of a headline.

(viii) Single quotation marks (' ') should be used in headlines, since double quotation (" ") marks consume more space. Single quotation marks are more attractive.

(ix) Articles much as 'the' 'an' and 'a' are generally not used in headlines.

(x) Above all, common sense should remain the primary rule in determining clarity.

Kicker: Kicker is another conventional headline, usually a one-line heading with a second line (Kicker) above it in a different style and half the type size. It extends no more than midway above the main line. Kicker headlines are used to dress up a page by lending variety.

Hammer: Hammer is the reverse of kicker, but, usually, in all capital letters. The big type is the hammer and the smaller type the main headline. One word, or two at the most, will suffice of the hammer. By virtue of their size, hammers impress the readers with their importance. But too many hammers on one page may dilute that significance, and destroy the look of the page.

This main news lead is different from the one we have already talked about above. Suppose there is a train accident at Aarah, about 60 km. from Patna. Just an hour before the first edition of a newspaper goes to the press. The first information reports from the Railways, or any other sources, convey the news about the accident but give scanty details. There is no precise mention about assaults. It will take about two hours for a reporter to reach the scene to get the first hand details. But we cannot wait till the reporter telephones from the spot or comes back to file the story. We must cover the story in the first edition. The story may be written thus:

Patna, Oct, 15-at least five passengers were killed and several wounded when three bogies of the Magadh Express derailed tonight at Aarah, about 60 km. from here, the railway sources said.

Details are awaited.

Details will pour in once the reporter reaches the site, and a composite story would crystallise besides, the Railways Ministry, in New Delhi, will give the official version. There shall also be eyewitness accounts. Hence, many news items are bound to flow in on the same event. All these are tied together, highlighting the major facts, and the Lead is written for the newspaper's city edition. A Lead is a device, used mostly in the case of developing stories, for updating the top or changing the story's emphasis in the light of new information of facts as these unfold.

Such stories include a strike, a 24-hour bundh, a river flood, an air crash or a train accident or other mishaps, a conference or a political meeting, an election, a visit to a state by a VIP such as the Prime Minister or the President. As the story - advances with the day, all these may require one or more Leads, like the Second lead, Third Lead and finally a Lead all.

Besides, a Lead is used to tighten loose ends of a dispersed story. A tie-up will provide a combined top for different items relating to a single subject or related development, namely, the Independence Day or Republic Day celebrations, religious festivals, etc.

A copy editor or sub-editor is a bridge between a reporter and the reader. He/she need not execute all these functions simultaneously. But, on any given day, he/she will be required to play all these roles.

A copy editor, generally know as the sub-editor or desk person, is a gatekeeper and image builder who protects a newspaper's reputation. He/she is a surgeon who performs surgery, and a priest who conducts a happy marriage between speed and efficiency. He/she is a tailor, too. He/she is an unglamorous backroom worker, who does a thankless but stupendous job, and represents the last stage. No one can see his/her edited copy except the proof readers, who, if smart and vigilant, may detect faults with subbing (editing). A desk person takes all the blame; he/she rarely gets any credit and remains anonymous.

A copy editor or a sub-editor receives, sifts, processes and issues news items after, giving them a final shape.

A copy editor:

(i) removes rough edges from the copy and polishes it to make it presentable; (Any story that comes into the newsroom is often raw, blunt, and rough edged. The first task or a sub is to remove rough edges so that the copy makes sense. This will make the copy pleasing and presentable to the readers.)

(ii) adjusts the copy to the style of his newspaper;

[Style is essential, particularly, to a newspaper, and every news organisation follows its own style. It is a device to maintain consistency and, thus, the credibility of a newspaper.]

You may ask what difference would it make if "P" is parliament" is written in the capital letter at some places and in small letter at other. It does make, for at least two reasons: style lends a sense of craftsmanship, and it affects the reader at two levels - consciously simplifies, and clarifies and corrects the language.

Hong Kong	Hongkong
Fertiliser	Fertilizer

Only one of the above should be followed consistently.

(iii) A reader who scans through his morning newspaper is in a great hurry. Hence, a copy editor should carve out each story in a familiar language so that it runs smoothly through the average reader's mind. Smooth writing ensures smooth reading. Simple, direct sentences are more directive. Also, he/she should delete cliches, extraneous words, jargon, ambiguities, non-descript adjectives and adverbs.

As far as possible, the predicate should be close to the subject. If an intervening clause removes the verb too far from the subject, the reader could lose track of the sentence and its meaning.

(iv) Tailors story length to space requirements.

(v) Detects and corrects errors of fact.

(vi) Simplifies, clarifies and verifies meanings.

(vii) Adjusts stories to make them objective and fair.

If a controversial matter is reported, then there are bound to be two sides or different points of view. Hence, all the points of view must be fairly presented. Carrying only one version and ignoring others in the coverage will amount to taking sides.

(viii) Adjusts stories to make these legally safe.

You should avoid using adjectives of pejorative nature with respect to persons. However, unpopular a person might be the law will protect him against defamation.

In matters before the courts, the cases of both the petitioners and defendants must be given space in the report.

For example,

When reporting an accident between a car and a bus, avoid writing who hit whom, unless it is established through a judicial inquiry. It should be described as a "collision".

(ix) Rewrites and restructures stories extensively, where necessary. As far as possible, the sub (editor) should look for errors in spelling, grammar and syntax, and clear the copy. But, an instant second look may sometimes compel him/her to rewrite it. The opening para may lack the punch, the copy may seem confusing, or the news may be hidden below. Hence, rewriting may become necessary for the sake of clarity.

Highlight the news-point, taking care to avoid distortion and respect the facts produced by the reporter. In case the copy is badly written, show it to the reporter. Sometimes, the reporters obtain the information, and fail to exploit it. This could happen while reporting the press conferences and major tragedies such as plane or train accidents.

(x) Follows the policy of the newspaper.

Sometimes a newspaper may support the policies of a particular political party, and, hence, would avoid criticising it. Even though you have a different opinion, you shall have to follow the paper's policy.

(xi) Corrects copy in the interest of good taste.

(xii) Avoids sensation.

(xiii) Removes those points that could be called undue publicity or 'puff'.

(xiv) Deletes doubtful words and sentence, following the thumb rule "when in doubt, leave out". Every story does not require all these treatment. But, every day, some story or the other will require any or most of these operations; a sub frequently performs these functions.

A copy editor /sub-editor should make sure that words are spelt correctly. A spelling error is a major effort, and reflects badly on the credibility of a newspaper. A few moments spent on checking the spelling of a word will keep the reader's mind at ease.

The Concentration : The production of a newspaper calls for undivided attention of 200 to 300 people in different departments, as it is delicate and complex process. There is tension since a deadline is to be met. In a news agency, the deadline in 'now'. Amidst this tense atmosphere, the sub-editor has to perform his job meticulously. He should possess certain qualities to discharge his functions efficiently.

The sources of the essential qualities of a copy editor/ sub-editor are:

Calmness: Be calm and composed, come what may. You should not get excited when a big story breaks-be it a disaster, calamity, the

	assassination of a big political leader or the collapse of a government.
Decisive:	Take quick and correct decisions. The editorial department has no place for indecisives.
Non-partisan:	Never take sides; be non-partisan.
Memory:	Have a sharp memory for counter-checking facts, if necessary.
Grasp:	Size up the situation as it unfolds, and estimate its relevance.
Know your reader:	Know the particular readership. This means you should engage one hand with subbing, and the other with the pulse of the reader.
Self-confidence:	Have confidence enough to correct a bad copy written by anyone, even the senior most reporter or the paper's editor.
Mature:	Be mature enough to correct only bad copy, and not just make changes for the sake of changing.
Sceptical:	Do not accept anything at face value. You should approach everything as a source of potential error.
Knowledge:	Be a jack of all trades, because a sub handles a wide range of stories (from killings to oil prices to satellite launch). You are required to have some knowledge about these, including how these compared with the past events, how the names of different nationalities are spelt. A good editor should store most of the information as it comes across, and search for more.
Stability:	Have enough stability to work under pressure.

Supporting Items : The copy editor will require a set of tools, the lack of which may lead to loss valuable time while subbing the copy. These aids are indispensable. Often, you may come across problems of spellings and facts, arising out of an average day's handing of the news. You should focus on the errors, and correct the name.

The Vocabulary

The basic building blocks of journalism are words. You should respect the words, and follow the way these are arranged and strung together. Any Misplacement of words could twist the meaning. Hence, you should pay attention to punctuation marks, grammar and syntax. All these are important in the sentence construction.

Punctuation Marks: Punctuation problems start and almost end with a comma. This little mark causes more trouble than the rest put together. Consider these examples:

Ram says Raj is an idiot.

Ram, says Raj, is an idiot.

Observe how the placement of the comma has changed the meaning. Remember that commas define relationships within a sentence.

Punctuation marks bring in clarity and better readability. At the same time, too many of these clutter a story.

There should be no comma after a verb unless it is immediately followed by a parenthesis.

One of the areas of punctuation in which mistakes are often made is the dash and the hyphen. These serve two nearly opposite purposes, but are often mixed up.

A dash is used to create a pause for emphasis, or to provide an abrupt change of thought, or to introduce a phrase or clause in parenthesis. Thus, a dash separates, and is spaced; the whereas, a hyphen joins the two, often unconnected, ideas. It is not spaced, and is half the size of a dash.

The Indications

Slug: A news item or story may run into several paras, and also exceed one page. If running into pages, a news story has to be kept track of from amongst various stories, and chronologically arranged. Hence, these paras, in a page, are divided into two of three parts. Then, these parts are 'slugged' and numbered, i.e., given a label, which identifies that story for that particular day, and helps the editor on duty to bring different parts together. Related stories are slugged to make the relationship clear.

Slug is an identification mark or tag. It is often the key word in a story and written on top left or right of a page. For example: On a day like 15th August, 26th January, festivals, disasters and press conferences, there are bound to be several stories related to the same subject. So, "Day' will become the Master Slug'. And for each story a "Sub-slug' shall be used. e.g., 'Day-PM' will be the slug for the story relating to the Prime Minister's speech on the occasion. Thus, PM is the 'Sub-slug', with 'Day' serving as the 'Master Slug'.

Editing Symbols: As soon as you start editing a copy, the first symbol you use is for paragraph indentation. Even if every para is indented, you should mark this symbol on every para. This would help the typesetter in knowing that you want paragraph to begin at that spot.

Pictures submitted for publication in the newspapers and magazines have to be edited to fit into the layout of the page, and also the unnecessary portions cut off, which the photographer night have added in the actual composition. The competent photo-editor's job is to see to it that he does not waste space, and trims a picture keeping the main essence of the subject intact. This reduction process, keeping the essential parts of the photographs intact, is called cropping. Since the photographers are emotionally involved in shooting their pictures, they might think whatever they have added in a picture would be published. This aspect is left to the judgement of the photo-editor, when the final composition of the photograph for publication is made.

A photographer might have given a group picture of the newly appointed ministers. The clever photo-editor might use only the heads of the ministers and cut off the rest of the portion in order to economize on space. A narrow strip of the faces of the newly elected ministers is certainly of more interest for the readers, and definitely not the dress they are wearing! Just as the editor edits a story by cutting the irrelevant portions, the photo editor also crops the picture, bringing out the emphasis of the photographic message as effectively as possible. To improve the look of the newspaper or a magazine, the photo editor might opt for vertical or horizontal pictures depending on the layout of the page make up, and, in the process, mar a picture drastically, keeping the main subject in focus. Unless he has the freedom to crop the pictures, he will not be able to introduce new ideas for improving the look of the page.

A good photographer must be able to handle every assignment the editor gives him to his own satisfaction. Pictures are in everything around us. Each one of us sees different pictures in the same object and situations, owing to the different background and experience each of tis have. You must have seen a lot of photographers which have won prizes. The subjects of these pictures must have been very ordinary or common. But, the way the photographer's composed them, and brought forth the essence, made a difference. Didn't they? Probably, you might have tried a picture or two on the same subject. But the judges were not excited. Why? It is not that you are wrong, and they are right; it is just that your vision is different. There could be as many photographs on a particular subject as there are journalists. You will be most successful when your vision is in tune with that or your editor. It does not mean that you will have to suppress your creativity. It is only to channel your creativity to achieve certain goals.

One has to work with great speed on a location. This is significant. On location, no one will wait while you try to figure out your shutter speed and lens aperture adjustment in your camera. Even as you get out of your vehicle, you should be setting your apperature for the type of lighting available on the location or what you intend to use (like an electronic flash), and be ready to focus to an average distance. You should actually shoot a news event from several different angles, and let your photo-editor decide which picture to use. But when everything starts happening, at the same time, you must be quick enough to do your own editing on the spot. Your grasping power must be like quick silver. You must decide which picture from what angle would be the best, and then get yourself in position to shoot it.

The newspaper photographs are based on factual situation. The photographs illustrates an event, bring depth into it, and probably comment on it. Usually, the photographer is given only an idea to work with, and is expected to create an appropriate photograph to illustrate it. This is where a good memory or a notebook will come in handy. The photographic techniques involved in shooting for magazines are not much different from those in newspapers. The technical skill is again taken for grated, and your primary concern is to illustrate the story clearly and completely.

Is a caption a must for a picture? Yes. Even though the news picture is supposed to tell a story on its own, one should say where and when the incident took place. Caption writing is an art by itself, and it comes with experience and aptitude. It is, generally, the job of the new editor. The picture and its caption are complementary to each other, and it is very essential to mention when and where the picture was taken, and who the persons seen in the picture are.

When a picture shows a VIP getting down from a car, the caption instead of saying that such and such a person is 'getting down' from the car should rather say so and so is 'arriving' at the particular venue or place for doing a particular activity, as the case might be. There is, for example, no need to say that a person is eating when the picture is showing it. One should say why, where and what he is eating, and on what occasion. A caption reading 'under the clutches of a monster', showing the picture of a scooter trapped under a huge lorry, is a good one.

If photograph is described in the body of the story, then there is no need for a separate caption and the picture could hang in between the paragraphs. Sometimes the News Editor might prefer to box a powerful picture with just a detailed caption to brighten the page. A really good picture could express the equivalent of a thousand words! Captions for the sports pictures are very important, and most of the photographers simply prefer to say something like a melee in the goal mouth which should actually say who is doing what. For example, it should read as 'Mr. X, who scored a hatrick, scoring his third goal in a row beating the defender Mr. Y'. This applies to all games. Sometimes the news editors prefer to give no captions, and the pictures simply hang under the headline, which itself serves as the caption. 'Queen Ann wins the Derby, 'Kapil clean bowled for a duck' and 'Mr. X takes over as Chairman, are some examples.

In most news coverages, the photographer reaches the spot only after the incident takes place, and is able to take only the result of what had already happened. In such special cases the newspaper or magazine might have to depend upon graphic illustrations to detail the activities that had taken place on a particular spot earlier.

From the information available, the entire incident in the original sequence could be sketched out so as to give the reader a clear idea of what the news story is about. Such graphic illustrations have been used time and again of depicting incidents of varying degrees. For most of the mountaineering expeditions, the routes taken by the mountaineers could be sketched out, adding all the necessary information regarding the routes. In an assassination case, a graphic illustration could show the position of the assassinator, the victim and others in the vicinity.

The graphics come in handy for the tabloids and magazines, where detailed stories are published with lots of illustrations-pictorially and graphically. With limited space, the newspapers go in for graphics, but not as a routine.

Knowhow of Techniques : Though the newspapers and magazines we read today have gone through several stages of developments, more changes are taking place as new techniques and technologies are introduced. The first newspaper in India was published on January 29, 1780. It was called the Bengal Gazette. Later, it also came to be known as Calcutta General advertiser or Hicky's Gazette. James Augusts Hicky was its founder, editor, printer and promoter all in one. The Bengal Gazette was a weekly. It consisted of two pages, measuring 12" × 8".

The Bengal Gazette of 1780 was a one-man show. Large newspaper establishments today employ thousands of workers, and use most modern equipment worth crores of rupees. Skills and inputs from many specialists in different areas are essential to produce a newspaper today. In India, we have over 27,000 publications, in this field, in more than 90 languages. The newspaper composing and printing methods have gone through major changes during the past few decades. However, the basic function remains the same, to convert the printing matter into printable format.

An understanding of the printing-matter composing methods would help in better understanding the limitations as well as advantages of each composing process, in designing the page.

To create the desired amount of leading or space between lines, he/she inserts metal strips called leads. When the composing stick is full, the lines of type are transferred to a long shallow tray, called a "galley".

After taking out proofs and carrying out the necessary corrections, the next step is to make up the page. i.e., to assemble various elements such as the text type, display type, picture blocks, according to the designed layout. Since the composed matter consists of hundreds of individual pieces, it is essential that it is held together securely or locked up. This may be done by tying up the type with a string, or by surrounding it with furniture strips of wood, metal or plastic. These, in turn, may be held firmly in place with metal strips. The type may be locked up on the galley in a metal frame, called a "chase" or directly on the bed of the press.

Collectively, type and other printed matter locked tip and ready to be proofed or printed is called a "forme".

Machine Setting : This method involves casting type from molten metal. For this reason, machine-set type is also referred to as hot type. There are four popular type casting machines-Linotype. Intertype, Monotype and Ludlow.

Linotype and Intertype : These are mechanical methods of composing and casting type in one piece lines called "slugs". Since these machines cast lines of type rather than individual characters, these are called "line-casting" machines.

The name Linotype is derived from casting a line-of-type. In both systems, the operator sits at a keyboard, not unlike that of a typewriter. The machine is adjusted to set type to the desired pica measure and leading. The upper front section of the machine carriers a magazine, a slotted metal container, which holds the "matrices", or letter moulds, of the type to be set.

When the operator strikes the keys, the matrices fall into positions to form a line-of-type. The operator sets as many characters and Wedge-shaped space bands as possible within the given line measure. The space hands are used for the word spacing. When the operator is ready to cast a line, he/she pulls a lever which sets off a series of event. The line, made up of matrices and space bands, is transferred to the casting mechanism. The wedge-shaped space bands are driven up between the words to justify the line. Molten, metal is forced into the matrices, and the trimmed line of type or slug is ejected onto a pan or galley tray. As soon as the type is cast, the matrices are returned to the magazine with the help of a mechanical distributor, and the space bands to the space-band box, ready for the next line.

After the matter is composed, the type is locked up on a galley. Line-casting machines can set type and leading as one piece. For this reason, it is impossible to reduce the amount of leading, the space between lines and words, once the type has been cast. However, leasing can be increased by inserting leads between lines by hand. The cost of corrections is reasonable. Any change a within a line means that the entire line, or even all the succeeding lines in a paragraph, have to be reset. The basic difference between linotype and intertype is that the intertype of matrices. They can be used for casting headlines as well as body matter.

Monotype: As the name suggests, "monotype" casts the characters one by one rather than as a complete line. It is a combination of two machines, a keyboard or perforator and a typecaster. It is a two-step or two-machine method of casting individual type characters, mechanically.

To Set Type : The machine is adjusted to the required pica measure and leading. As the copy is typed, it produces a perforated paper roll, which is used to drive the typecaster. A combination of holes dictates the letters, spaces and punctuation marks to be set. Normal spacing is punched into the roll between words. A calculator, measures the amount of unused space at the end of the line, and the operator then punches the holes to indicate the amount of additional space to be given between words to justify the line. When the roll is fed into the casting machine, it is fed in backwards so that the machine "memorizes" the amount of space to be added between words, as the letters are cast.

To set type, the perforated roll is fitted on the typecaster, where it directs the casting, mechanism by means of compressed air. The air passing through the perforations brings the matrix holder and the specific matrix ready to be filled with molten metal into proper position. Once the type has been cast it is ejected onto a galley, one character at a time.

Ludlow: This is a combination of handsetting and machine-casting operations. Like linotype, it produces a slug, but in a different way. The operator sets the type matrices and leading in a composing stick by hand. The composed matrices are then locked into a casting machine, where they are filled with molten lead to produce the slug. Ludlow was designed primarily to cast display type from 12 to 72 points, but it is mostly used for the newspaper headlines.

Phototypesetting: It is also known as photocomposing, or cold type setting. All the other methods stated above involve hot type. That is, they require the use of molten metal. Since photocomposing does not involve metal casting, it is also called a cold type-process.

The first phase of photocomposing resembles that of monotype setting. Unless the perforator is attached to a video display unit (VDU), the operation is limited to conversion of copy matter into a coded perforated tape. This perforated tape is then fed into a programmed computerised unit, which projects the desired images of type characters onto photosensitive film or paper.

This paper is then made up in mechanicals or photomechanicals from which printing plates can be produced. Photocomposing provides a fast, flexible and reasonably economical method of setting type. This method offers several advantages over other methods. In handsetting and casting, type is to be inked in order to print. The pressure of the metal type against the paper causes ink squeeze, which tends to make the edges of the printed forms irregular. Offset plates produced from art pull's tend to have rough edges. In phototypesetting, on the other hand, individual letters are projected and exposed directly on to photosensitive paper of film, resulting in the sharpest possible letter forms.

As long as type is on a piece of metal, there is a limit to just how close the letters can be set. With phototype setting, it is merely a question of projecting the letters, where one wants. Letters can be set touching, overlapping, in fact, in any way one wishes. Another advantage of phototypesetting is that type can be set and matter made up directly on photosensitised film or paper. This means that it is possible to go directly from film to plate-making. This process saves time for the designer as well as the printer. A phototypesetting unit with a visual display terminal (VDT) offers the additional advantage of providing a visual display of the composed matter.

Phototypesetting is done through the computers, which are essentially electronic equipments capable of logic functions, according to predetermined programmes. The computers can carry out programmed decisions and eliminate errors caused by human judgement. The programmed decision-making process can be used advantageously to reduce pre-press time. This is one of the major crisis areas in newspaper production. In hand or machine setting, the speed of compositors is restricted because of the requirements of proper word-spacing and the line alignment process. In computer setting, these functions can also be programmed to carry on predetermined page make-up.

The computer input is text set on tape, and the output is a coded tape, including format and typographical instructions. Just as the compositor, composing by hand or by machine, has to think of the text as type in a specified type face of a certain size, of a certain line length with all the spacing, word breaks italics, capital letters, and other textual conventions, the computer programmer has to design his programmes to convert straight input tape ("idiot tape", as the computer experts picturesquely call it) in to the typographically stylised output.

The computer contains, within its stored programme, all or most of the typographical decisions an experienced compositor takes as a result of his knowledge and experience in typesetting. The programme may be written to produce the required kind of text-setting. The output of the computer-coded paper tape can be used to control the actual typesetting equipment, including the conventional automatic composing machines using hot metal or any phototypesetting system. The outcome of the total system is dependent on the computer programme employed.

The programmes used in computer typesetting do not differ in principle from those used for many other computer operations. That is to say the computer obeys the programmer's instructions by performing a series of calculations, in accordance with the needs of the output, which in this case is the tape used to operate a typesetting machine. A computer can be programmed to carry out all the calculation needed to establish wordspacing within acceptable limits, and, beyond these, a word-break is required to break up a word and place part of it in the next line. Photo editing and page designing can also be done on the computers. Now a days, almost all big newspapers in India are using the computers for composing purposes.

As you know, different editorial components of a daily newspaper or a magazine are generally news reports, special reports, photographs, book reviews, are reviews, are reviews, film reviews, feature articles, interview stories, investigative and interpretative reports. Along with these, newspapers also publish advertisements, with display and classified public information, notices and jobs/employment advertisements. In addition, newspapers also publish the stock market information, weather reports, radio, television, cinema and theatre charts.

The newspapers operate in a competitive world. In addition, these have to compete with the radio and television.

Also, as living styles and product consumption patterns of the readers improve, the newspaper editors and proprietors have to improve the quality of their product.

Therefore, to keep up with the times, there has been a marked improvement in the use of the typography and newspaper design in the newspapers during the last few years. More improvements are bound to take place with innovations in newspaper production. If you take a closer look at the newspapers being published from different centers in India, you will notice many differences in their use of typography, design and production techniques. Several newspapers have started using colour printing for improving their appeal to the advertisers and readers.

At any newspaper stall or shop, you will notice a large variety of newspapers and magazines. Newspapers come in different shapes and sizes. There are newspapers that provide general public interest news to the readers. There are other with cater to the needs of the specialists. Every newspaper has its own way of presenting news, views and features. In a competitive market, it is essential for each product to have "uniqueness" or an individual identity. By appropriate use of typography and layout design, each newspaper attempts to require and perpetuate its unique identity.

Even if the contents of two papers are similar, the use of different typography and design can given the newspaper two distinct identities. For example, take a daily English language newspaper published from Delhi, and compare it with a newspaper published from Patna, Jaipur, Madras, Bombay, Calcutta, Chandigarh, Hyderabad, Trivandrum, Lucknow or Bangalore. The page one design, layout of the news items, pictures, box items type faces, even display of news items will stand out prominently. Besides, the newspapers from Delhi will carry more national and international news. Others will emphasis more local state, regional, national and international stories in that order. Almost the same criteria apply on other pages, including the edit page. The reasons for these varied emphasis are the needs of the readership.

The front page of a newspaper is like the face of a beautiful woman. If it is attractive, it will hold the attention. You may have heard the expression, "the front page news". For a newspaper, to report news is a normal function, but there is something special about the fact that the news is printed on its front page. The front page is the "face" of a newspaper. Let us take a closer look. Carefully, read the news items printed on the front page of your daily newspaper, and try to find reasons for these items being printed on the front page, of your daily newspaper, and try to find reasons for these items being printed on the front page. Remember, front page is normally the page that is read first, or, at least, looked at first.

We all acquire a unique identity by our own name. The uniqueness gets reinforced by the unique way we write our names, i.e., the signatures. Many other distinct features add to our individual identity. Similarly, newspapers have a name. If you observe the front page of a newspaper closely, you will see that the masthead of a newspaper is much more than just the name of the newspaper. To understand the significance of masthead, you should take as many different newspapers and magazines as you can, and see how newspapers and magazines try to acquire a unique identity by their mastheads or names.

Newspapers sell news, Headlines are a means to attract the readers towards the news items. For a page designer, each headline is a new and unique challenge. For him/her, the headlines of the news items are much more than just a set of words. It is the responsibility of the page-designer to make each headline as distinctive as possible within the given newspaper format and its policies with regard to the use of type faces and type sizes. These policies evolve over a period of time

To get a better understanding of the concept, let us again go back to our newspapers, and examine how the headlines are made distinctive and used to provide an eye-appeal or an attractive page design. The task of the page designer or make-up person is to decide whether he/she wants to give more news items and shorter coverage of each, or less news items and emphasise them with greater details. A headline can be made bold (big typeface), a single line and run horizontally across columns, or short with width: small typeface two lines and one column. Carefully notice these variations in the headlines in your paper. Each, page designer uses his/her own experience and creative genius to make the page attractive and give each news item an appropriate placement on the page.

Headlines are given generally by the sub-editors/ copy editors. The page make-up person cannot change them, but he/she can increase or decrease the display value, readability or importance of the news item by using different techniques at his/her disposal such as type face and size, placement, making it run horizontally across more columns of less. You will find that most newspapers every day give a four or five column bottom spread on their front page; it is down to give a solid base to the whole page.

It is said that a picture is worth a thousand words. On the same basis, it can be extrapolated that a good cartoon is worth at least two thousand words. From a page designer's point of view, it is important to realise that photographs, cartoons and graphic have a special significance. Placing a picture or cartoon at wrong place may not only reduce its utility, but also reduce the design appeal of the total page.

A page designer has to examine whether the picture, cartoon, graphic, chart, has an independent value or it has to be juxtaposed with a particular news story. The size may have to be adjusted due to placement or space considerations. Having closely examined some of the major components of the front page of your newspaper, individually, let us now take a look at the architecture of the page or the overall page design. For this, we have look at the page from some distance. One way is to do a comparative study of two or more papers.

Hang two or more papers of the same date on the wall, and stand at a distance to take a critical look at these. As you look at these pages, study the structural outline-of the news stories, bold headlines, pictures, cartoons, placement of box items, etc. Take a look at the whole page from the masthead to the bottom line. Look at the page, as if you were trying to study a painting or a sculpture. You will notice that there is a design in the page, a form and a structure. Each page designer has his/her own concept of beauty and page structure. To bring it out, he/she uses different type sizes, white spaces, placement of pictures, graphs, charts, cartoons, etc. Inside pages of a daily newspaper differ from the front page in their format, structure, and presentation of contents. If you open a daily newspaper, you will see that on top of the page, there may be indications about the topic covered on that page - international news, national news, state news, sports news, city news, business and economy news, etc.

Even if there is no indication on the top, you will notice that the news items on that page have a common link. It helps the readers in their search for a news item. Also by grouping news items on specific pages we are able to give the newspaper a structure. The inside pages under one-group often tend to cover as many news items as possible. Hence, often these pages may seem cluttered.

One common feature in all daily newspapers is the editorial page. The format of this page looks similar in many newspapers in India and abroad. On this page, you will notice that there is a section where the editor(s) write their analysis of the major national and international news items. These are often referred to as the "newspaper's point of view". Along with that, there may be one or two articles written by prominent people on current topics. Also, a demarcated section devoted to "letters to the editor", giving reaction of the readers to the news/views, which might have appeared in the newspaper, or items of concern to the readers but not covered in the paper.

Each newspaper has, usually, a fixed spot for general information items such as the weather forecast, entertainment, cinema, radio, television, etc. The design of the inside pages of a newspaper is relatively much more structured than the front page, which is dependent on the major happenings during the past few hours. Advertisements have special significance for commercial publications. The very existence of newspapers and magazines depends on the revenue from advertisements. Hence, special care must be taken with regard to placement of advertisements along with the news stories on the pages.

There are some important factors, which influence the effectiveness of advertisements in a newspaper. Therefore, in many cases, advertisements are placed on these pages according to the product or services to be advertised. For example, advertisements of sports goods such as shoes, wear, equipment or sports programme are generally placed on the sports pages. The advertisers often request for such placements, and even pay extra for such favours. Advertisements, in a way, are paid for news items. Large colour advertisements have special significance in page design. Page design can be made more attractive with colour advertisements.

Newspapers are meant to be read. Anything that obstructs or reduces the convenience of the reader must be avoided. As far as possible, the news item should be contained in a neatly defined area. Look at the page of a newspaper as a reader, and ask yourself: Are the news items displayed in a nice, readable manner? Could you suggest any improvements?

Each letter, each word and each story has special significance. Headlines, photographs, cartoons, box items, charts and graphics - all these are important ingredients of the newspaper page design. Readability for a page designer has a different meaning than that for a reporter, sub-editor or proof reader. Readability for a page designer has more to do with its visibility and the convenience of its reading for a reader than the actual contents. Readability from a page designer's point of view depends on placement of the news stories, typography and the overall page layout.

Daily newspapers and periodicals differ in their size, format, page layout, overall design, and printing techniques. While pages of most daily newspapers measure 41 cms x 56 cms, magazines or periodicals tend to be around 27cms x 20 cms. However, there are weeklies such as the Sunday Mail, the Sunday Observer or even the weekly editions of daily newspapers, which are registered as weeklies. They are also of similar size, look and design as the daily newspapers.

The cover pages of periodicals have special significance from the editorial and newspaper's policy. While about 85 per cent dailies are subscribed to and delivered at homes or offices, more than 50 per cent magazines are looked at before being bought. Hence, the magazine covers have special significance. Next time you go to a magazine stall, take a critical look at the arrangement or display of magazines. You will see how each magazine tries to attract attention. It is the cover of a magazine that holds your eyes, makes you pick it up and compels you to purchase it. Generally, the magazine covers have photographs of women. It is said that the readers like pictures of women on the cover of a magazine, but no cover on the women.

Now, if you take a few magazines of the same kind such as Business India, Business World and Business Today or India Today, Sunday and The Week, put them side by side, you could examine the difference in cover contents, price and design strategy to attract readers' attention. Limits of imagination of a page-designer determine the limits of page design for a magazine. However, there are a few factors that make some designs more suitable than others.

Every magazine has history behind it, which gives in a tradition in cover-design. This tradition or the past pattern of the cover-page design tends to set the standard for selection of the alternatives, which may or may not be suitable for particular magazine.

To attract the new readers, a magazine will need to adopt unconventional designs, but too much variation from the past may also tend to alienate the regular readers.

To study the design-pattern trends, take a look at three or four issues of the same magazine. You will see some common or regular features in the designs. Study the format and the items displayed on the cover page.

The final test for a magazine is at the newspaper or magazine sales stalls. The success is measured by the number of readers willing to pay for it, and that determines its paid circulation.

To understand the sales promotion strategy, we have to find out first the readership profile that an editor and publisher of a magazine have in mind. The readership profile is defined in terms of age group, educational level, marital status, disposable income, nature of job, quality and place of residence, consumption pattern, etc. Most general interest magazines are read by a wide spectrum of people in different age groups, income levels, educational standards, etc. The readership profile is defined in terms of groups and percentages.

Another factor that tends to influence the price and cover design of a magazine is the long term sales promotion strategy of the newspaper management, i.e., editor and publisher. The most important question can be: Is the management trying to build a long-term (one to three or five years) subscription and distribute the magazine through mail, as is down by the Reader's Digest, or, is the main emphasis on sales promotion through newspaper and magazine stalls. In case the management adopts the sales promotion policy of promoting newspaper though open sales, i.e., through newspaper stalls, the magazine cover design acquires strategic sales promotion importance. The cover designs, in this case, should be critically evaluated with the cover of other magazines in the same genre.

Instant Alterations : Change is a way of life in journalism. No two editions of a newspaper or magazine are alike. Whenever a reader picks up a newspaper or magazine, he/she expects to find something new in it. However, in newspapers and magazines, changes take place within the predetermined format. Formats provide a sense of continuity. Format, may be viewed as a rough outline of the newspaper or magazine, its shape and size, placement of its masthead, and the typeface used for it; placement and presentation of the news, views and other contents. Presently change in a continuous manner is the skill that makes design layout a challenge for each item, on each page, of each publication.

At the first glance it may seem obvious that the change is inevitable, so the question of "need" may seem redundant. However, it is essential that we understand the areas of change that influence the very existence of a newspaper of a magazine and also determine its readership growth pattern. While incorporating changes in page make-up or design layout we must keep in mind a few factors:

(a) While bulk of the readers will remain the same, some new readers, however small, may be added with each new edition.

(b) Some readers dropout and thus change the overall readership profile.

(c) Newspapers and magazines operate in a competitive environment, hence new challenges from competitions have to be met.

(d) Tastes, information requirements and entertainment requirements of readers keep changing.

To respond to change one must understand the compelling reasons for change to incorporate meaningful and effective changes. The Readership in newspapers and magazines is built up slowly. It is a painfully slow marketing and editorial effort.

With passage of time most readers get "addicted" to the nature and quality of presentation of the news, the views and the format in which the newspapers and magazines present their contents. Yet as we saw in the previous section there is a need for change. Hence, the question crops up "how much and how" the change should be incorporated in each issue?

Since each publication is a unique entity, there can be no simple clear cut answer. However, generally, it would very much depend on the subject matter of the topics to be covered. In most cases the change would be reflected in the treatment of topics, language, the quality of illustrations, allotment of space, positioning of articles, typographic changes etc. With the common observation that a picture is worth a thousand words - the nature of pictures selected to accompany the composed matter often indicates the degree of change. Pictures or illustrations used indicate the degree of change. Pictures or illustrations are usually the first to be noticed and often draw relatively strong reaction from readers. Hence it is important that the quality and contents of pictures or illustrations selected should not have to vary from the earlier issues. However, on the other hand, it may also be necessary to keep up with the competing publications.

A cautious approach may be to stay within the bounds of past practices of the publication and the standards of lead publication in that genre of publications. Some leaders, tend to lead in bold ways and later make amends under pressure from readers.

It is not uncommon in the newspaper industry that changes have to be incorporated when the total publication is almost ready or at times under print. In daily newspapers it is almost a way of life. Whenever last minute changes have to be incorporated-the effort is to incorporate the required changes or include the new items with minimum disturbance to the overall page layout. However, some sudden events may warrant total change in the front page layout or cover design of a magazine. Even in case of the most drastic situation, the important factors to be taken note are the time required to bring about the change and the impact of changes on the printing process and schedule. Each printing process and schedule, has its own advantages and limitations. While bringing about changes in the editorial matter their impact on the printing time should also be considered. Events, which demand last minute changes usually require prominent display.

For an editor or reporters of an English newspaper there are only twenty six alphabets with only two symbols each-one-as a capital letter and the other in its small form, for he page make-up man the choices are almost unlimited. Today with the help of computers one can develop new type faces by incorporating variations in size, form and shape of each letter. It is the size, from and shape that determine and distinguish the type face of a letter.

For a page layout designer, letters become a visual framework that gives readers their first overall impression of a printed page. As page designers, we must select type by analysing its visual appearance as well as readability of its type face.

While the choices may be many, editors of daily newspapers for the sake of economy, workability and convenience to its readers, make deliberate attempt to limit the variations of type faces used in their page makeup. Many newspapers adopt just one type face in different sizes throughout the newspaper.

However, magazines and advertisers tend to experiment

with typography to give their pages and messages an eye catching quality.

Speedy Transfer

Speedy transmission of news is as important as the actual news gathering. It has been made possible by the advanced electronic equipment. Increasingly, apart from the speed of the delivery of the information, serious thought is being given to the aesthetic presentation of the textual and visual material on a printed page. This is being treated on par with the editing of information, for both content and language.

The computers and word processors are being used in page make-up. The painstaking manual typesetting and page layouts are a thing of the past. The expertise of the graphic designers and the options made available by the computers have together provided a variety of page designs to choose from.

The facsimile machines, popularly called the 'fax machines,' have proven themselves to be indispensable in reporting back to a newspaper office from the location of an event. These facilitate faster despatch of news from the newspaper office too. Let us now see what functions the electronic equipment must perform to meet the requirements of the newspaper office.

Working Characteristics

The newsroom is a place in the newspaper office, where the news items arrive, and are sorted our. The faster the incoming flow of news, the greater the speed of production of the various pages of the newspaper. The photographs and illustrations need to be quickly located or prepared to supplement the information in the text.

News is a perishable commodity. The newspaper staff have to be on their toes to ensure that important news items are processed quickly, to meet the deadlines of publication. Speed is a prerequisite of the newsroom, and its importance in the production of a daily newspaper could not be emphasized enough. Speed is essential in the following aspects of the, newspaper production: in communicating information; in processing information; in page-designing and layout; in printing and production; and in packing and distribution. Rapid transmission of news becomes meaningless, if information being imparted is inaccurate. This might even affect the paper's credibility. In this context, the accuracy of the data and apparently minor details of spellings and language, assume importance. Such correction work is done with the help of the computers and 'fax' machines.

Sometimes, to give in-depth treatment to an issue, complete information might have to be provided in the form of the historical data or facts about the events preceding the current ones. The computers are an ideal system for storing data in, their memory and this data could be retrieved at a later stage. The computers act as the data banks, and are very useful sources of reference for the newspapers.

The computers permit data maneuverability to suit the needs of the page designers. This might become necessary in the presentation of the same news item in a different format. The computers could even be programmed for an unlimited supply of type faces. Software for a variety of page designs exist and continue to be invented. The typography, thus, is another requirement of the newsrooms.

Presenting Art

The arrangement of captions, photographs and graphic on a page would have to facilitate easy reading, besides being visually appealing. Certain parameters of format are fixed for any newspaper, such as those of the page size, print area, number of columns, positions of masthead, allotment of articles according to their categories and page titles. The page make-up artist works both independently and with the software packages to give a variety of options for the design of pages or their layout.

The Desktop Publishing, the DTP for short refers to both hardware and software that are involved in preparing high quality prints of pages, once these are composed satisfactorily. The prints are used as artwork, and the actual duplication is done by offset printing, owing to the high costs involved in the DTP operations. The hardware of a DTP includes a large-sized colour monitor of the VDU and a laser printer apart from the CPU, which is programmed to suit the DTP software. The laser printer involves a high-speed, high-quality printer technology. The DTP software consist of programmes to compose pages and their layout. These perform the function of the word-processing and automatic margin alignment, providing a variety of typefaces, page-numbering, etc.

2

Art of Learning

Definition and Scope

Teaching-learning process is as old as human beings are on earth. It has been carried out not only by human beings but also by animals to teach their young ones to adjust themselves successfully with their environment. With the passage of time, it has undergone revolutionary changes.

If the teaching-learning process is effective, then the child is able to make the best use of the things in the world around him. If a child has not learnt the art of living harmoniously with others, he will find himself beset with more difficulties than the person who has learnt how to establish social relations with his fellows. So the acquisition of knowledge, skills and attitudes which enable us to adjust ourselves in an effective manner to the environment may be said to be the aim of teaching-learning.

Teaching-learning process is a means whereby society trains its young ones in a selected environment (usually the school) as quickly as possible to adjust themselves to the world in which they live. In primitive societies this adjustment meant conformity with the things as they were. In advanced civilisation of the modern times, effort is made not only to adjust to things as they are but also to make an advance in the improvement of conditions of life by training the young in the modes of thinking and acting which will help to improve the conditions of living that surround them.

Teaching-learning has four aspects: teacher, student, learning process and learning situation. The teacher creates the learning situation for the student. The process is the interaction between the student and the teacher.

Teaching-learning process is a means through which the teacher, the learner, the curriculum and other variables are organised in a systematic manner to attain pre-determined goals and objectives.

Teaching-learning process simplifies the various elements of the teaching-learning situation have to be brought into an intelligible whole. The teaching-learner activities which are varied and complex have to be harmonised. These elements and activities induce learners and their individual differences, the methods of teaching, the material to be taught, classroom conditions, teaching devices and aids, questioning and answering, assignments, thinking, enjoying, creating, practicals skills, discussions and many others.

Teaching-learning process is influenced by the totality of the situation. Teaching learning is fruitful and permanent if the total situation is related to the life situations. Teachers can play an important role in, facilitating learning when they take into account the needs of the learners.

Communication in three Dimensions

Interaction between the teacher and the learners is the core of the teaching learning process. This interaction through a sort of three way communication, results in behaviour changes in the learners.

A learner needs the help of a teacher when he wants to learn any subject and to solve any problem. The process of guiding the learner involves eight steps—communication from the teacher to the learner (steps 1 and 2), from learner to teacher (steps 3 to 5), and again from teacher to learner (steps 6 to 8). Through this 3-way communication, teacher could direct his course of teaching concretely. On the other hand, learner can know how well his learning is progressing and how sure he can make his way of learning. So teacher should establish firmly this 3-way communication between many learners and himself.

The formative evaluation in step 7 and KR in step 8 are important to conduct the effective teaching learning processes. KR is a kind of feedback information which has many types. For example, in responding to his behaviour, teacher, says: "good," "wrong," "no," "well," "hum," "wonderful," "interesting" and some times repeats and summarizes learner's opinions. Sometimes teacher gives many non-verbal KR, nodding, smiling, winking, and making gestures.

Major Characteristics : Teaching and learning are interlinked. We cannot think of teaching without learning. The teacher teaches and the students learn. Teaching is not in a vacuum. It is therefore obvious that for making teaching learning sound and effective in our educational institute the teachers must look into its various aspects very carefully and critically so that they contribute in making teaching-learning inspirational and relevant. Following are the chief aspects:

Command, planning and organisation of the subject matter or content and activities : There are no two opinions about the important factors that the success of the teaching-learning process greatly depends upon the thoroughness of knowledge of the subject matter to be taught by the teacher. The soul of effective teaching learning is good command of the subject matter. The next aspect is to present the subject matter to the class. Here we enter into the field of organisation of the subject-matter and the use of methods of teaching and teaching technology. The teacher's endeavour will be to use different dynamic and progressive methods of teaching and learning. He should encourage the students to develop proper habits of learning. He should stress self-learning on the part of the students.

Class control and discipline : Appropriate class control and discipline is one of the most important characteristics of a successful teacher. A good teacher is one who can control his class not through fear or high-handedness but by virtue of his interest in the learner, good command on the subject-matter and the ability to present it interestingly and effectively. The learners also appreciate good teaching and cooperate with the teacher in the teaching-learning process.

Psychology of learners : It must be realized by a teacher that all his knowledge of the subject-matter, his ability to present it methodically and effectively and his ability to control the class situation ably, while teaching will be effective only if he takes into consideration the interests, abilities, aptitudes and limitations of the learners. A teacher must learn to understand his learners and encourage them. He has to be sincere and honest towards his learners. An ideal teacher is always humble. He has to practise tolerance and patience in dealing with the learners. The participation of the learners is very important and necessary if the teaching learner has to have a broader and meaningful process.

Evaluation : Evaluation has an important place in the teaching learner process. A teacher should carefully evaluate his students to find out how they can make more progress. He may use a variety of methods for this purpose. Self-evaluation by both the teacher and the student is very important.

Evaluation Exercise

Teaching remains central to both learning and evaluation. There is an interrelatedness between teaching objectives (ends), learning experiences (means) and evaluation (evidence of what is taught and learnt). Evaluation is the process of determining (1) The extent to which an objective is achieved (2) The effectiveness of the learning experiences provided in the classroom and (3) How well the goals , of teaching have been accomplished.

In evaluation one has to know where students were at the beginning if we are to determine what changes are occurring.

In evaluation one has to obtain a record of the changes in pupil by using appropriate methods of appraisal.

In evaluation one has to judge, how good the changes are in the light of the evidence obtained.

Evaluation may lead to changes in teaching technology and also in learning technology.

Thus, evaluation comes in at the planning stage when teaching objectives are identified. At every point of learning, evaluation is an attempt to discover the effectiveness of the learning situation in evoking the desired changes in students.

Evaluation is integrated with the whole task of teaching and learning and its purpose is to improve learning and not merely to measure its achievement. In its highest sense, evaluation brings out the factors that are inherent in student growth such as proper attitudes and habits, manipulative skills, appreciations and understanding in addition to the conventional acquisition of knowledge.

It has been rightly observed, "The definition of evaluation places it in the stream of activities that expire the educational process; these activities can be reduced to four essential steps: identification of educational objectives, determination of the experiences students must have to attain these objectives, knowing the pupils well enough to design appropriate experiences and evaluating the degree to which pupils attain these objectives."

Objectives provide the starting point on which are based all the learning experiences which in their turn are the material of evaluation.

Teaching objectives : Our teaching objectives are the changes we wish to produce in the child. The changes that must take place through education are represented in:

1. The knowledge children acquire
2. The skills and abilities children attain
3. The interest children develop
4. The attitudes children manifest

If education imparted is effective, then the child will behave differently, from the way he did before he came to school. The pupil knows something of which he was ignorant before. He understands something which he did not understand before. He can solve problems he could not solve before. He can do something which he could not do before. He revises his attitudes desirably towards things.

Specific classroom objectives : These objectives must involve points of in formation, the skills and attitudes to be developed and interests that could be created through the particular topic or subject taken up for work in the classroom:

A statement of classroom objectives:

(1) serves as a basis for the chores of classroom procedures that should provide for suitable experiences to the children.

(2) serves as a guide in seeking evidence to determine the extent to which the classroom work has accomplished what it set out to do.

Learning experiences : A learning experience is not synonymous with the content of instruction or what the teacher does. Learning results from the active reaction of the pupil to the stimulus situation which the teacher creates in the class. A pupil learns what he does. He is an active participant in what goes on in the class. Changes in a pupil's way of thinking and developing concepts, attitudes and interests have to be brought about gradually. No simple experience will result in the change. Many experiences, one reinforcing another, will have to be provided. They may have to be repeated in increasing complexity or levels in meaningful sequence extended over a period of time. A cumulative effect of such experiences will evoke the desired change of behaviour with reference to a specific objective.

The following considerations will be useful in the selection of such experiences:

1. Are they directly related to goals?
2. Are they meaningful and satisfying to the learners?
3. Are they appropriate to the maturity of the learners?

The Improvement

It is worth bearing in mind that learning is what students do, teaching is what the academic staff does and that improvement in teaching can only be demostrated if there is consequential improvement in learning. On the other hand, improvement in learning may occur for reasons that have nothing to do with teaching, for example, students are able to spend more time, gain better access to libraries and become more strongly motivated.

As observed by prof. R.S. Adams and others, "Students may learn what the teacher intended them to; they may not. Furthermore, teachers, like others, are fallible, they may not always teach correctly. It follows then that in any learning situation, students may learn correctly what the teacher taught incorrectly or may learn incorrectly what the teacher taught correctly-or fortunately, the opposites."

Finally, although students certainly do learn because of the instructions they receive, they also learn in spite of the instructions they receive. In the process of accommodating to what is being taught students attempt to 'fit' the new experience—into their past experience in to the knowledge, insights and understandings that they have accumulated previously. It is this capability of human beings to transcend their immediate circumstances, to, add into their 'learning' their past experiences, that complicates the instructional process and makes it difficult for teachers to tailor the learning experience appropriately for their (unusually diverse) students. As a consequence, the instructional strategies are often based on different assumptions. Some deliberately set out to exercise control over the learner by :

(i) either trying to exclude outside influences; or
(ii) by trying to build beyond them; or
(iii) by trying to overpower them.

For example some earliér attempts at programme learning tried to confine student attention precisely and exclusively to the material to be mastered. Other more sophisticated mastery learning programmes attempt to both discover and start from what the learner's basic knowledge is and to provide 'branch' programmes catering for individual differences. Operant conditioning, of course, has always represented an attempt to 'override' other influences, however powerful they might be. Outside these more mechanistic strategies, other instructional strategies have been based on other assumptions. For example, where students are expected to learn by emulating their instructors (e.g. as in medical and veterinary training) reliance is placed on observational 'learning.'

Learning Operations

Teaching operations and learning operations are interlinked. Nevertheless teaching operations to be successful must take into account the learning operations needed to accomplish the teaching objectives which themselves are based on learning objectives. It is therefore, desirable to consider the learning operations first. Learning operation are as under:

1. Discrimination of stimulus situation.
2. Response or cognition.
3. Assimilation of relationship between specific elements of the situation and the response.
4. Developing application and control over the environment.
5. Definite behavioural changes.

Teaching operations may be enumerated as under:

1. Presentation of stimulus in a specific control.
2. Bringing suitable responses by organising appropriate learning experiences.
3. Elucidation and elaboration.
4. Setting up drill and review exercises for fixing up the behaviour in the repertoire of learning.
5. Evaluating learning outcomes.

Variables and Components in the Learning Process

1. Task to be learned.
2. Characteristics of the task to be learned.
3. Characteristics of the learner.
4. Conditions under which effective learning takes place.

Components of the Teaching Process

1. Instructional goals

2. Entering behaviour
3. Instructional procedures
4. Performance assessment

A close review of the components of learning and teaching processes reveals that there is a close correspondence between the two. Performance assessment becomes a part of the teaching process so as to confirm whether or not the instructional objectives are realised and it provides a feedback to other components and also supplies data for developing teaching technology.

Dual Processes

Modern teaching-learning process assigns an important place to student-activity. It calls for a child-centred approach. The most distinctive feature of modern society is its science-based technology which has been making a profound impact not only on the economic and political life of a country but also on its educational system. The changes that occur as a result of the impact are broadly described as 'Modernisation'. This modernisation has affected the teaching-learning process in many ways. The recent changes in the concept of teaching-learning process have led to the development of newer areas of educational endeavour. In a traditional society the aim of teaching-learning was the assimilation of the accumulated-stock of knowledge. But in the modern society, the main aim of teaching learning is not acquisition of knowledge alone. It is the awakening of curiosity, the stimulation of creativity, the development of proper interests, attitudes and values and the building of essential skills such as independent study. Teaching-learning process has to serve as a powerful instrument of social, economic and cultural transformation .of the society. Teaching-learning process is conditioned by the nature and demands of society to which the learner should get adapted and attuned. One of the main aims of teaching-learning in the modern society is to keep pace with the advancement of knowledge and skills.

For a pretty long period, the teaching-learning process has been by and large, a process dominated by the institution of professional teachers. Now, the process is to be replaced to a great extent by a process in which the individual learner is expected to take up challenges through an inevitable intellectual revolution. The intellectual revolution has been enabled further by forces of hardware technologies at low cost, socialization process due to interdependence. Besides, projects, farms, factories, markets, excursions and playgrounds will become classrooms in the new teaching-learning process.

3

Media's Effect on Learning

Masses and Technological Media

Among the most significant forces for change in recent years is the technological sophistication we now possess, for this sophistication not only affects our lives in profound ways but also seems to hold tantalizing promise for increasing our efficiency in education (Kinder, 1973). The last 80 years have seen the development of steam-driven, high-speed rotary presses, advanced optics, films, wire and tape sound recordings, simple and complex duplicating and copy machines, radio, television, computers, and communication lasers.

This technological escalation has bestowed upon education proliferation of equipment and materials which can assist in the reorganization and redefinition of educational experiences. In the past, most teaching depended almost entirely on verbal communication between teacher and student, or written communication to the student from printed materials. Although, these communication channels continue to play important roles in the learning process, today's students are learning facts, skills and attitudes from pictures, television, recorded words, programmed lessons, and other media. Once technology enters the school building, dramatic renovations usually begin. With the technological magic touch, a simple school-house turns into a systematized learning centre.

Today, many countries around the world use some form of technological media in education. In a few countries, the use is fairly widespread. Most technological devices and programmes, however, are structured around the needs of the teacher and are employed as teaching aids in the classroom. In other words, most educators are using technology to answer the question : how can technology help the teacher? In a few areas, however, focus is on the needs of the student. There, educators ask the question : how can technology help the learner?

In the instances where the student is the centre of attention, technology is catalyst for educational change. Its absence would made a significant difference to the educational process, because technology is an integral part of a well-throughout system, not merely a teacher's aid:

Locatis and Athinson (1984) define media as the means (usually audio-visual or electronic) for transmitting or delivering messages. Media includes such things as prints, graphics, photography, audio-communication, television, simulating games and computer.

Schramm, Wilber (1973) in his book *Big Media—Little Media, Aid Studies in Educational Technology*, categories computer, VCR, TV as 'Big Media' and 'radio, filmstrips, graphic, audio cassettes and various visuals' as 'Little Media'.

Meaning and significance : Nelson Henry has very rightly observed in *Media and Symbols*, "Educational institutions, left to themselves may not be successful in achieving the educational objectives of the developing societies without the support of the new media." New media, implying mass media, as channels of education gain relevance from their capacity to disseminate information to a great number of people (masses) and make the present educational programmes more effective and meaningful.

According to Dr. Marshall McLuhan whose books *The Gutenberg* and *Understanding Mass Media* throw a lot of light on the subject of mass media, it is the medium which is the message. This means that the medium by which a piece of information or knowledge is communicated to us exerts a profound influence on us. The effectiveness of a piece of information depends upon the medium through which it is imparted.

Dr. McLuhan thinks that electronic media affect the sensibilities greatly because they tend to massage the sense. Thus, the medium is not only the message but also the massage because it massages the sensory organs and stimulates them to respond actively. Therefore, it is important that the mass media be utilised in the classroom teaching so that the students may obtain sensory stimulation as a part of the process of instruction.

As observed by Wilbur Schramm in his book *'Big Media-Little Media'*, mass media can be made use of in education "as support models in two basic but overlapping ways."

(1) They can beamed part of environment into which learning activities are designed as seen in distance teaching institutions.

(2) They can be brought into the environment as indirect partners or as tools in the hands of the teachers, by supplementing additional or supportive information that is educationally important and useful.

Mass media are means of impersonal communication via some medium, imported through mediated situation. Mass media are means or instruments of communication that reach large number of people or pupils with a common message. The matter may be printed like newspapers or it may take the form of radio, television and cinema. Carlton W.H. Erickson observes, "In recent years technology has swept through society from research laboratories into manufacturing communications, the space age, and finally now, into education."

In early times, the teacher was the only medium of communication for children. He taught his students orally. During the course of time the invention of the printing press, led to the printing of books. Then came newspapers. Now for quite some time new mass media like radio and T.V. are increasingly used in education. They reach large members and also help in improving the quality of education.

Schools and colleges for long have been the sole medium for imparting information and aiding in the acquisition of knowledge. But with the technological development and fast expanding knowledge, new avenues of education have come up. These media disseminate information which the schools can no longer ignore but needs to be integrated into the teaching-learning process.

The National Policy on Education 1986 and modified policy, 1992 has observed, "The media has profound influence on the minds of children. The mass media make the constraints of time and distance manageable. Modern educational technology must reach out to the most distant areas and the most deprived section of beneficiaries simultaneously with the areas of comparative affluence and ready availability."

Mass media serve some important functions. They are helpful in reaching large number of people. They are helpful in the spread of compulsory education and adult literacy. Recently their use is being made increasingly in distance education. They are useful in making instruction more effective and meaningful.

The use of radio, supplemented by correspondence programme has proved to be very successful in Kenya. Radio forums as a means of adult and continuing education have proved to be extremely successful in Canada, India, Nigeria, Sweden, Tanzania and many other countries.

It is sometimes felt that the mass media tend to diminish the importance of the teacher. It is also claimed in certain circles that they are likely to replace the classroom teachers. A close look at the use of these media of education indicates that they are supplementary media. A lot of work by way of pre-telecast, during telecast and post-telecast remains to be done by the teachers. Many gaps are to be filled up by them. In spite of the explosion of technological media in the developed countries, they still occupy the place of importance. Fears about the replacement of teachers are unfounded.

How Broadcast Programmes Benefit Schools ? : There is hardly any doubt regarding the potential of the radio as an instructional aid. Frederic Wittis has rightly remarked : "I like to think of education by radio as a timely, vital and dramatic thing; a system of learning or acquiring more information, a means of widening one's horizon or enriching one's life and breaking down prejudices through inspiration and not perspiration; an education by desire and not by discipline; a pattern of swiftly changing pictures, events with keen interpretations, not statistics and formula's; a moving panorama of the world in which we live—right now, while we are living in it—not a dreary drill of textbooks and tests. In short, I feel that one of broadcasting's most helpful contributions to education and one of its real responsibilities to itself and its listeners is the popularising of education itself."

R.G. Reynolds writes: "Radio is the most significant medium for education in its broadest sense that has been introduced since the turn of the century. As a supplement to classroom teaching its possibilities are almost unlimited. Its teaching possibilities are not confined to the five or six hours of the school day.

It is available from early morning till long after midnight. By utilising the rich educational and cultural offerings of the radio, children and adults in communities, however remote, have access to the best of the worlds's stores of knowledge and art. Some day its use as an educational instrument will be as common place as textbooks and blackboards."

Merits

1. Bringing the school into contact with the world around.
2. Helping in the spread of elementary education.
3. Helping in the promotion of adult education.
4. Assisting in the spread of non-formal education.
5. Enrichment of school programme.
6. Furnishing up-to-date material.
7. Developing critical thinking.
8. Developing leisure time interest and appreciation.
9. Providing opportunities for student participation.
10. Providing an alternative approach to the education of out of school children.
11. Imparting vocational skills.
12. Popularising science with a view to developing scientific outlook.
13. Promoting emotional and national integration.
14. Providing information about population education, energy conservation, preservation of wild life etc.
15. Serving as a training component for teachers.

Limitations

1. Radio broadcast is a one-way communication. Students cannot put questions to the broadcaster.
2. The educational value of radio broadcasting depends merely on the use of sense of hearing.
3. The students have little opportunities to participate in the instructional activity. They are passive listeners for most of the time.
4. In several cases, broadcasting time does not suit all educational institutions.
5. The number of receiving sets is not adequate in the case of several educational institutions.
6. It becomes very difficult to integrate school programmes which radio broadcasts.
7. A continuing listening on the part of the students may make them inattentive and uninterested in the task of gaining learning experiences.
8. Usually there is paucity of adequate pre-information, manual or guides regarding radio broadcast with the result that the students and teachers both face difficulties in making necessary preparation for the utilisation of these programmes.

Suggestions for effective broadcasting

1. The school broadcasts should not be merely course lessons but should have a wider horizon of application in day-to-day life.
2. The school broadcasts should be planned according to the needs of the syllabus, students and concerned teachers.
3. Teachers should occasionally meet, discuss and plan the type of assistance required on mass media instructional facilities.

4. The radio programmes should be intended to give supplementary information to the various topics in the syllabus.
5. Good planning and administration is highly needed so as to make the programmes effective and worthwhile.
6. Broadcasting time should be suitable to schools.
7. Adequate feedback should be provided.
8. There should be proper follow-up on school broadcasting programmes.
9. Adequate listening facilities should be provided in schools.
10. Broadcasts should be made in easy and simple language.
11. Broadcasts should be made in a pleasing style.

In short all the six main stages of a radio broadcast namely, production, preparation, listening to the programme, feedback, consolidation of acquired knowledge and evaluation should be carefully attended to.

History of school broadcasting : Ever since the start of school broadcasting by British Broadcasting Corporation (B.B.C.) in 1920, it has made rapid strides in making sound contribution to formal education, In the U.S.A., in 1923, there were programmes in accounting from New York: programmes in arithmetic and literature from Oakland in 1924, 20 States in U.S.A. had provision for educational broadcasting.

Around the same time about 98% of the schools in U.K. were equipped with radio and there were regular daily programmes. Bombay Station put out items of special interest to school children. Madras had regular school broadcasts for half an hour on all weekdays. Similar programmes were introduced by Calcutta Station in 1932. The programmes for schools produced by Akashwani Stations are for the following categories of people:

(a) Children of primary classes;

(b) children of secondary and higher secondary classes;

(c) Preparing lessons for secondary and higher secondary classes near examination times;

(d) Teachers;

(e) General enrichment programme for children.

These broadcasts can either be 'live' or 'transcribed' depending on the physical presence of the person broadcasting or his recorded speech. Broadcasting organisations throughout the world, including AIR, include in their output various school broadcasts. Such programmes are normally arranged in consultation with the heads of various institutions. This liaison between the radio and educational authorities helps in bringing out effective and useful programmes for the pupils. The planning of such talks is undertaken with great care and by persons of repute. The programmes are prepared termwise and copies are supplied to schools sufficiently in advance to enable the teachers to discuss the subject with the pupils.

Educational Television (ETV)

ETV in the world : TV has become child's third parent and a first teacher. The history of television shows that it is a very powerful, informative socializing and mobilizing force. Most of the countries of the world have gone for television to solve their difficulties and problems relating to education. Direct television instruction started four decades back in progressive countries like UK and USA The regular programmes were sent on air in November 1936 by BBC. Remote areas were provided with television sets. By 1958 more than 98% of the population was covered by television transmission. By 1961 Moscow and U.K. shared the programmes with each other. By 1962 American engineers, succeeded in bouncing television waves across the Atlantic on a Satellite-Telestar. In 1967 the first regular service of coloured televisions in Europe began on BBC-2.

For the first time, television for instructional purposes was used in the USA. A large number of experiments in instructional television were conducted there. In 1958, a project entitled continental classroom started instructional television for the whole of USA. It telecasted a programme "Physical of the Atomic Age" for science teachers. About 40,000 teachers received instruction through this programme. Later on, several programmes such as modern chemistry, contemporary mathematics and new biology were also telecast by this project. In 1961, a project called "Mid-west Airborne Instructional Television" started instructional television. About 13,000 schools received the programmes benefiting about five million students, at a cost of 7.5 million dollars or at an expenditure of 1.5 dollar per student. At present there are hundreds of instructional television programmes being telecast in USA and other countries.

Significance of educational television : Television is the most potential instrument in educating masses and thereby narrowing down the gap of progress between the developing and developed countries of the world. For a country like India which has vast and inaccessible areas, different climatic conditions, large and ever growing population, TV can be an important central media in providing functional, formal and non-formal education to the masses. It can also help in bringing about social and cultural changes bearing on art, music, drama and literature. It is through television that stimulating and thought-provoking views of renowned statesmen, scientists, educationists, artists and teachers can be shared by all. Television helps in enforcing the public understanding of social, political and scientific advancement of a country. Following are the important merits of television.

Chief merits

1. It permits the use of the best available teacher to teach a subject for a large number of student viewers. It

preserves the expert teaching skills of such teachers on video tape or film for later use.

2. It provides a common experience to all students when they all see the same basic ideas or techniques on television.
3. It provides the teacher an opportunity to observe the instructional methods and ideas of their experts and to increase his own knowledge of teaching methods and stimulate new ideas.
4. It provides technical advantages not readily available in normal classrooms for illustration or demonstration.
   (a) It makes possible close-up magnification of small objects, components, intricate mechanisms, diagrams, etc.; giving student a "front-row seat."
   (b) It allows instantaneous change of perception by switching from a wide camera angle to a close-up or by "zooming" in.
   (c) It permits relationships between two illustrations or time lapse between two stages of a process by dissolving one picture into another.
   (d) It provides for comparison of two or more illustrations by superimposure or 'split screen' effects.
5. It directs the attention of the student to the exact detail of object which he should see by eliminating distracting surroundings.
6. It makes quick and lasting visual and rural impressions which can often reduce the time necessary to teach an idea or technique.
7. It makes it possible to bring large, scarce, new or refined equipment "into the classroom" electronically.

8. It incorporates useful film sequences, slides, graphic art and makes available teaching aids within a television presentation, tailored to meet the needs of a particular course or subject.
9. It saves time, effort and cost of setting up classroom projection equipment.
10. It brings instructional films into classrooms as needed with no special classroom preparation, no darkening of rooms or use of special ventilation in the room.
11. It provides more "immediacy" than instructional films.
12. It brings live demonstration, video-tape or film presentations to the classroom at the instant or immediately after they occur.
13. It permits inclusion of up-to-date information, modification, new equipment or techniques into the classroom instruction.
14. It allows the teacher time to observe individual students or to assist them during the television presentation, or to determine what needs further application after the presentation.

Limitations

1. The medium is limited to one-way communication from teacher to students. Students cannot put any question.
2. The total cost of teaching by television is more than normal classroom instruction, unless television is used to reach large number of students at one time or sequentially over a period of time.
3. Television has special and unique techniques and requires occasional re-arrangement of subject sequence.
4. Individual differences of the students are not attended to in a TV lesson.

5. TV lessons may not suit the school timings.
6. TV lessons are not flexible.
7. Instruction through TV is not child or learner centred.

Kinds of educational

1. Total TV teaching.
2. TV as a complementary basic resource.
3. TV as a supplementary environment.

Kinds of educational TV

Open circuit television : It is the usual type of telecast by commercial or non-commercial stations.

Closed circuit television (CCTV) : It is the selective telecast which can be used only by specially equipped receivers. Its range is limited to the length of the cable. CCTV can be used to great advantage in educational institutions. Its capabilities are as under:

1. It increases the range of instruction to one or more locations beyond the classroom.
2. It enables institutions to present televised instruction in accordance with their specific needs and schedules.
3. It provides opportunities for the exchange of professors and courses between one institution and another linked to a circuit.
4. In teacher training institutions CCTV with video-tape-recorders can be used to record performance of the teacher trainee during micro-teaching lessons. Video-tape provides the necessary feedback.
5. CCTV is used in many medical colleges in developed countries. The entire operation can be covered by using a single television camera or a battery of cameras located at vantage points.

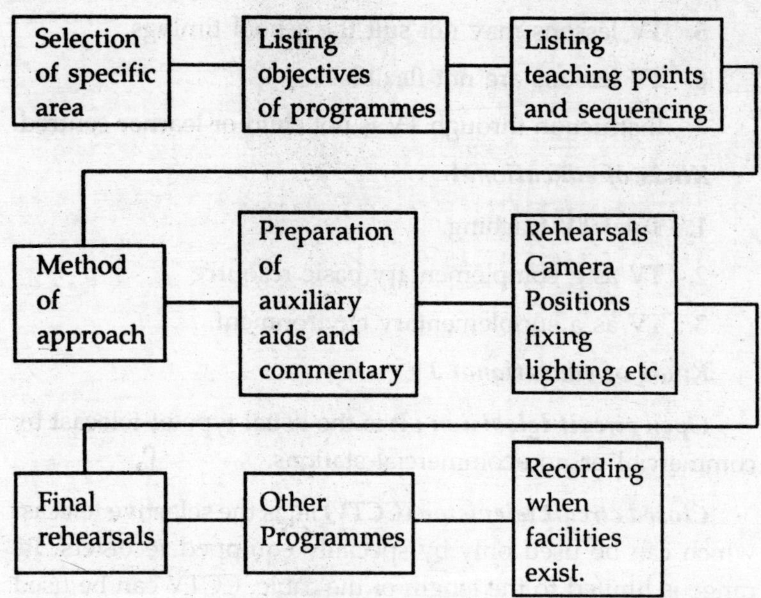

Fig. : Basic procedures in programming ETV.

Part Played by Teacher

School TV programmes have five main stages and it is necessary that the teacher should be associated with each stage.

1. Planning and Preparation
2. Presentation
3. Production
4. Utilisation
5. Evaluation

Teacher in the planning and preparation of TV programmes: No TV programme for schools can be planned and prepared unless the classroom teacher is effectively associated with this work. To plan and prepare a good TV lesson, a thorough knowledge of the requirements of the students of different age levels, the suitability of the materials, the sequence and the contents are very vital and this can be met fully only by the classroom teacher. Experience tells that the classroom teacher can contribute effectively in this area if he has a good grounding and knows very well the mechanics of a good TV lesson.

Teacher in the production of TV programme : Production is a technical thing but the knowledge about the mechanics of production must be known to the classroom teacher if he is to appreciate a good lesson, i.e., to locate its strong and weak points and suggest improvements.

Teacher in the presentation of TV programme : Again, in the presentation of a TV lesson it is only the classroom teacher who can deliver the goods—no doubt a teacher with initiative, imagination and subject competency. The presentation involves only a selected number of teachers but the scope of selection involves all the teachers of a subject. A good selection can be possible only from a TV trained group. It is noted that without necessary training in this field even a very good and competent teacher in a school fumbles and stumbles in the studio.

Utilisation of TV programme and the teacher : Pre/post telecast utilisation is the area where the teacher is the master of the situation. It may be emphasised that no TV lesson is complete without the introduction and follow-up exercise in the classroom by the subject teacher. An average lesson with proper and well thought introduction and follow-up can become a very effective lesson whereas a good lesson in the absence of one or both can go flat. The teacher has to inspire the students, prepare them and arouse their curiosity before the telecast of the lesson and afterward has to clarify the doubts, if any, provide the missing links and re-inforcement in the follow-up. He has also to integrate the TV lesson with his classroom teaching. He has also to take care of many other factors and provide congenial conditions to enable his students to really benefit from a TV lesson.

Teacher in the evaluation of TV programme : Evaluation is another important area. If tackled properly, it contributes considerably to the quality and usefulness of TV lessons. No evaluation is possible or worthwhile without the involvement of the classroom teacher. Moreover, simply involvement of the classroom teacher does not help much unless he is fully conversant and properly trained to evaluate and assess the TV lesson from all angles and has acquired competency to do the job well. Without proper training the teachers even fail to fill up the check-sheets properly—an exercise to be completed by the classroom teacher after every lesson.

Facilities of Physical Nature

Once the television becomes an integral part of classroom teaching, the physical facilities available in the schools are as important as the quality of the programme, from the utilisation point of view. No matter how rich and valid the TV programmes are, they cannot reach the audience unless optimum physical facilities are available to the viewers. The availability of physical facilities appears to be quite simple yet it requires a constant vigil to keep them all in operational readiness.

Broadly speaking we can classify the physical facilities into three categories : (a) Space and seating arrangements. (b) TV sets, Antenna and other accessories. (c) Literature.

(a) In each TV viewing school, suitable space area must be earmarked for television viewing depending upon the number of viewers. Ideally speaking each class that has to view a TV lesson, should have TV set, fitted in the classroom itself but it is not possible. Therefore provision of a room, which can be converted into a TV room should be made, Hall is another alternative for large number of viewers. Other points to be taken care of are: (i) Placement of TV set and its adjustment, (ii) Seating arrangement, (iii) Lighting, (iv) Ventilation, (v) Space for demonstration, per-telecast and post-telecast activities.

(b) It is needless to say that the TV sets should always be in operational condition so that these can be switched on at a very short notice. The various factors that put operating off are: (i) Defective power points and plugs, (ii) Defective Antenna, (iii) Misadjustment of TV controls, (iv) Major defect in the TV, (v) Voltage fluctuations, (vi) Operational procedures like locked cupboards etc.

(c) The school television programmes by and large are syllabus based programmes and therefore the students must know the connecting links between their classroom teaching and the television programmes. These should reach the classroom teacher in the beginning of the session or term as the case may be.

Relevance of Films

Broadly speaking, a film is a· multiple media of communication. It presents facts in a realistic way, dramatizes human relations, arouses emotions and transmits attitudes. It may be used for the communication of ideas, attitudes and experiences to the masses of people. It is very effective in adult education. An educational film has been described as the greatest teacher because it teaches not only through the brain but through the whole body. It has a very powerful influence on the minds of children and is shaping their personality. The main aim of educational film is to elevate and educate them according to the patterns and principles set by the society. A good educational film should help the students to develop a sense of citizenship. A film on national integration can be prepared to help inculcate ideas of oneness and unity. 'Live and let Live' can be that theme. A variety of topics—historical, biographical and of current interest can be covered.

Some of the main advantages of motion pictures are given below :

Increased reading interests of the students : Various investigations conducted in USA. show that film producers arouse increased reading interest in children. They are stimulated to get more information about the fact they have observed in a film show.

Real learning situations : The film puts before us the learning situations which look to be quite real and actual. The child sees something happening and his experience is direct. Therefore, he is deeply impressed.

Selected learning situation : A child learns from his actual life experience more than he learns from the lessons which he gets passively in the school. But life experience comes as a routine.

Sometimes it has no educative value. Sometimes it may have adverse influence. But in an educational film, all the learning situations are selected ones. They have a great educational value.

Quickness of movement : The events in a film show run very swiftly but without losing continuity and essence of development. Therefore, the effects are also received swiftly in a concentrated form.

Vividness : The learning situation is quite vivid. Everything is happening in such a way as if it is more than living and actual. All the activities are quite vivid.

Motivation : The film motivates teaching. The child takes a great interest. A long study of many weeks may not be able to bring home the acts of the French Revolution to a child but he will at once understand and learn everything about the movement if he is shown a film of the events.

Recreation : A film show is recreational also. It is a play for the child and not work. Thus he learns through playway. He feels light and happy after the show.

Development of study habits : Educational films develop study habits as children like to know more about the facts they have learnt in the show.

Illustration of all the learning situations : We cannot give an .adequate idea of an ocean to a child who has never seen a lake even. A child cannot understand what a mountain is like if he has never even come across a hill in his life. But it is not possible for us to take every child to the ocean and mountains, to the deserts and valley, to the Tundras and the Tropics. The film serves us here wonderfully. It brings the ocean, the mountains, the deserts, the valleys the Tundras and Tropics, all in their form and with all their grandeur into the school hall.

Charles, F. Hoban and E.B. Ormer summarise the educational advantages of films as: means of imparting information, development of skills, development of attitudes, enlarging interests and development of the will to solve problems.

The Odds

1. Educational films sometimes include an element of fiction in historical events.
2. Recapitulation in not possible on the spot. Sometimes the teacher likes and the pupils too wish to dwell longer on a particular shot in the show. But the film does not wait. It goes no.
3. Really good educational films are not available in our country.
4. The whole process is very costly. All the schools cannot afford to have good halls, projectors and other equipment for the purpose.
5. It may have some bad effect on eyesight.

6. Generally teachers are not trained to handle the projector and organize the show.
7. It needs electricity. Many village schools have no electricity.

Suggestion for making the optimum use of Educational Films.

The most important point to be taken into consideration is that the film must be relevant and purposeful.

When a film show is going to be arranged, the teacher should see that it is really needed in connection with the studies which are going on. He must discuss the background of the learning situations to be presented in the film show, previous to presentation. It should serve the purpose of recapitulation. The whole process may be arranged in the following steps :

1. Preliminary talk about the film.
2. Presentation of the film.
3. Discussion and follow-up on the film.
4. Recapitulation and recording of salient features.

Film Society for Children

The Children's Film Society India (CFSI) was established in 1955 as an autonomous body with the objectives of promoting and encouraging the Children Film Movement in the country. It also aims at providing children and the young people, films with clean and healthy entertainment. The organisation is engaged in production, acquisition, distribution and exhibition of the films suitable for the children and young people. The main office of the Society is at Mumbai and Zonal offices are at New Delhi, Chennai and Kolkata.

Since its inception, the society has produced and purchased about 100 feature films and 104 short films.

A pilot project to reach the rural children in Maharashtra by means of Mobile Film Unit has been in operation for a number of years.

Four children film clubs are functioning, viz., one at Kolhapur (Maharashtra), two at Porbandar (Gujarat) and one at Mumbai.

The society organises film festivals and participates in important international films festivals abroad. In India, the first international film festival was arranged in Bombay in 1979.

In the year 1981, the Indian festival was accorded 'A' Category status by the International Centre of Films for Children and Young People (ICFCYP), Paris.

The society has set up a National Centre of Films for Children affiliated to the International Centre of Films set up at Brussels under the sponsorship of UNESCO. Some of the important films a teacher can make use are : (1) *Scout Comp,* (2) *Guru Bhakti,* (3) *Ganga Ki Lahren,* (4) *Bachon se Batten,* (5) *Gulab Ka Phool,* (6) *Ekata,* (7) *26 January.*

Medium of Newspapers

The press is an informal but very influential agency of education. The press includes newspapers and magazines. They provide a variety of information. They cover almost all areas of knowledge. They keep us well-informed. They are very useful in the teaching of various subjects. Instruction through newspapers introduces variety and an element of 'playway'.

The newspapers are very useful for the study of languages. Pupils learn many new words and many new expressions. They learn how to express themselves and how to follow the expression of others. As regards social studies they learn how the society is developing day by day. They learn a lot about the society. There is much geographical and scientific information also in daily papers and magazines.

For international understanding the study of newspapers is essential. Children come to know how the world is progressing, how we are woven internationally, how the events occurring in one country affect all the other countries of the world and how we shall have to suffer if the Third World War breaks out.

In the teaching of arithmetic, the newspapers can furnish examples concerning banks, interest on savings accounts, deposits is also very helpful in the teaching of economics and commerce. Likewise a lot of information on various subjects is available form newspapers which can be used in daily teaching.

4

Media Issues

The Idea

Communication is an integral part of one's life. We constantly exchange our ideas, thoughts and emotions with others, in our everyday life, to satisfy our physical, emotional or other needs. Infect, it is impossible for the society to survive in the absence of communication.

There are various meanings to the word 'communication', like "sharing of experience on the basis of commonness" (Wilbur Schramm); "one mind affecting another" (Claud Shannon); "the transfer or conveying of meaning" (Oxford Dictionary).

Communication is a dynamic process of action and interaction towards a desired goal. Thus, it is "a process of sharing or exchange of ideas, information, knowledge, attitude or feeling among two or more persons through certain signs and symbols."

Practical Characteristics

Communication needs a sender, a receiver and a channel,

be it language, paint, song or anything. Being at the heart of all social action and interaction, communication is a relating tool that creates understanding, facilitates work, and strengthens collective living among people.

The primary function of communication is to inform, educate, entertain and influence people to make them function smoothly. It also has a secondary function to perform as well through debates and discussion, cultural promotion and integration; it fosters creativity and understanding among people, groups, and societies so that they live in peace and harmony. These functions have been discussed below:

Information : Information is regarded as power. The more informed you are, the more powerful you become. Communication provides us enormous information about the environment in which we live. Information such as news of war, danger, crisis, famine etc., is important for that helps us in taking appropriate steps to safeguard our interests.

Instruction : Instructing, educating and socializing the members of the society is one of the major functions of communication. Communication creates awareness, provides a fund of knowledge, expertise and skills, gives direction and opportunity to people so that they can become an active member of the society.

Persuasion : With the passage of time this has become one of the major functions of communication. Persuasion helps in reaching decision on public policy in order to make possible to control and govern.

Entertainment : Entertainment is the need of every individual in order to break the monotonous routine of daily life and to divert their attention from the troubles and tensions. It not only revitalise our personality but also educate us. Communication provides entertainment through films, music, drama, art, literature, comedy, sports etc.

Debate and Discussion : Debate and discussion are the two ways in media through which public can clarify different viewpoints on issues of public interest and come to a general agreement on matters that concern all.

Integration and Cultural Promotion : Communication is a great integrating tool. It enables different individuals, groups or cultures to come to know each other, and appreciate others, way of life. It also provides opportunity for culture to be preserved and promoted.

Varied Formats

All of us are engaged in a variety of communication acts. There are:

Intrapersonal Communication : It is talking to oneself, listening to oneself and relating one to oneself. This helps us contemplating, conceptualizing and formulating our thoughts or ideas before we actually indulge in overt communication.

Interpersonal Communication : This is the universal form of communication that takes place between two individuals. It is person-to-person contact, which includes everyday exchanges that may be formal or informal by means of words, sounds, facial expressions, gestures, postures etc.

There is face-to-face interaction between two persons in interpersonal communication and so it becomes very effective because one gets immediate feedback. It is also possible to influence the other person and persuade him or her to accept your point of view. It also has an emotional appeal and can motivate, encourage and coordinate work in a much effective manner than any other form of communication.

Group Communication : This is an extension of interpersonal communication, where more than two individuals are involved in exchange of ideas, thoughts, skills and interests.

This kind of communication provides an opportunity for people to come together and discuss topics of common interest.

Communication in a group serves many goals like collective decision making, self expression, increasing one's effect, elevating one's status, relaxation etc. On the other hand it also has many limitations, as it is time consuming and often inefficient. In addition imbalances in status, skills and goals may distort the process and the outcome sharply.

Mass Communication : Another form of communication which involves communication with mass audience in Mass communication and the channels through which this kind of communication takes place are referred to as mass media. But both mass media and mass communication are generally considered synonyms for the sake of convenience.

Any mechanical device that multiplies messages and takes it to a large number of people simultaneously is called Mass Communication.

Thus, it is clear from the above definition that mass communication is a special kind of communication in which the nature of the audience and the feedback is different from that of interpersonal communication.

The two main components of mass communication are thus audience and feedback.

Audience : Whosoever is the recipient of mass media content constitutes its audience. Here the audience is large, heterogenous and anonymous in character. Heterogenous in the sense that messages are sent to people in all walks of life, each person with unique, characteristics. By anonymous, we mean that the receivers of the messages tend to be strangers to one another and to the source of those messages.

Feedback : Feedback in mass media is slow and weak. It is not direct as in face to face exchange and is invariably delayed. Considerable time and money are required to process the feedback received from the audience.

Streams of Different Nature

Mass media is broadly divided into print media and electronic media. Print media has a history of about 500 years. Whereas the electronic media are products of the 20th century.

Print Media : It includes newspapers, magazine, books and other printed matter. Their growth was slow in the beginning but as the demand for education and information increased, they evolved quickly and flourished greatly.

Electronic Media : It includes radio, television, satellite TV, cinema etc. They provide instantaneous communication and their impact is greater. This differentiate it from print media. Electronic media are quicker than print media as the latter takes more time for mass production and delivery to a widely dispersed population.

Radio : Time of its inception is in 1920s. And since then its network has expanded a great deal. One of the best advantages that radio has over other media is that it can serve and entertain an audience which is otherwise occupied. However, the radio has suffered a setback in the recent times because of TV, which has attracted especially the urban population.

Television : With a modest beginning in the 1930s, it has become a powerful media of mass communication. It has grown into a massive network of mass information and mass entertainment.

The newer development in network technologies is that of satellite-Cable television. Audiences now have multiple choices ranging from news and information to entertainment of wide variety.

Films : Films are considered a major mass medium because of their mass appeal and influence on society. They set trends in styles and tastes, dominate the popular radio and television entertainment programmes.

There has been rapid expansion of mass media all over the world in recent times. People now have more access to mass media whose reach is getting wider due to technological advancement. The mass media are now not limited to urban population but have made inroads into small towns and villages. People now have more access to information and thus have become better and more informed and educated. However, despite the growth of media, its reach is largely limited to urban areas in India.

The Print Media, although a powerful means of communication cater only to audiences that are literate. There are about 20,000 newspapers and other printed matter produced in major metropolitan and big cities in the country but only a small fraction of reaches the rural masses.

The television network has also increased tremendously covering 80 percent of the, population. But again TV is out of reach of the majority of the rural masses. Only the few in the village have access to it. The new development in this direction have been the linking of satellites via cable to the TV at home. Again even if audiences in small towns and villages have access to these sophisticated media, the messages are lost on them because they are not area specific and lack local cultural flavour and relevance, which is very necessary for audience to identify with and understand.

Radio is one of the significant media of mass communication. Government owned All India Radio covers 80% of the area and 90% of the country's population. But again the broadcast receiving facilities are limited. There is also a vast imbalance between the availability of radio sets in rural and urban areas. Inspite of the imbalance, radio is the only medium which is said to be truly a mass medium in India because it is a low cost mobile means of communication.

Films has become a major medium of popular entertainment. But again film exhibition facilities in the country are limited. Most of the cinema houses are in the metropolitan cities and towns.

Affection Reality

Our age is the age of mass communication and mass communication performs certain functions that are useful to us. Millions are exposed to a variety of messages each day. But the question is what is the extent and nature of its impact?

By and large mass communication messages are positive i.e., Pro-communal harmony, anti-drugs, anti-AIDS, anti-war, anti-terrorism, pro-national and so on. Infect, it has helped in promoting national integration and has created awareness among people about the socio-economic and political development of the country.

But the adverse effects of mass communication have also been felt and that to not so much from print media as from television and cable T.V. and overdose of T.V. is bad and gives ideas about a materialistic culture that doesn't exist.

A model is an abstracted representation of a reality. It only represents the reality of communication for better understanding of the communication process and is not a reality. Models are based on assumption that theorists make as to how communication functions and what effect it has upon individual and society.

Development of Models : The earlier models of communication were simple but inadequate. Aristotle constructed a model which had only-speaker-speech-audience-these three were elements, and the basic function of communication was to 'persuade the other party'.

By 1950s models became more elaborate and adequate. The universally applicable models of communication are those of Shannon and Weaver's.

Some Examples

Harold D. Lasswell's Model (1948) : Lasswell presented a strictly verbal model which takes the form of a question:

Who

Says what

In which channel

To Whom

With what effect?

Identification of source, analysis of message content, choice of channel, characteristics of audience and evaluation of effects are the 5 components of communication process. It is the 'effect' that the model emphasizes the most change in one of these elements will lead to a change in the effect.

Claud Shannon and Warren Weaver's Model (1949) : They were the first to develop an engineering model of human communication based on telephone communication. In this model communication begins with an information source who creates the message, he transmits it by means of his vocal apparatus which acts as a transmitter, through the air as the channel with noise interference to the hearing mechanism of the person he is communicating with acting as the receiver which recreates the message so that another person, a receiver, can receive it.

Their model is important as it introduces the concept of 'Noise'. Noise refers to channel that may interfere with the signals transmitted and produce different signals.

Charles E. Osgood's Model (1954) : His model is different from the earlier attempts in the sense that it doesn't follow the conventional pattern of communication from source to channel to receiver.

He emphasized the point that each participant in the communication process sends as well as receives messages and as such encodes, decodes and interprets messages. This is particularly true in interpersonal communication.

Wilbur Schramm's Model (1971) : He adopted Shannon and Weaver's model and introduced two concepts of encoder, decoder, redundancy, feedback and noise into his model. He stressed the importance of feedback and noise, where feedback refers to response that a receiver makes to a source's communication.

According to him in a conversation between two people, one is constantly communication back to the other. The feedback obtained in such situation plays a very important role in the communication process as it tells the source how his messages are being received and interpreted. The 'Noise' may contaminate the message and make communication ineffective. In many instances a message is likely to suffer deterioration before it is decoded and interpreted by a receiver.

Wilbur further viewed the communication process as a complex one in the context of personal, social and cultural factors. Communication, according to him is a process of sharing of experience. The source can encode and the destination can decode only in terms of experience each has had; for e.g., if we have never learned German, we can neither encode nor decode in that language.

He further elaborated this model by bringing into focus the frames of reference of persons participating in the communication process. A (source) and B (destination) have the same kind of situation, have the same social resources and face similar constraints. If the destination decides that the message is interesting and promising enough, he selects some of it or all of it, interprets it according to his frame of reference and disposes it according to his needs, values, social imperatives and constraints.

George Gerbner's Model (1956) : In his model communication is seen as a transmission of messages. There are three stages in his model. The first stage is horizontal. It starts with an event E as perceived by M (Human being directly or through a Machin). M selects E according to his perception of the event. Thus, the process involves interaction and negotiation.

In the 2nd stage, which is vertical dimension, converts whatever we have perceived into a signal. This is called message. Here, it is also important to select the appropriate 'means'-the medium channel of communication.

The 3rd stage is again horizontal. Here the meaning of the message is not 'contained' in the message itself, but is the result of an interaction or negotiation between the receiver and the message.

Theodore M. Newcomb's Model (1953) : This model tries to explain the role of communication in a society or a social relationship. According to it, communication maintains equilibrium within the social system. This model assumes significance in the light of people's increasing need for information. Infact, in a democracy people need adequate information about their social environment so that they can identify their problems and share with their group, and know how to react.

Bruce H. Westley's & M.S. Maclean's Model (1957) : This model is an extension of Newcomb's model and specifically adapted for the mass media. It is based on the assumption that messages in mass communication pass through check points called 'gatekeeper' before they are actually received by audience. They decide on which messages are to be transmitted and how their content are to be modified. Thus, the audience's exposure to an event's reality is in the gatekeeper's hands.

But this model also has a drawback and that is that it applies only to mass media and fails to take account of the relationship between the mass media and the other systems through which we fit into society like family, work, friendships, school, trade unions etc.

Every communication order is ultimately conditioned or influenced by the political system and cultural milieu and the ends and purposes for which it is to be used. What could India's freedom mean to the concept of mass communication? What could be the type of new orientation for individual media, their functional roles and dimensions, their goals and priorities?

With the dawn of freedom, the Indian media were delinked from the apron-strings of British political and cultural imperialism. As part of the sovereign national system, they could now be used to serve the people and the nation according to new visions and national goals, policies and targets set by the new architects of the nation, the media managers and experts.

However, when the Britishers left, India was emaciated by the Partition and was left at the lowest level, politically, economically, socially and communication wise. There were yawning gaps in the communication infrastructure. India's tryst with its new density was therefore very uncertain.

Politically, the Constitution of India, enforced on 26 January 1950, the first Republic Day, had granted to every citizen and media the freedom of speech and expression and to every adult the right to vote and elect legislators. The establishment of a representative system of government, gave the right to every citizen to be informed, that is to have reasonable access to social, political, aesthetic, normal and other ideas and information vital for the grooming of enlightened voters and inculcation of democratic citizenship. It also implied the right to reasonable access to competitive sources of information and media. These rights which flowed out of democratic citizenship enjoined new obligations on the communication media and government to inform and educate the citizens and children of the country and at the same time stimulate awareness about fundamental and other civic and social duties. It was generally agreed that mass media of communication would have a key role in the building of our democratic polity and illumination of our social fabric.

With the beginning of the era of planned development since 1950-51, another role of the media of mass communication came to the forefront. It would provide communication support to the plans and inform people about the philosophy and objectives of plans, about the targets and benefits accruing to them as also about their responsibilities involved in the planned efforts. The other demand on communicators was to enthuse and involve people by removing ignorance and superstitions, by changing their negative attitudes and motivating them into purposeful action, all through persuasive and two-way communication.

The dimension of their task was underlined by the Study Team on Mass communication sponsored by Ford Foundation, which observed that "India's development task is so great and her population so large that only by the most efficient possible programme of public information necessarily emphasising mass communication can communicators hope to reach people often enough and effectively enough to activate, on the needed scale, discussion process and subsequent action in the cities, towns and villages." In this context, the Vidyalankar Committee stated that the principal aim of publicity or communication was to prepare the minds of the people to meet the challenges of these new problems.

On the basis of studies on development and communication done in India, UNESCO and various developing countries, as also on the basis of field-based experience and communication and promotional research studies and surveys, a new professional thinking on the concept, role and process of relevant communication gradually emerged. Broadly speaking, the purpose of communication came to be understood as :

(1) politically to create, inform and enlighten public opinion, the basis of a democratic developing society to create awareness among individuals as also about their fundamental duties and obligations to promote scientific temper and national cohesion in society and inculcate the spirit of cooperative partnership among all sections of people, and to foster the establishment of feedback loops and research methodologies to assess public opinion and interpret it;

(2) economically, to act as an activist in the extension of technology transfer among various sections of farmers, workers and other members of the working force, to provide a supporting pad to efforts at modernization and economic growth, afford market and tourist information and to stimulate advertising and promotional campaigns; and

(3) culturally to foster individual and community expression, discovery, enrichment, creativity and enlightened reaction.

This type of purposeful and dynamic communication system couldn't grow out of the mass media-oriented Western concepts, models and theories, which were not very relevant to rural areas in India or any other developing country. It had to be evolved out of a process of trial and error, experimentation and deliberation. Conceptually it had to be envisaged and shaped by professional committees or bodies especially to be set up for the purpose and reinforced by the directions and guidelines of intentional, regional, national and local seminars, conferences or memorial lectures. Such a system could not grow it was sustained and nurtured by the committee, trained and socially and professionally oriented practitioners and their managers as also by a competent research base. But above all, none of these things would happen unless the efforts in this direction get the policy backing and financial and administrative support of the government and proper appreciation and cooperation of the media and their organisations and the people.

Common Point of View

After Independence, challenges and experimental opportunities came in quick succession. Rehabilitation of refugees, the problem of integrating the recognised states, the Kashmir issue, green revolution, communal disturbances, strikes, inflation, abject poverty, colossal unemployment, malpractices in the public distribution system, corruption, shortage of essential commodities and housing facilities, wars, local and general elections, student unrest, gheraos, walkouts and many more problems constituted serious challenges. Fortunately, policy support and communication aid sanctions flowed from the dynamic and supporting leadership of the various Indian Prime Minister's and their governments.

New dimensions of importance were given by these personalities. As a supporting measure professional introspection, trend setting and guidelines came from the various mass communication and professional bodies and media commissions and committees set up by the government from time to time. Eminent among the bodies which left their impress on the communication scene of India included the first Press commission, UNESCO sponsored Evaluation Study Team on TV, the Study Team on Mass Communication sponsored by the Ford Foundation, the Vidyalankar Committee for the Study of Five Year Plan Publicity, the Chanda Committee on Broadcasting and Information Media. All these bodies were set up or functioned in the sixties and seventies. The Verghese Committee on Autonomy for Akashvani and Doordarshan, the Kuldip Nayar Committee on News Agencies, the second

Press Commission, Satellite Instructional Television Experiment evaluation teams and the Joshi Panel on TV Software deliberated and submitted professional guidance emerged from the numerous UNESCO or international, regional and national communication and media seminars, conferences and evaluation and promotional surveys and reports undertaken by various research teams.

Political Viewpoint

A look into the visions and dynamic and supporting leadership of the various Indian Prime Ministers and their governments would reveal that without them many Indian communication systems and patterns or strategies of mass communication would have remained still-born. In fact, the individual trend and directional setting in the communication process by each Prime Minister has been pronouncedly significant. For instance, Pandit Jawaharlal Nehru, India's first Prime Minister, sought to make mass communication a process of dialogue more than a merely to and fro communication, and certainly more than downward communication. A builder of modern India, he was also a builder of the communication system and media in our country. His package contribution was the laying of the foundation, securing extension a modernization of media, introducing professionalism, tempering of media freedom with social responsibility and giving a rural and research orientation.

The second Prime Minister, Lal Bahadur Shastri, reinforced Pandit Nehru's directional and managerial model by adding a focus on professional integrity and dedicated service. The third Prime Minister, Indira Gandhi and her government have provided a thrust for sophisticated multi-media technology. Blending and balancing with the resurgent indigenous technology, it aimed to ultimately strengthen and streamline the entire communication network to make it more rural service worthy, elastic and effective enough to offer services of international standard to prestigious international meets in India as also to provide communication support to the implementation of the 20-point programme. The new technology helped in rearing the confidence building-role of the electronic media which operate in the public sector. Smt. Gandhi's government also recognised the importance of a free press but insisted on its responsible functioning and observance of a code of ethics in the discharge of its professional and social responsibilities. There was a focus on the need of the Indian media and practitioners to play a leading role in the New World Information and Communication Order to seek a balanced and two-way flow of information in the world, so as to contribute to the maximum extent possible to the South to South cooperative communication efforts and programmes. There was an emphasis on using media for national unity and integration. Liberalisation of the import policy for facilitating media machinery and material for faster mechanisation of the media units, ensued while offering encouragement to communication research and training and media development programmes.

The fourth Prime Minister, Morarji Desai and his government sought to emphasise on autonomy of media, including that of Akashvani and Doordarshan, austerity and professional integrity. The fifth Prime Minister, Choudhary Charan Singh and his government, during his short tenure, endeavoured to bend the functioning of the media primarily for the benefit of rural areas and agriculturists. The seventh and the present Prime Minister and his government are additionally focusing on the application of computer and other modern technologies and are emphasising on open university educational aspect of mass media and better professionalism and programming.

There is a consensus of media experts, however, that the real architects of India's present modernised, multimedia, integrated, development oriented system of communication were Pandit Nehru and Indira Gandhi—as a matter of coincidence father and daughter. If India has entered the satellite, electronic and modern visual communication age, it is primarily for the vision and dynamic leadership of these two Prime Ministers. If our country has developed and revitalized traditional and other indigenous media, and made them in conjunction with modern mass media as instruments of innovative and development communication, specially in the areas of family welfare, health, agricultural extension and eradication of illiteracy, the credit for this too goes primarily to the incisiveness and initiative of these two leaders and their governments.

Apart from bequests of national leaders, there are existent visible and invisible contributions of several other professional and individual entrepreneurs, exponents, trainers and researchers who have helped individually and co-operatively in making our communication system what it is.

Modern Viewpoint

Since Independence, the concept of mass communication in India has been transformed. From the Western theories-based hypotheses it has now become most flexible, relevant and development-oriented. Now, a participatory type has been envisaged by the 7th Plan for a decentralised form of planning system at the district level. Four stages have marked this transition in our country:

(1) communication considered as a process of transmitting information, ideas, thoughts, feelings and attitudes to large anonymous audiences with an accompanying hypodermic model of who says what in which channel to whom with what effect;

(2) a distinction being made between informational communication and persuasive communication seeking

to influence the behaviour or attitudes of the respondents;

(3) focus in media strategies shifting from mass media to media mix or relevant communication technologies. Experience and research revealing that with literacy, financial and technical problems rampant in a country, there could be very little success by adopting only big media strategies. Attention thus started being fixed on low cost small media such as low powered radios and indigenous or folk form of channels as well;

(4) communication being accepted as a multi-disciplinary science or a distinct discipline supported by its own hypotheses, systematic knowledge, research methodologies and trend and case studies.

This nebulous concept of positive, multi-lateral promotional communication of participatory type came to be known by different names, such as development communication, development support; communication, integrated rural communication, participatory communication and the like. The philosophy behind these themes was to provide a meaningful system in developing countries to harmonise development and communication efforts aimed at giving the rural and urban people a better deal. While the relationship between the two was accepted by all, the issue of cause and effect has remained still unresolved. In other words, which is the mover and which is the moved, remains a chicken and egg question. Whatever the perception, both development and communication are now considered engaged in a reactory system, one helping the other, complementing and supplementing each other in the process of fostering balanced growth and progress. If people have access to mass media, and the messages are segmented and relevant, even rural people with low literacy rates and per capita incomes can be sensitised, motivated and changed.

Being considered different from terms like advertising, public relations, propaganda, agriculture extension, rural communication, promotion, marketing communication and even the Western concept of mass media-oriented communication, the term 'development communication', in the Third World countries has acquired a more positive and pragmatic role and result-oriented connotation. As explained by Nora Quebral of Indonesia, this brand of communication implies "the art and science of human communication applied to the speedy transformation of a country and the mass of its people from poverty to a dynamic state of economic growth that makes possible greater social equality and the larger fulfilment of human potential." This development support concept of mass communication is thus dynamic, purposive, practical and promotional in approach and nature. It is a new hope for development and social change in the Third World. Though not a panacea for all ills, it is one of the vital components in any development planning and implementation. This science and art of communication views an individual, a society or a nation in its totality, transcending thereby from a piecemeal or a segmented view of rural or urban society, economic and human development. In our country development communication combines in it the philosophy of humanism of Pandit Nehru, intending to achieve a better, richer and fuller way of life, along with the growth and development of the country as a whole. Another strand of the concept which is typically Indian is that development communication should grow mostly out of people's participation and people's satisfaction, the essential ingredients of which are:

(a) a sense of feeling to have actively participated;

(b) a sense of pride in evolving co-operative solutions to the problem in hand;

(c) a sense of achievement, reflected in the concrete betterment of poorer sections of the people and of backward areas.

Research studies based on Western models ascribe to mass communication different roles in development, varying from nil to the enthusiastic, from a cautious to a pragmatic position. Lloyd Sommerlad a UNESCO expert projected a balanced and pragmatic picture about the role which communication can play in national development. In his view "communication is an important element in the matrix of influences which lead to innovation and modernisation of a society. If used constructively, the media can help create an environment favourable for change and development. They can enlarge horizons, bring information about the experience of others, raise aspirations and help to provide the motivation for improved practices and social conditions. They are part of the process of teaching new and better ways of working and living. The extent to which communication, both interpersonal and mediated, contributes to development depends on the policies and strategies adopted and the skill with which the tools are used. Essential will be the planned use of extension services and the media, co-ordination of the parallel channels of communications, co-operation between various government and private agencies involved in the development; a programme appropriate to the cultural background and provision of participation, feedback and a multilateral flow of information."

The communication revolution in India is experiencing the confluence of three stages of technological growth: wire, wireless and integrated. True to its tradition of assimilation of foreign and indigenous elements, India is pressing into service the earlier and modern media and using high cost and low cost communication technologies. Her Song and Drama Division, Field Publicity units and extension agencies, padyatras, folk media and human activist system on the one hand and satellite, colour TV, video, cassette, computer, electronic and digital technologies used in press communications and telecommunications on the other indicate the balance the country holds so as to meet the needs of her mammoth, multi-media mass communication exercises, movements and campaigns. Some of the innovative multi-media programmes involved in the green and white revolutions in the northern states, TV coverage during the course of SITE, Kheda, on-going SITE and INSAT—IB experiments and the 9th Asiad, 7th Non-aligned and recent Commonwealth Summit and Namedia meets are pointers to the evolution of the spirit and urge for innovation and experimentation. Similar trends were visible in the video technology based experiment for intercommunity communication near Delhi, the Farms School programme of All India Radio and the newspaper communication support for Chattera Village initiated by the Hindustan Times, a Delhi English daily.

Apart from these illustrations, the government sector publicity media units provide more robust and wider display of media mix. For instance, outside publicity done through Field Publicity units undertake a variety of publicity programmes like film shows, group discussions, talks, seminars, song and drama programmes and photo displays. These pertain to major national themes like national integration adult education, child welfare, family welfare, agriculture and agro-based small-scale industries. Similar programmes are also organised to make people aware of social evils like untouchability and drinking. The Song and Drama units utilise live entertainment media to make the masses aware of the various national programmes and objectives. It has a wide range of stage forms like puppet shows, plays, dances, dramas, ballads, harikathas and sound and light shows.

The mix used by the Directorate of Advertising and Visual Publicity is a visual package. It comprises press advertisements, illustrated printed material like posters, folders, leaflets, cinema slides, metallic tablets, radio and television spots and photographic exhibitions.

Another set of print medium mix for mass circulation is brought out by the Publications Division of the Ministry of Information and Broadcasting comprising books, pamphlets and journals in Hindi, English and other Indian languages on a wide range of subjects including art and culture, history and tradition, political evolution, democratic process, economic development and social resurgence.

Thus we see that whether it is the sphere of agriculture, family planning or government publicity India has been pursuing the policy of appropriate mix of media and technologies. This has entailed the use of face to face, group, written, printed; visual, folk, computerized electronic, outdoor or even a mix of them. The approach has been multi-media and cross-disciplinary, goal and result oriented. Centralisation in core programmes have been successful in so far as it has sought to stimulate unity in basic plan programmes or achieving integration in national cultural programmes, but it has equally underlined the importance that at grassroots level the development programmes should be localised and area specific and implemented as far as possible by the involvement of local people, but you need to support decentralisation which has inherent value, by an integrating system. Here the challenge to media practitioners and managers is in finding ways of making satellite and other big media an integrating force, at the same time making them help to knit together several decentralised activities at the grassroots level.

The family planning communication package is an example. It envisages an all out effort at dovetailing of population education in the formal educational system as also in the non-formal training programmes of functionaries of development departments. It has centralised programmes integrated with decentralised activities. Its media package is wide complexioned and involves a still more dynamic package comprising radio, TV, colour films in 16 mm film strips, cinema slides, exhibitions, tape recorders, newspapers, magazines, posters, folders, brochures, leaflets, hoardings, wall paintings, bus boards, match box labels, dramas, puppet shows and other local folk art media. Its symbols and slogans are splashed all over, from mud walls in villages to telephone and telegraph poles in cities, reminding people that family planning is an intrinsic part of the environmental scene and an aid to family welfare.

Alongwith discovering new media mixes, strategy of field publicity or extension is also changing. The necessity of people's involvement and obtaining their feedback is calling for modification in the strategies known by various names as area approach, pooling plans or district-level decentralised plans.

India has made use of another multi-dimensional, multimedia and demonstrational audio-visual aid called exhibition. In size, stature and character it varies from stationary to mobile or even exhibition on wheels; from simple village exhibitions, trade fairs and a seasonal market to very big, modernly designed multi-levelled complexes, known as national and international exhibitions or world trade fairs. These exhibitions use a package of communication media ranging from spoken word, exhibits or visuals to video, TV, films, radio, projectile aids, traditional media, promotional literature, outdoor publicity aids, balloons, neon light and sky splashed advertisements. Cumulatively these exhibitions draw large crowds and their impact differ from creating awareness and publicity to more dramatic results in terms of transfer of technology and sale of goods and machinery. Policies and programmes of government are also publicised through photographic exhibitions. Art exhibitions and gallaries promote education about art forms of various kinds.

Whatever form that these innovatory types of communication strategies may take-person-to-person or group, written, printed, visual, folk or electronic, indoor or outdoor, hot or cold, or even a mix of them-the basic feature is that these programmes are goal oriented, research fed, professionally planned and executed and assessed. They are pragmatic and multi-media and disciplinary in approach. They are fairly sensitive and alive to criticism and suggestions and in a sense quite responsive and flexible.

The dimensions of integrated communication system which are found relevant to rural India warrant closer relationship between the administrative and communication agencies; credible and knowledgeable sources; segmentation of messages for different audiences; linkage of information to the felt needs of the people; and projection of timely usable, solution-oriented and people-beneficiary messages. The other requisite preconditions of a successful system of communication are management decentralisation for effective participation of people and the inculcation of the philosophy of empathy among the media practitioners and managers and policy makers.

Despite a large measure of success in mass communication, one big lesson that emerges out of the Indian scene of communication is that we must continuously rediscover the goals and dimensions of mass communication and its media. To this end, our communication system, our postulates, our media's role and their functions need to be periodically or as a part of inbuilt research, assessed, modified or revamped. This would help us realise our cherished dreams of a sunny future without being swept off our feet or alienating us from our fundamental values. Here the application of feedback research is significant. So is the contribution of a professionally and media-oriented and socially activising training system, which can strengthen the country's capacity for attracting to the communication, advertising and public relations professions, man of vision, integrity, independent judgement and professional aptitude. This would help equip them with media climated and field based knowledge and skill to serve our society.

5

Significance of Learning

Kid's Importance

A Dictionary of Education (1981) by Derek Rowntree considers child-centred approach to education/teaching, as, "Rather wordily slogan, but its main point is made by teacher who claims 'I teach children, not subjects'. Implies care for the 'whole' child-his Personality, Needs and Learning Style and not just for his or her academic process."

The Concise Dictionary of Education (1982) by G.R. Hawes and L.S. Hawes defines child-centre education as, "An educational theory or system that emphasises the pupil and his or her individual characteristics as central in conducting instruction instead of focusing on subject matter, external authority, and educational requirements. Curriculum is constructed according to the pupil's interests and needs."

In their book *A Critical Dictionary of Educational Concepts (1986)* Robin Barrow and Geoffrey Mitburn observe, "The essence of child-centred education is, self activity, that the child should be at the centre of concern. ...Explicitly or implicitly, child-centred educationalists tend towards a view of *Education* being a process of leading out rather of imparting knowledge."

Child-centred education stresses the need for taking care of the child, its growth and development. It requires 'individualisation' of approach, so that one must study each child carefully, keep observations over a period of time, study the growth and development in sensory—motor area, intellectual area, emotional area, social area, language area, and so on.

The Aim : The aim is development of the total personality of the child.

Programme : Programme is to be activity-based with different teaching strategies.

Pace of learning : It is to be based on children's needs and abilities.

Teaching-learning : Teacher's role is that of a facilitator in learning and development.

Discipline : It is to be achieved through the maintenance of positive human relationships between teachers and pupils.

The need

1. The child is agent in his own teaming. Out of the three components of a learning situation; the child, the teacher and the components of a learning situation environment, pride of place is to be given to the child. He must become the most important agent in his learning. It means that curriculum must be thought of in terms of activities and experiences which appeal most to the child.

2. Children learn best when they are active. When we

consider the child an agent in his own learning, we must provide for him to be active. The medium of learning is the activities undertaken by the child. Learning takes place through a continuous process of interaction between the learner and his environment.

3. Knowledge or information is not the goal. Self-realization is the goal. Personality and character are more important than the subject matter. To possess all the knowledge of the world and lose one's own self is an awful fate in education.
4. Child-centred approach is more psychological than logical. It emphasises the process rather than the product.
5. Child-centred approach gives freedom to the child under the creative and sympathetic direction of the teacher.
6. One single exposure to an experience does not affect all the necessary coordination of the physical and mental faculties of a child to preserve the net value of exposure. Hence there has to be repetitive exercises and drills to give a certain knowledge and the efficiency and tenacity of a skill and value. It is here the child becomes a trainee and the teacher becomes a trainer or the child an educand and the teacher as an educator.
7. A child is a unique being and can function only by remaining in the world in which it has a specific role to play. The teacher's role in the world in which it has a special role, both in its spirit, is to help the child to conform to its unique habitual values, choices and consistent behaviour patterns.
8. The child's sense of wonder and astonishment and his natural curiosity lead to a learning process which should be encouraged by teachers.

The limitations : Child-centred education has a few limitations which must be taken care of by the teachers. Too much freedom is likely to engender ego-centricism in children. Children may grow to be unwilling to accept reasonable authority. If all the times and at all places, likes and dislikes, preferences, whims and interests of children are elevated above the mature judgements of parents and teacher, it may result in undesirable outcomes. Adams, therefore, wanted that both the children and their teachers should be on the same footing of importance.

Pragmatically speaking, learning cannot be child-centred always in absolute terms. Child-centred education implies that each child may have a separate learning activity besides a few group activities. Perhaps no nation can afford to spend so much money, resources and time on child centred education. Child-centred learning is confined to the learned discourses of educational thinkers. There are so many children under the charge of a teacher that it is rather impossible to attend to the specific needs of children individually.

Corrective measures : Of course emphasis on child-centred education tends to free the child from the tyranny of the traditional approach to education which meant 'chalk and talk', 'bookish knowledge' and the 'supremacy of the rod'. Implicit in all the positions of child-centred education is that the teacher must be prepared to give initiative to the learner in the educational encounter. The teacher as well as the child must remain active in the teaching-learning activity. The teachers must take the initiative and find out the limitations of the learner's own spontaneous and undirected activity. The teacher has an obligation to assess the limitations of child's choice of educational activity. The teacher's legitimate role in encouraging self-disciplinary function cannot be over-emphasised.

The role of the teacher in child-centred education.

1. Motivation of children.
2. Developing trust and confidence in children's capacity to learn.
3. Becoming as a resource for creating meaningful learning experiences.
4. Accepting the individual and the group.
5. Participating as a member of the group in guiding learning.
6. Becoming sensitive to the child's needs and interacting in a way that would provide a sense of feeling and security.
7. Recognising and reinforcing the individual contribution. Principles of Teaching

The educators and philosophers have emphasised certain principles of teaching which the teachers are expected to bear in mind for making their teaching effective, efficient and inspirational. Sometimes these principles are classified as psychological and general principles. This classification is however very arbitrary and both types overlap.

Psychological Principles

Principle of activity or learning by doing : Children are active by nature and any process or method that is not based upon the student activity is not in accord with the progressive educational theories. Rousseau considers the child as a "hero" in the drama of education and as such he must be allowed to play the dominant role. So the first principle is to keep the class active.

Children have been endowed by nature with tremendous vitality. In the words of T.S. Avinashilingam, "The great Ganga of life flows majestically on. But if anyone tries to retain and dam it, the dam will break unless attempts are simultaneously made to divert it into other channels. The waters can only be diverted, but cannot be dammed indefinitely. If anyone tried to do the impossible, it would be at his peril, for the dam will break, sooner or later. So is the nature of children. The great vitality of our children cannot be permanently restrained without providing a positive purpose. Thus, providing for various types of activities which will interest the children and give them opportunities for observation and the use of their hands is to offer them the fulfilment and satisfaction which nothing else confers."

Activity does not mean mere physical activity. If a pupil is to develop all sides of his personality, then it is necessary for him to be active in all ways, to exercise all the powers he has.

Principle of playway : This principle is closely related to the principle of learning by doing. According to Froebel play is the chief activity of childhood. It gives joy, freedom, contentment and inner and outer peace. It holds the source of all that is good. But "without rational conscious guidance," says Froebel, "childish activity degenerates into aimless play instead of preparing for those tasks of life for which it is designed."

Play is a natural activity just as a poet cannot refrain himself from writing a poem, a musician from singing, a dancer from dancing and an actor from acting, so too a child cannot refrain himself from playing. Play comes from within. It is a voluntary activity and is the manifestation of creative urge. It gives joy, freedom, contentment, inner rest and peace with the world. This implies that a spirit of playway should prevail in classroom work.

Principle of motivation : The teacher will do his best to motivate all children in the lesson. Motivation arouses the interest of children and once they become interested, they are willing to concentrate and work. Motivation is developed by the following techniques:

(i) Utilising the instinctive tendencies of the children in an effective manner.

(ii) Satisfying the curiosity of children.

(iii) Utilising all the senses of children.

(iv) Relating closely body and mind.

(v) Linking teaching-learning with life.

Principle of self education : Best teaching is enabling the child to learn by his own efforts. Teachers must fire the imagination of their students. Children, we are told, must be left free to express themselves, for the best education is self-education. Teachers, we are told, must stand aside. They must talk less, explain less and direct less. Adamson states, "The whole business is between the individual and his world's and the teacher is outside it, external to it. He may facilitate it, turning his attention to one or other member of the wedded pair. He may approach the individual and his avenues of approach will be one or other of the instincts or emotional dispositions which are the prime movers of mental life. He may try fear, pugnacity, curiosity, or sympathy or a combination of them, to quicken the current which seems to him sluggish or he may approach the factor truth, whichever of the three words it belongs to, and see whether anything can be done by lighting it up, or lining in main features and blotting out detail to facilitate adjustment.

But whatever he tries, subject or object or both together, he remains outside the process, a spectator, a manipulator, perhaps a disturber; he is never in it and of it. Within that mysterious synthetic activity through which the individual is at once appropriating and contributing to his environment, forming and being formed by it... the teacher has neither place nor part."

The statement implies that the essential activity in teaching is not the adjustment of child to teacher but is to enable him to adjust himself to the environment and also to change the environment to adjust himself. Teaching must enable the child to work independently and without the teacher at a later stage.

Dr. A.G. Hughes and Dr. E.H. Hughes remark, "It must be emphasised, however, that teachers are not as superfluous as some enthusiasts suggest, teaching is not the baneful evil it is sometimes represented to be. It is true that children are by nature curious, assertive and creative, but they are also submissive, imitative and ready to appeal for help. It follows, therefore, that we are not necessarily working contrary to child nature when we teach. We must, however, know when to teach and when to stand aside, when to explain and when to leave children to make discoveries, when to demonstrate and when to leave children free to experiment, when to require children to listen and when to give them scope for free expression."

The two important aspects of teaching are stimulation and inspiration. The teachers must fire the enthusiasm of their pupils. They must encourage them in the development of their natural desire to work and to be active and guide these desires into worthwhile channels. The late President Eliot of Harvard once said, "The supreme value of a teacher lies not in the regular performance of routine duties, but in his power to lead and inspire his students through the influence of his own mental and moral personality and examples."

Principle of individual differences : No two children are alike. Teaching to be effective must cater to individual differences of children.

Principle of goal setting : A definite goal must be set before each child according to the standard expected of him. Short-term or immediate goals should be set before small children and distant goals for older ones. It must be remembered that goals should be very clear and definite and the children must understand these goals.

Principle of stimulation : Burton has said, teaching is the stimulation, guidance, direction and encouragement of learning. Ryburn emphasises this aspect in these words, "the guidance of the teacher is mainly a matter of giving the right kind of stimulus to help him to learn the right things in the right way."

Principle of association : Thorndike points out that things we want to go together should be put together. Many different things or ideas which we want to go together should be associated with each other. They should form a part of one process. Then it becomes easier to make the students understand their relationship.

Principle of readiness : This principle is indicative of learner's state of mind to participate in the teaching-learning process. Readiness is preparation for action. A teacher must be alive to this principle.

Principle of effect : This principle states that a response is strengthened if it is followed by pleasure and weakened if followed by displeasure.

Principle of exercise or repetition : According to it, the more a stimulus induced response is repeated, the longer it will be retained. Other things being equal, exercise strengthens the bond between situation and response. Conversely a bond is weakened through failure to exercise if it is the principle it has two sub-parts:

(i) Principle of use and

(ii) Principle of disuse.

Principle of change and rest : Psychological experiments in learning have demonstrated that fatigue, lack of attention and monotony can be overcome by making appropriate provision for change, rest and recreation. While framing the time table it is kept in view that subjects and activities are provided in such a way that the students do not experience boredom and fatigue. Usually two consecutive periods of a subject are not provided in a class.

Principle of feedback and reinforcement : Learning theories point out that the immediate knowledge of the results and positive reinforces in the form of praise, grade, certificates, token money and other incentives can contribute to make the task of learning joyable.

Principle of training of senses : Senses are said to be the gateways of knowledge. The power of observation, discrimination, identification, generalisation and application can only be appropriately developed through the effective functioning of senses.

Principle of group dynamics : Under the influence of group behaviour, appropriate changes in the behaviour of the members of the group can take place. Individuals composing the group think and feel as the group feels, do as the group does. A suitable climate for group dynamics is to be created in the classroom environment.

Principle of creativity : Opportunities should be provided to the students to explore things and events and find cause-effect relationships. This principle envisages that every student possesses some element of creativity which must be explored and developed to the maximum extent.

Principle of correlation : Gandhi Ji was of the firm view that Correlation should be the basis of all work. He advocated that correlation of the learning task should be established with the craft, physical and social environment.

General Principles

Successful teaching necessitates that the teacher comes down to the level of the pupils and at the same time assists them in rising above it. To a great extent, the principles of teaching to be followed depend upon the age of the pupils, the subjects and topic of the lesson. However, there are certain general principles which should underline the teaching of all subjects. As already stated, there is no clear-cut dividing line between psychological and general principles of teaching.

Principle of definite goals or objectives : Destination or goals of teaching-learning must be clear to the teachers and students. Goals and objectives keep the teachers and students on the track. Definiteness of goals helps in planning executing and evaluating every step, phase or act of the teaching-learning process.

Principle of child centredness : The entire teaching endeavour is for the child. Therefore, it is essential that teaching strategies should cater to the aptitude, interest and abilities of the students. In the drama of education, child should be assigned the role of 'hero.'

Principle of linking with life : Teaching can never be performed in a vacuum. It is always in a social context. In the teaching of all the school subjects, examples from everyday life should be given their due place.

Principle of correlation : Knowledge is one 'whole.' Various ideas and events are interrelated. There exist links among various subjects. Correlation of the present events can be made with the past. Similarly future can be visualised on the basis of the present happenings or state of affairs. Gandhi Ji propounded his system of Basic education with correlation as its cornerstone-correlation with the craft, correlation with the physical environment and correlation with social environment.

Principle of active involvement and participation of students : Teaching-learning is a two-way traffic. Traditional teaching was almost teacher-centred. There was very little scope for the involvement of the students. The teacher taught and the students listened to him passively. The new teaching emphasises that the students must actively participate in all the stages and steps of teaching-learning.

Principle of cooperation : Classroom environment becomes lively when the teacher and the taught work in unison, helping each other in carrying out the task of teaching and learning. All the participants have the same common interest. Naturally, they must cooperate with teacher.

Principle of remedial teaching : All students do not learn with the same speed and accomplishment. Some lag behind and need extra coaching. The teacher has to find out where the fault lies and think for positive measures. He may have to arrange for remedial or compensatory or extra teaching for any particular group of students for removing their specific difficulties.

Principle of creating conducive environment : Physical as well as social environment of the classroom plays a vital role in motivating the learners. Arrangement of light and furniture etc. should be properly attended to. There should be proper discipline and order. The teacher should be sympathetic but firm.

Principle of planning : Planning determines the quality or success of any task. Planning in teaching involves the preparation of the lesson notes, provision of teaching aids, and working out strategies to be adopted in the delivery of the lesson.

Principle of effective strategies : Teaching process to be effective must adopt proper means, strategies and tactics. A teaching strategy is a generalised plan for a lesson which includes structure, desired learning behaviour in terms of goals of instruction and an outline of planned tactics necessary to implement the strategy.

Principle of flexibility : Strategies should serve as guides for effective teaching. Strategies may have to be changed if the classroom situations so warrant. Teaching is a complex task and a live phenomenon. The possibilities of alternation in planned strategies cannot be ruled out at the execution state. A teacher must be quite imaginative and resourceful for adopting himself and his teaching to the requirements of the teaching-learning environment.

Principle of variety : A variety of teaching aids and strategies should be adopted to motivate and sustain the interests of the students. Variety serves as great tonic for creating fresh environment and checking boredom and lethargy.

Great Adages

Significance : The maxims of teaching are very helpful in obtaining the active involvement and participation of the learners in the teaching learning process. They quicken the interest of the learners and motivate them to learn. They make learning effective, inspirational, interesting and meaningful. They keep the students attentive to the teaching-learning process. A good teacher should be quite familiar with them. Now we proceed to discuss them.

Proceed from the known to the unknown : The most natural and simple way of teaching a lesson is to proceed from something that the students already know to those facts which they do not know. What is already known to the students is of great use to the students. This means that the teacher should arouse interest in a lesson by putting questions on the subject matter already known to the pupils. The teacher is to proceed step by step to connect the new matter to the old one. New knowledge cannot be grasped in a vacuum. A civics lesson on the powers of the President of India may start from the powers of the President of Municipal Board or of the President of Village Panchayat. A lesson on profit and loss in arithmetic can easily be taught to the pupils by referring to the shopkeepers who make profit. A history lesson on Lord Ram may be taken up with the celebration of Ram Lila.

Proceed from simple to complex : The simple task or topic must be taught first and the complex one can follow later on. The word simple and complex are to be seen from the point of view of the child and not that of an adult. We would be curbing the interest and initiative of the children by presenting them complex problems before the simpler ones are presented. In a lesson on nature study, for instance, a child will understand the concept of a flower first and thereafter its various parts. Similarly in a geography lesson the teacher will take up the general study of a region or country first and later on a detailed and specific study.

Proceed from easy to difficult : We must graduate our lessons in order of ease of understanding them. Students' standard must be kept in view. This will help in sustaining the interest of the students. In determining what is easy and what is difficult we have to take into account the psychological make-up of the child. Logically viewed one skill may be easy but psychologically it may be difficult. There are many things which look easy to us but are in fact difficult for children. The interest of the child has also to be taken into account. Lines are very easy to draw but a child may not like to draw lines. He may try to draw an animal. There is no doubt that it is difficult, but it is more interesting to him and so is easy for him. We should encourage him to do so and our approach will be psychological instead of logical.

Proceed from the concrete to the abstract : A child's imagination is greatly aided by a concrete material. "Things first and words after" is the common saying. Rousseau said,

"Things, Things, Things." Children in the beginning cannot think in abstractions. Small children learn first from things which they can see and handle. Very young pupils learn counting with the help of pebbles, etc. A child understands an aeroplane with the help of a model. Actual visits to canals and rivers provide a clear idea of them.

A lesson in geography can be made interesting with the help of models, pictures and illustrations of bridges, rivers and mountains, etc. Care must be exercised to ensure that the students do not remain at the 'concrete stage' all the time. This is only the initial step for children with a view to reach the higher stage of 'abstraction' as they advance in age.

Proceed from particular to general : Before giving principles and rules, particular examples should be presented. As a matter of fact a study of particular facts should lead the children themselves to frame general rules. The rules of arithmetic, of, grammar, of physical geography and almost of all sciences are based on the principle of proceeding from particular instances to general rules.

Proceed from indefinite to definite : Ideas of children in the initial stages are indefinite, incoherent and very vague. These ideas are to be made definite, clear, precise, and systematic. Effective teaching necessitates that every word and idea presented should stand out clearly in the child's mind as a picture. For classifying ideas, adequate use must be made of actual objects, diagrams and pictures. Every possible effort should be made to make the children interested in the lesson.

Proceed from empirical to relational : Observation and experience are the basis of empirical knowledge. Rational knowledge implies a bit of abstraction and argumentative approach. The general feeling is that the child first of all experiences knowledge in his day to day life and after that he feels the rational basis. For instance, plane geometry makes better sense when taught in the context of everyday life instead of it in the format of a highly abstract theory. It is always better to begin with what the children see, feel and experience than arguing and generalising.

Proceed from psychological to logical : Logical approach is concerned with the arrangement of the subject matter. Psychological approach looks at the child's interests, needs, mental make up and subject logically. When we treat a subject logically, we re usually thinking of it from our own point of view and not from the point of view of the child. In psychological approach, we proceed from the concrete to the abstract, from the simple to the complex and from known to unknown. We start reading by teaching the child to read a whole sentence, as for him, the unit is the sentence, not the word or the letter as it is for the adult. This is psychological approach. In a drawing lesson a child has little sense in lines and curves. Logically we start with simple lines and curves but psychologically we start with drawing a whole animal.

Proceed from whole to parts : Whole is more meaningful to the child than the parts of the whole. J.P. Guildford, E.B. Newman and May Seagoe conclude after their research that the 'whole' approach is generally better than 'part' learning because the material to be learnt 'makes sense' and its parts can be seen by the learner as interrelated. The learner sees a relationship between the central idea of the material to be learned. The 'whole' unit or passage for slow learners should be smaller than the 'whole' for the fast learners.

From near to far : A child learns well in the surroundings in which he resides. So he should be first acquainted with his immediate environment. Gradually he may be taught about things which are away from his immediate environment. In a geography lesson we start from the local geography and then take up tehsil, district, state, the country and the world gradually.

From analysis to synthesis **:** Analysis means breaking a problem into convenient parts and synthesis means grouping of these separated parts into one complete whole. A complex problem can be made simple and easy by dividing it into units.

From actual to representative **:** When actual objectives are shown to children, they learn easily and retain them in their minds for a long time. This is specially suitable for younger children. Representative objects in the form of pictures, models, etc., should be used for the grown ups.

Proceed inductively *:* This maxim includes almost all the maxims stated above. In the inductive approach, we start from particular examples and establish general rules through the active participation of the learners. In the deductive approach, we assume a definition, a general rule or formula and apply it to particular examples. An example will make this distinction very clear. 'The farmers in India are very poor' is a general statement in the deductive type of reasoning. The inductive will follow thus: Ram is a farmer. He is very poor. Shyam is a farmer. He is very poor. Krishan is a farmer. He is very poor. In this way from several such examples it will be evident that farmers are poor. Thus, we derive generalisations. Both of the approaches i.e. the deductive and inductive have their own importance. However in general, inductive approach is considered a better one.

Conclusive Part

In the ultimate analysis it must be observed that the maxims are meant to be our servants and not masters. Moreover, by and large all are interrelated. It is also to be kept in view that children differ in their aptitudes, capacities, interests, mental and physical make-lip. Different maxims suit different situations and different children. It is, therefore, essential that a judicious use should be made of each maxim.

6

Magic of Media

In scientific journals sections of the scientific community are talking to themselves, much as a nation talks to itself in its newspapers. But the relationship between journal editors and their readers is a more intimate affair than national newspaper editors could ever achieve with their readers. Journal editors need their readers in a unique way, because those readers are also authors who supply all, or nearly all, the material published in the journals. Journal editors should therefore conduct the relationship with their reader-authors as carefully as they would conduct any personal relationship that they hope will continue and grow into something valuable, enjoyable and of lasting significance to both parties.

A new journal, in particular, depends enormously on how skilful its editor proves to be in shaping, balancing and developing the contents so that people not only read the journal but also subscribe to it. Eventually the journal will gather its own momentum and will be able to maintain its individuality when a new editor takes over. But however well established the journal may be, the editor should at all times exercise firm but flexible control over what goes into it and how the material is processed and presented to readers.

Many questions specific to these aspects of journal editing have so far been touched on only lightly, if at all. This chapter therefore considers editorial responsibilities in general; the mix-of contents; archival information; and the journal as a forum. Under these main headings the points covered include rapid publication, the structure of research articles and priority dates for them, Letters to the editor, editorials and book reviews, anonymity (or otherwise) for the writers of these items, and the time lag in the appearance of book reviews are also discussed, together with society business/professional news, and corrections.

The Journals : Most sponsors endow editors of their journals with considerable autonomy and the responsibility for observing scholarly traditions as they apply to publication. Autonomy allows or stimulates editors to produce successful journals; it also leaves room for the occasional failure. With an eye on success rather than failure the wise editor takes an active interest in helping to define or redefine the journal's aims, policies and editorial coverage, and in recruiting members for the editorial board or for the regular panel of referees. Associate editors and board members should be chosen for their ability to provide support and seasoned advice. For society-sponsored journals the editorial committee should meet regularly and have clear responsibilities in decision-making on general policy matters. This also makes it easier to find a natural successor when an editor resigns or retires.

For any journal to succeed, the editor must aim to publish research articles of exceptional quality. The publisher of a new journal will probably press they editor to accept papers that are rather less than excellent at first, in order to fill the pages of the early issues. Non-descript or third-rate papers should nevertheless be rejected: better a slim journal of reasonable quality than a sub-standard, fat one.

Of course, the more successful a journal is in attracting papers, the higher its rejection rate will be: 80% is typical for weekly medical periodicals, falling to 45-60% for specialist biomedical periodicals though rates differ in different disciplines. Some well-regarded journals in fact accept only those articles rated as outstanding by referees—a policy well worth considering.

To attract large numbers of papers from which the best can be selected for publication, a journal needs a wide scope. On the other hand, if the scope is too wide, it will be difficult to identify the readers and promote the journal to them; and readers will not subscribe to a journal for the sake of one or two articles in each issue that might interest them. The right balance has to be found for this as well as for other aspects of editorial work.

Rapid Publication : One of the editor's main responsibilities to authors and readers is to arrange for papers to be published as promptly as possible. Many journals build up a backlog of accepted articles to give the editor and publisher some leeway in filling issues of a standard size and to allow the editor to balance topics in each issue it is journal policy to do this. Although extra articles that are ready for publication can usefully go to proof stage, forming an emergency reservoir for each issue, the manuscript backlog should not be allowed to grow to an unhealthy size. Most authors would prefer immediate rejection to acceptance if there is to be a year-long lag while papers work their way through the pipeline.

For the editor, a giant backlog produces the risk that authors whose work and ideas have progressed during the waiting period will make numerous changes in proof. To avoid this, editors can offer authors the choice of acceptance with publication within a specified period, or the opportunity to submit their work elsewhere. A better method is for the editor to accept only the most exceptional papers as they arrive, publish them quickly-in issues of uneven size if practicable and return the other papers to their authors immediately.

Some journals have experimented with accelerated refereeing (or no refereeing) and fast production for certain papers only. The editor may have a hard time deciding which articles deserve such treatment and coping with the consequent disruption of printing schedules, but the results for the journal are often worth the extra trouble. Better still is to publish all the accepted paper very quickly, omitting one or more proof stages but maintaining the overall quality of the journal.

Faster publication can also be achieved by reorganizing procedures in the editorial office and-if it seems necessary and if funds are available-by obtaining extra editorial assistance. It is worth discussing the production timetable with the printer to see whether and where any of the printing and proofing procedures could be speeded up (or omitted). Camera-ready copy can of course save time as well as money if authors can be persuaded to prepare it to the editor's and printer's satisfaction.

Wise Aspects : Most journals include both archival and current-awareness elements in their make-up. It is in mixing these elements to match readers' needs and wants, while fulfilling the journal's aims, that editors give their publications a distinctive character. The list of items that may be included in journals is a long one. In a new journal the mix will depend on the journal's cope, on the interests of the editor and editorial board or committee, and on the publisher's assessment of the market.

Editors of weekly journals tend to place more weight on news worthiness when they consider publish ability than do editors of monthly or quarterly archival journals. In the medical field, of example, Sir Theodore Fox argued that in a weekly Journal such as The Lancet, which he edited for many years, the research articles might well be dropped, as they were read by only a small number of subscribers. Ingelfinger disagreed with this view, arguing that part of the function of a weekly medical journal is educational, and that doctors ought to be informed of current research activity even if it is not of immediate practical value to them. In fact, the Lancet continues the mixed tradition with much success.

The sequence of the various sections in each issue of a journal is an indication of editorial priorities. In medicine, for example, the New England Journal of Mèdicine (a society-sponsored journal) publishes original scientific articles first in each issue and has the editorials in the middle, after the case records of the Massachusetts General Hospital (i.e. 'local society' activity) and before the letters to the editor. The British Medical Journal, on the other hand, with editorials that are often on medico-political as well as scientific issues, puts these first, followed by the original scientific articles and, towards the end of the issue, official reports of the British Medical Association. The Lancet (independent) begins with major original articles, hypotheses, review articles and the like, then launches what may be called the 'commentary' side of the journal with the editorials (leaders and annotations), followed by the letters to the editor. The society-sponsored New England Journal of Medicine is, therefore closer in arrangement to the independent Lancet than to the society-sponsored British Medical Journal, and it seems likely that the editors rather than the sponsors or publishers chose the sequence of sections.

It is also interesting to look at Science (society-sponsored) and Nature (commercially published), which both begin with editorial pages. Science confines itself to a one-page editorial before printing major scientific articles and reviews, followed by lengthy news features and commentary. In both journals the short scientific contributions are relegated to the second half of each issue. The arrangements are subtle announcements of editorial purpose, not dictated by pressures from the sponsoring organization, and new editors may learn something from them.

Archival Information : The description 'archival', applied here to research articles, brief communications and review articles, means that the information is expected to have lasting value, not that it is expected to be dull, But unless journals can afford to pay editors or copy-editors to rewrite papers skilfully, in cooperation with authors, there is not much that editors can do to make papers more lively, apart from exhorting authors to take courses in scientific writing, if any are available, and to study they style manuals recommended in the journal's guidelines for authors. The convention IMRAD structure Introduction, Methods, Results and Discussion) of articles in the life sciences is often blamed for the dullness of the average scientific paper. The real reasons is more likely to be that many scientists, however much they want to see their work in print, regard writing up completed studies as a chore for which they have little patience and which gets in the way of the next piece of work.

The IMRAD structure is in fact suitable for many articles and provides novice authors, in particular, with a comforting and familiar framework for their papers. But editors should be flexible and encourage variations on or departures from the conventional structure. The historical-survey type of Introduction, in which 'the problem' too often remains undefined, could well be replaced by an outline of the hypothesis tested, followed by the reasons for examining the hypothesis. Methods and Results can usefully form a single section, and many Discussions would benefit from less rigorous editing, as ideas thrown out casually may spark off new trains of thought in readers minds.

Experiments with journal conventions could inject much-needed life into scientific writing and show that scientific work, like much else, has exciting moments that compensate for the daily slog.

Another tradition worth breaking is the one decreeing that negative results are not worth publishing. Publication of these results would often prevent the work from being repeated needlessly. This is especially true of work showing that statistically significant correlations were not found when these were a reasonable expectation. Editorial policy on publication of negative results was changed in two journals in the early 1970s (Journal of Experimental Education and Journal of Education Research) after Walster & Cleary published an article in defence of negative results.

Interest Creation for Journals

A good way of creating interest in a new journal, or any journal, is to include a few solicited review articles on subjects of topical interest or in a new field or a neglected one. Review article are often what readers want most. Solicited reviews, of course, bring with them the problems common to all solicited articles, Unsolicited -review articles in a new field or presenting an unusual synthesis of ideas, perhaps covering several disciplines, should be considered sympathetically. Established review series tend to be conservative in their choice of topics and authors, and journals can provide a useful service by occasionally publishing more unorthodox reviews. An example of a journal whose editor took on the role of scientific critic and interpreter, a role too often forgotten or neglected, is provided by the Journal of the Royal College of Physicians (London), launched in 1966. This journal aims to publish review articles which synthesize information gleaned from many scattered articles, and to present that information gleaned from many scattered articles, and to present that information in a form helpful to physicians who are too busy to find and correlate all the primary research articles.

An experimental method of generating review articles, or surveys, in an inter-disciplinary field has been described by Jesse. An extensive bibliography was compiled and copies were given to a number of scientists in disciplines related to quantitative microscope. These workers modified the bibliography and prepared papers which were first presented at meetings and then published in The Microscope, together with the revised bibliography which was basically common to all of the papers. The method seems especially promising when information retrieval services can be used in compiling the bibliography.

Priority Dates : A final point about research articles is that priority dates are important to authors and can be vital in some fields if a claim for priority has to be established inside or outside the law courts. Editors have a responsibility for protecting authors' claims to priority by assigning dates to articles. Several dates can be used the date the typescript is complete; the date of submission, taken from either the covering letter or the postmark; the date of receipt in the editorial office; the date a manuscript is provisionally accepted; the date a revised version is received; and the date a final version is accepted. Martinsson has suggested that authors should give the date of completion at (for example) the end of the abstracts submitted for publication with their articles. This is a useful idea but may not be acceptable in some cut throat fields of science. The most practical dates to print for published articles are the dates of receipt in the editorial office and of acceptance in the form in which the paper is printed (ignoring copy-editing changes). (Editors who run their offices single-handed could, however, base the date of receipt on the date of the covering letter for articles that arrive in their absence.) If a paper is heavily revised the date of receipt should be the date of receipt of the revised version. If the author makes substantial changes in proof, of adds new material after the final manuscript has been accepted, the additions should be called a 'Note added in proof ' or should be distinguished in some other way so that readers realize that the material is never than the main part of the paper.

The year in which an article is published is the date used when an author's work is cited, but if questions of priority arise the published dates of receipt (year, month and day) of the manuscripts make it clear who has absolute priority. Editors or publishers should also record the dates on which journal issues are delivered to the post office or other agencies for distribution to subscribers, as these dates can be important in patent disputes and for establishing priority for taxonomic descriptions. The date on the journal cover may be quite different from the date on which the journal actually appears, as well as from the date on which it reaches subscribers-though editors should make every effort to match the printed date with the actual date of issue.

Traditional Aspects : A conventional archival journal which never publishes anything but original research lacks an important dimension. Many journals therefore publish one or more sections providing for comment, criticism, feedback from readers, discussion and controversy. Editors of new journals have a wide range of items to choose from, including Letters to the editor, Editorials (or 'leaders'), Book Reviews, Hypotheses, Speculative articles, Controversies, Current concepts, Personnel views, Seminars, Case conferences, Open letters to public bodies and so on. Editors of established journals may add to, or change, the mix of ingredients from time to time. For example, in 1976 the British medical Journal introduced five new features: Condensed reports, Side effects of drugs, Where should John go? (For would-be emigrant doctors), Views, and Briefing-a balanced mixture of science with practical professional matters.

It is sometimes argued that self-criticism by scientists in their journals may encourage the general public and lay press to criticize scientists unnecessarily. Some editors have therefore discouraged discussion of professional ethics, the environmental dangers of some kinds of experimentation, potential cruelty to animals in experiments, and even standards of scientific writing. But the answer to this is fairly obvious: the public will criticize science and scientists from time to time anyway, and if there is something to criticise it is better for scientists to put their own house in order first.

The recent rash of new journals on the philosophical, cultural and ethical implications of science, which Ingelfinger has commented on, perhaps reflects the failure of established journals to accept enough articles on these implications. The segregation of subjects like this into a sub-speciality may mean that fewer scientists than before will reflect on the raison d'etre of their profession and its contribution to civilization. The blame for this will be laid at the door of shortsighted editors.

Among the many possible discussion and opinion-forming sections of journals, Letters to the editor, Editorials and Book reviews are the ones that appear most often.

Letters to the Editor : Many letters to editors are badly presented, in spite of being written with an eye to publication. Even if an assistant deals with the Letters section, the editor should read all the letters, either before or after the assistant has worked on the selection to be published. Most journals that publish correspondence point out that the editor reserves the right to reject, shorten, excerpt or edit the letters for publication. Editing should, however, be restricted to removing intemperate statements or examples of bad taste. Spelling mistakes should be corrected but the grammar should not be changed unless the writer's point is unclear. Letters should be published as soon as possible after receipt and, except in rare cases, they should be signed. Readers, attacks on an editor's own editorials or on editorial policy should be printed whenever possible- either with a reply if a reasonable one can be given or an apology if one is needed.

The time to announce 'This correspondence is now closed' is when letters on a given topic begin to repeat points made earlier, or when the letters are from the same two or three correspondents. At this stage the writers who disagree can be left to carry on their correspondence privately.

Letters to the editor rarely need to be refereed. Any letters criticizing a previously published article should be shown to the author of the article, whose reply should preferably be published in the same issue as the critical letter.

***Editorials (leaders) and Anonymity*:** Editorials, often called 'leaders' in British journals, are statements of point of view. They deal with one of three types of subject: a new research advance (perhaps underlining the importance of an article in the same issue or putting it into a broader context); a statement of position on some aspect of one of the scientific disciplines represented in the journal or on the interaction between science and society at large; or a discussion of the journal itself-its objectives and editorial policy.

Some journals never publish editorials or any kind, but even archival journals ought to explain their editorial policy at least occasionally, so that contributors, potential or actual, know where they stand. The guidelines for authors, if well constructed, state the purpose and scope of the journal and describe referring procedures and the criteria for selection of papers, but the purpose and scope should not be static and any change in editorial policy should be brought to readers' notice in an editorial.

Editors who want to know whether readers think the purpose of their journals is being achieved can most easily find this out by writing appropriate editorials. Readers will certainly react and if their letters are published they will feel that they are influencing the direction a journal takes. Even the unpublished letters can give editors food for though. The days of authoritarian journals with the attitude. 'The editor and the editorial board know best' are surely over.

Not all editorials are written by editors and not all editorials are signed. Is this anonymity justifiable? Shouldn't the authors be named, to make it clear that they are real people whose judgements may be fallible rather than superior beings making ex cathedra pronouncements? The standard answer to this question is that the editor takes responsibility for all editorials, whoever writes them, and takes the blame for any that seem unacceptable or in accurate to readers. But this is carrying editorial responsibility too far. If the argument were extended to its logical conclusion, no papers in the journal would bear any authors' names, since the editor ultimately assumes responsibility for the papers too.

There are several better arguments in favour of anonymity, as pointed out in a recent anonymous editorial. One is that editorials are sometimes the work of several of the editorial staff, who could not sign en masse. Other editorials may be based on the advice of one or more experts who would not necessarily agree wholeheartedly with the interpretation-perhaps a political one—expressed in the final version. A third kind of editorial may have been provided by a well-informed expert but may need to be heavily rewritten before it can be printed. Or a prominent scientist may be unwilling to sign an editorial because the position it takes either compromises or preempts the stand of the writer's professional organization on that issue. Anonymity also gives younger or less well-known scientists an opportunity to speak freely without fear of being harmed in their careers or having their views discounted because readers have not heard of the writer before.

Although signed editorials are to the preferred anonymity can therefore sometimes be tolerated. In addition it might improve the situation if a new distinction were to be drawn between leading articles and editorials in scientific journals leading articles by experts who are asked to comment on the scientific content and significance of work by other people should be signed, while editorials that are the work of editor is and/or their editorial staffs need not be signed. If the distinction proved difficult to make, editors could allow the outside consultants to decide whether they would sign their work.

Statements of opinion about or on behalf of the profession should usually, be signed, whether written by the editor or by an outside consultant, since the opinion may be against what most people in the profession believe, and an unsigned editorial may carry too much weight with the lay press, the public and too government. Similarly, in a society sponsored journal an anonymous editorial might be taken as reflecting the society' collective opinion of policy. Either a disclaimer should be included or the editorial should be signed.

Editorial comment on research articles in the same issue is particularly valuable a journal of wide scope whose readers may not immediately recognize the importance of every piece of work described or its potential application to them own or another field. To obtain expert comments which can be published at the same time as the article commented on, the editor should first telephone the potential writer to ask whether the leading article (or editorial) could be completed within, say, two weeks. A copy of the final manuscript of the research article can then be sent to the commentator, who may well have been one of the referees. Since it is usually considered an honour to be invited to contribute a leading article, most people will produce it in time. The leading article, could every be accelerated through the printing process to avoid any delay. Or the authors of the research papers may accept a short delay if it means that their article receives greater prominence.

An interesting use of an editorial is to comment unfavourably on an article that the editor has nevertheless decided to publish. The Lancet of 17 September 1977 published an editorial on Bladder cancer and saccharin' which listed what the editor countered to be faults in the research design of an epidemiological study reported in the same issue. The editorial made clear the editor's reasons for accepting the article for publication despite its faults: rumour about the study's results were already circulating and were influencing public policy on whether saccharin should be banned, but since the design of the investigation was open to criticism the study, with its detailed description of the design, had not been accepted for publication elsewhere and could not be judged objectively. The authors agreed to this procedure and their reply to the editorial criticisms was published in a later issue. It would not be good policy to print many editorials of this kind but the example shows how effective it can be to throw away the editorial rule book. Editors should assess their work often, asking not 'Will this set an awkward precedent? But 'What, in this particular instance, will be most conducive to the public good?'

Book Reviews : Anonymous book reviews provoke the same objections as anonymous editorials. The answer is much the same, too; signed reviews are preferable from many points of view but anonymity allows people to write freely when they might not otherwise do so in reviewing books by their friends, enemies or colleagues. Editors who want to be flexible on this point could state that reviews will normally be signed but that the writers may remain anonymous if they insist.

Book reviews can be either descriptive or evaluative. Descriptive reviews, which merely recast the blurb and the list of contents, help to make a book's exigency known but do not help anyone to decide whether to buy it. All list of books Received is more useful then a collection of descriptive reviews, since many more books can be listed than can be reviewed.

Evaluative reviews are helpful to both readers and authors provided that the reviewers in fact discuss the books named: Some reviewers take advantage of their platform in the journal to publicize their own thoughts on the subjects covered, with hardly a mention of the books themselves. This essay type of review is encouraged in journals devoted to book reviews, such as the American Sociological Review, but is inappropriate in journals with short book review sections.

Guidelines and or review forms can be used to set the tone

of the book review section and to discourage reviewers from writing essays instead of evaluating the books under review. The guidelines should state the word limit or range, the time allowed for writing the review, whether it will be signed (as discussed above), whether the reviewer will receive a fee, and what the review should ideally include. Good reviews state the contents of the book, convey its flavour, evaluate it critically, then 'stop' though 'depth and extent of coverage' might be substituted for 'flavour'.

Book reviewers should be as carefully selected as referees are but good reviewers are hard to find. 'The qualities that make for a good critical reviewer are to a large extent the same qualities that make for a good editor, or a valuable member of an editorial board, or a helpful dissertation adviser. Editors should impress on reviewers the necessity for speed, and should telephone beforehand to make sure that the reviewer can take on the work and write the review by the date required. The book review section might also be given preferential treatment, with accelerated production for all or most reviews.

Although reviewers are not usually responsible for the whole of the lag between publication of book and publication of a review, delay by reviewers is a major headache for editors as well as exasperating for authors and publishers. It is unfair to authoress if reviews do not appear for months after publication, especially if the book is about a fast moving subject. Editors can compensate for this by listing 'Books received' as soon as they arrive, whether or not they are going to be sent out for review. Some editors print lists of 'delinquent reviews'; this shows that the editor considered the books worth reviewing but was let down by reviewers.

In newspapers and magazines the apparent zero lag between publication date and review date is achieved for books of general interest by review copies being sent out before the official publication date. Even though publication dates are not usually set in the same way for most scientific books, and though their reviewers are rarely paid, the review lag for scientific books is disproportionately long; Chen found that among 3347 reviews published in 54 biomedical journals in 1970 the review lag ranged from 0-2 months to nine years, but the mean lag was about 10.4 months. In the two journals the Lancet and the British Medical Journal) with the shortest review lags the average lag was 5.8 and 6.6 months, while in the two journals with the longest lags (Acta Radiologica and Therapy, Physics, Biology) the average lag was 42 months.

Editors who can find a way of shortening the lag for evaluative reviews to weeks instead of months and years will be rendering great service to librarians and potential readers as well as to authors and publishers. Many publishers would be happy to help editors by supplying advance information about books in press, or even by providing sets of proofs if reviewers agree to read material in this form. It is worth writing to the major publishers to enquire about this and to establish a convenient mechanism of receiving review copies immediately after publication.

Editors can exercise flexibility and flair over book reviews as well as over other features. One interesting 'review' published not long ago took the form of a long letter to the editor declining the invitation to write the review and stating the writer's lack of qualifications for doing so. But in his letter the writer threw such interacting light on the booking question that many readers must have rushed out to buy or borrow it.

Unsolicited book reviews should be considered on their merits. Editors who don't want to receive such reviews should say so in their guidelines for authors.

Book reviews, like letters to the editor, should be edited lightly, if at all. Errors of fact, spelling and grammar should be corrected. Vituperative attacks on authors or publisher should be softened into something more civilized and not open to a libel action. Negative reviews, however, need not be avoided: readers want to know what not to read as well as what to read or buy. Comments on the price are superfluous is a review: readers should be able to judge from a well-written evaluative review whether a book is worth the money. Suggestions to the publisher that the reviewer would prefer a paper-back, or that the book might have been cheaper if glossy paper had not been used, are also redundant: a paper-back is only cheap if there is a large market for the book and coated paper, which for a short run- book may both be significantly more expensive than matt paper, may be essential for good reproduction of the illustrations.

Journals with Book review sections should always have a Letters to the editor section, and the author (or others) should be allowed to set the record straight on facts about the book or to point out cases where the reviewer has misunderstood the purpose of the book or its it ended audience. Attacks on the reviewer's evaluations are not, however, M order.

In the journal, each review should be headed with the full title of the book the name(s) of the author(s) or editor(s), date of publication, publisher's name and palace of publication, name of series, number of pages, number of tables and illustrations, price, and sometimes other information such as the size of the pages or the name of a translator (see Manten).

Book reviews are often badly indexed in the Contents lists of journal issues as well as in volume indexes. If there is space for all the books reviewed to be included in the Contents lists, the books and their authors should be given priority over the reviewers' names; if the reviewers, names can be included as well, so much the better. In the volume index, a list of book reviews is invaluable whether as a separate index or included in the subject index under 'Book reviews.' Reviews are then listed alphabet under the name of the first author of each book. The title and the date of publication should be given, and preferably the reviewer's name too, though this will appear in the author index. Editors should send two copies of every review printed in their journals to the publishers of the books reviewed. The copies should include the volume number, page number and date of the issues in which the reviews approach, as well as the journal's name.

Society Business and Professional News : Editors of society-sponsored journals may have to publish some or all of the following items of society business: presidential addresses (usually no editing allowed); abstracts or synopses of meetings (which should be edited, if only to show how abstracts of papers in the body of the journal should be presented); reports and resolutions from the society's general meetings; conference papers; and news and notes. If conferences have separate editors who suggest editorial procedures different from those usually applied to papers in the journal, the editor has to decide what the policy will be. If the conference papers are published in a separate issue with a guest editor, there may be delays and disagreement over copy-editing standards. For news and notes, editors must usually accept what their societies provide, editing only for grammar and technical points of style, but ensuring that the amount of material does not outweigh the scientific content of the journal.

A problem facing editors of some society-sponsored journals is that members may expect to have their papers published without any refereeing and even without review by the editor. This privilege is becoming less, common but older members of a few societies or national academies may still expect to benefit from out-dated rules. Editors should try to see that, when rules are revised, a procedure is provided by which the editor can appeal to an editorial committee if there is a dispute.

In both society-sponsored and commercial journals, especially weekly or monthly publications, a section on forthcoming meetings is useful to readers. This section usually needs accelerated production. It should include a note of the publication deadline for such announcements.

Corrections : From time to time, authors point out errors or commissions that they have noticed since their papers were typed or printed. It is more important to correct these mistakes for readers than to establish who was responsible for them. Corrections should be printed in type of normal size, with a heading clearly advertising their existence, and they should be listed as Corrections on the Contents page, preferably always in the same position and giving the full title of the article that is being corrected; corrections should also be listed in at least two places in the subject index of the volume. They should not be buried in an obscure place in the journal in the hope that nobody will notice that a mistake has been made; this practice goes against good scientific principles, though it is common in many leading journals.

This chapter has mentioned a few ways of handling some features in journals, but the best mix of articles and other items will always depend on the personality and ability of the editor and on the particular circumstances of the journal—the field(s) it covers, its readership, its state of financial health, the quality of its editorial board and referees. Three are no blueprints for producing successful journals, and even if there were, editors would be right to ignore them and create journals out of their own imagination, intuition, good sense and knowledge of the field. Some questions on a quite differing level still remain about editing. Will new technology, for example, help editors to cope with the more mundane problems of keeping their journals going in times of steeply rising costs? Or will that new technology instead destroy journals and books as we now known them?

Happenings and Seminars

Conferences have a special part to play in the transfer of

scientific information. Organizers and editors new to the work may also benefit from the advice of their predecessors on the organizing committees of conference series. This chapter deals with the questions: which conferences are worth publishing and how should they be published and edited?

The publication of conference proceedings is criticized on many grounds. The commonest objections are that 'routine publication... Clutters up the literature and overburdens library budgets', that published proceedings 'are not profitable to scientific endeavour', and that by the time they are published, many of the papers have already been printed with essentially identical data in academic journals as proper publications. Those that have not may have been disapproved by reviewers and editors. The symposia proceedings are not subject to review and there is no distinction between invited and proffered papers. Other objections are that proceedings volumes often sink into obscurity, are carelessly edited, and are published far too long after the conferences they record.

Decisions about whether to publish conferences are influenced by pressures on and from the many conference-goers who are apparently obliged to present papers to earn their travel grants, by the overt or covert aims of organizers and sponsors, and by the opportunism of certain publishers who view conference-goers and libraries as captive markets. "The first kind of pressure often results in many mediocre papers being offered at conferences. To counteract this, in their circulars and invitations the organizers should point out to intending participants and to grant-giving bodies that all kinds of communication at the meeting—contributions to discussion as well as formal papers-are important in their own right. The other two kinds of influence-the ambitions of organizers and of publishers-tend to encourage the publication of mediocre volumes of proceedings. Obviously, some conferences can be transformed into admirable books, and many publishers serve science excellently (and with little profit) when they produce these books. Equally obviously, other proceedings should never have reached the printing presses, and there are publishers who are seduced by guaranteed sales rather than the prospect of a worthwhile product. But while, good sales figures are a legitimate goal for publishers, the organizers, sponsors and potential editors must remember their wider responsibilities to science when they assess whether proceedings are worth publishing. It is not a good idea for editors to lend their names to publishing projects over which they may not have, or do not wish to take, full editorial control.

The Proceedings : Some clues about the content of conferences that succeed as books are provided by book reviewers. In a typical review the writer points out that although the material in the proceedings volume is available elsewhere, the juxtaposition of diverse, loosely connected topics is useful, particularly for someone tying to survey several fields of current interest quickly. I found the volume introduced me to interesting lines of work relevant to my own interests, and I suspect it will serve the same purpose for others. That, after all, is one of the things a good symposium should do.'

Another reviewer praises the clarity of the discussion sections and then says: 'At many meetings such discussion is more valuable than the formal presentations, for it brings out the points which the speaker may have passed over but which other participants do not follow; much of the disparity of research results between different centres can be resolved during such an interchange. As this review implies, the most important contribution from many smaller meetings is indeed publication of the discussions.

Organizers and editors can help to dispose of some of the objections to the publication of proceedings either by designing their conferences specifically for a well-defined readership or by considering carefully whether all or any of the work presented is worth publishing in collected form. If there is no editor on the organizing committee when (and if) publication is decided on, an experienced editor should be appointed as soon as possible after this decision is taken.

The criteria for publication of conference proceedings are, or should be, the same as for any other book namely that the work described is original, authoritative, up to date and readable, and that a need exists for the information offered. Not surprisingly, it is no easier to decide whether a genuine need exists for conference proceedings than it is for any other kind of book. The pressures mentioned earlier do nothing to smooth the decision-making path. One signpost may be found in the distinction between 'collegial' and 'a positional' conferences. Collegial conferences are those at which research findings are exchanged and their relation to other work is discussed. They are worth publishing if the subject and the size of the meeting are right. Even congresses with 1000 or more participants may be worth publishing in full when a field needs strengthening because it lacks funds or journals, or both. For large meetings of this kind, poor papers should be weeded out by a selection committee and/ or refereed before publication. It is easier to convert medium-size conferences with 100-1000 participants into good books than it is to make successful books out of vast congresses, but in both cases there should be some selection and plenty of guidance for contributors on what is expected of them.

The small specialist symposium of up to 100 people is perhaps the most promising source of a worth-while book. At meetings of this size there is usually plenty of time for discussion and criticism of the work presented, and poor papers cannot easily slip into print unnoticed. Contributors, Comments on each other's papers are in fact a good substitute for refereeing-though if there are no referees the speakers should be carefully selected.

On the other hand, small workshops held to resolve differences in methods or results between different research centres are probably unsuitable for full publication, especially as speakers at this type of meeting may not be keen to express their doubts freely or strongly if they are to be recorded in print. Similarly, positions conferences at which people try to reach a consensus on a particular issue are not suitable candidates for full publication. The appropriate product of a positional conference, if a consensus is reached, is an announcement in a journal, not a blow-by-blow account of how that consensus was won.

Chosing Articles : As duplicate publication does so much to give conferences a bad name, editors of proceedings must guard against it even more carefully than journal editors do. Ideally, papers destined for a proceedings volume should either (a) report completely new work that has not been and will not be published elsewhere by the same author(s), or (b) be designed specifically as conference papers related to the themes of other speakers at the meeting and differing from journal articles that describe the same work. For the second kind of paper authors might, for example, be encouraged to 'include new hypotheses or preliminary findings and to speculate on the significance of their own or other people's results. The two kinds of paper correspond to two different categories of meeting. The first kind of paper is more suitable for the large meetings at which people expect to hear the leaders in their fields describe new work. The second kind of paper is better for smaller meetings especially meetings where discussions as well as papers will be published, and where the papers are intended to form a provocative basis for discussion.

Principles and Rules : The guidelines for authors should tell contributors to both categories of meeting which kind of paper to prepare. Contributors should be assured that their contributions will be published quickly and distributed widely, and that the proceedings will be easy to retrieve that is, the papers will be published either in a journal or in a book that is adequately listed in catalogues and by the secondary services.

The organizers, sponsors and potential editor must first ask themselves seriously whether the subject of the meeting would be better dealt with in a multi-author monograph, where the structure, coverage and standards of presentation can be controlled much more closely than is possible for most conferences. If the answer is that it would, they should abandon the thought of publishing the proceedings, or should perhaps replying the meeting with publication in mind (which may make for a less successful meeting).

Another point to consider is that publication of proceedings as journal supplement or in regular issues of journals is often preferable to publication in book form: distribution is better, retrieval is simpler, production may be faster, and papers usually receive the refereeing that so many proceedings lack. Many proceedings are successfully published in journals, especially in well-defined fields where suitable journals exist and where editors were willing to donate enough space and then either hand over editorial control to the conference editors or undertake the work themselves. Alternatively the conference organizers may advise contributors to submit their papers in the usual way to one or two selected journals, in which case there will be no need for a conference editor.

For multi-disciplinary conferences it may be difficult to find appropriate journals to take a collection of the papers. The large circulation general journals rarely have space for more than a few papers from any one meeting, and other journals may be too specialized to reach the readership envisaged for the proceedings. If a multi-disciplinary symposium is worth publishing, it is therefore probably best published in book form.

When conference proceedings are published together in a

journal issue or supplement for which the organizers appoint their own editor, problems may arise when editorial policy for the proceedings differs form policy for the journals for instance over the type of article required. The conference editor should discuss policy with the journal editor and resolve major differences before telling contributors what kind of papers to prepare. If contributors are asked to follow the journal's guidelines for authors, minor problems over presentation of the typescripts should not arise.

For most large congresses, abstracts or synopses may be the best and only type of publication needed. If these are circulated before the meeting participants can use them to select the speakers they want to hear or try to meet. The collection of abstracts remains useful to participants long after the meeting, especially if the speakers' addresses are included, as they ought to be. Participants should, however, be asked not to cite these abstracts as if they were published papers: abstracts are often difficult or impossible to obtain after the meeting, and presentation of a paper at a meeting does not constitute publication of the full paper.

***Room for Privacy*:** Some conferences are published privately by their organizing committees or sponsors. Unless these bodies already have a publishing programme and an editorial department, the editor of a one-off conference will have to find and deal directly with the printer. Editors faced with finding a printer should look at the work of several printing house before asking one to produce detailed specifications. The organizing committee and the editor also need to agree on several questions to which the printer will want answers. How long is the volume (or volumes) likely to be? How many copies are to be printed Oust enough for participants; or are other sales likely?) Is the material highly technical (mathematical, chemical, etc.) or likely to be heavily illustrated? What date will the copy be ready for typesetting or printing? What kind of cover is wanted (hardback, paper-back or flexible)? Are there any special binding requirements (e.g. ring or spiral binding)? Can the material be supplied in camera ready form?

Camera-ready copy can be a good way of reducing costs ad publication time but it is not always the best solution to production problems. If the conference secretariat (the editor's secretary?) Has to retype all the papers this takes a lot of time and money; in extreme cases it can be more expensive than paying for professional composition, unless the cost is hidden in institutional over heads. On the other hand, if authors are expected to provide perfect typescripts, the editor is either unable to do any editing or has to persuade authors to have their papers retyped after editing and copy-editing are finished. The guidelines for authors must make these points clear as well as giving detailed information on how the desired appearance of the typescript is to be achieved and on the layout of titles, headings, references tables, legends and illustrations.

Promotion and distribution also present problems when proceedings are published by a sponsoring organization which has little or no previous publishing experience. The retrievability of proceedings published in this way is often law, as it can be difficult for librarians or anyone else to find the address, or even the name, of the publisher. Some journal editors go so far as to ban these semi-mythical volumes from reference lists. To counteract this kind of objection, editors of privately published proceedings should arrange for review copies to be sent out and for the book to be advertised and listed in appropriate journals and other publications. If the sponsoring society publishes a journal, free exchange advertisements might be arranged with other journals.

The main advantage of private publication is that the proceedings can cost much less than with commercial publication. 'The price is often fixed by ... dividing the sum of the paper, printing and binding costs by the number of copies printed; all others costs, such as salaries of copy editor, administrator and typist, being inconspicuously absorbed by the learned institution which employs them. If a small mark-up is added and all the copies printed are sold, the sponsoring organization may make a useful small profit. More often it will make a loss, unless the 'administrator' happens to be a hard-headed business manager who can deal successfully with costs and costing, and with promotion, sales and so on.

Much of the work of instructing authors, making arrangements with printers and promoting and selling retrievable information is lightened for editors and organizing committees by good commercial publishers. The criteria as applied of book is also applicable to conference proceedings.

The financial arrangements that the organizing committee makes with the publisher will vary, depending on the requirements of the sponsoring society, the market for the volume(s), and the publisher's usual method of handling conference proceedings. The organizers may, for example, arrange to pay the publisher an agreed share of the registration fees in return for copies of the proceedings being supplied to the participants, with the rest of the print run being sold by the publisher in the usually way; or the publisher may put all the copies on the open market, knowing from past experience what percentage of participants and how many libraries will buy copies.

Timebound Programme : It is worth repeating that the editor must draw up a firm timetable for receipt of synopses and manuscripts. The dates depend on what has to be circulated before the meeting,, what has to be ready (and in what form) at the time of the meeting, and what is to be published after the meeting.

Circulating reprographed copies of the complete papers beforehand, or printing them by the time of the meeting, may seem to free participants from having to make detailed oral presentations that cut into or do away with discussion time;

but both methods have drawbacks. Even for small meeting, copying and circulating all manuscripts is expensive; it is also wasteful, since not all the participants will bother to read the papers. Circulating the printed papers in proof form, however, may produce good discussions at the meeting, since more people read printed papers than would read reprographed copies. But if the discussions are to be included in the proceedings, special arrangements then have to be made with the printer.

The best solution seems to be to circulate synopses of informative abstracts about three to four weeks before the meeting and ask authors to supply manuscripts either shortly before the meeting or during it, to allow the manuscripts to be as up to date as possible. The deadline for submission of synopses or abstracts may have to be about 12 weeks before the meeting.

If there is a set date for publication of the proceedings, manuscripts will be needed some 5-12 months before hand unless there is to be no editing and papers are to be supplied as camera-ready copy. Except when papers have to be printed for circulation before the meeting, the deadline for their receipt should be not later than the last day of the meeting (or earlier if papers are to appear in a journal with an earlier deadline): even the best-intentioned authors lose much of their incentive to work on manuscripts as soon as they leave one conference venue for the next, or for home. If the discussions at the meeting are not being published, editors must be particularly strict with authors over the deadline for receipt of manuscripts: if there is no buffer period of essential editorial work on the discussions, the date of receipt of the last manuscript is what determines the date of publication.

For a small symposium where informal discussions as well as formal papers are to be published, the deadline for receipt of papers might be set at, for example, three weeks before the meeting. This allows the editor to deal with at least some papers beforehand. During the meeting the editor can discuss queries with authors and persuade any who haven't submitted their papers to part with them before the meeting ends. For this kind of conference, authors should be told that they may modify their manuscripts during the meeting, if they wish, to take account of what is said by other participants or to allow last-minute results to be included.

Debating Standards : Discussions at conferences are often more illuminating than the papers that provoke them. Formal papers nearly always report work that members of an invisible college already know through preprints and personal communication. During discussion, on the other hand, most people talk openly about their most recent work and lines of thinking; they are stimulated to discuss work in progress and to report negative results; and in the right atmosphere they speculate freely, in ways that can open up new areas of study. The best discussions take place at small informal meetings designed to include plenty of time for discussion and attended by some 15 to 25 people. The edited record can make stimulating reading. With good organization and thorough editing larger meetings of up to 100 or 200 people may also produce worthwhile discussion; large congresses never do.

Editorial Challenges

However good the discussion may be, they are never worth printing verbatim. When discussions are included the editor therefore has a heavier task, though a more creative one, than when papers alone are published. The guiding principle in editing discussions should be that whenever comments are attributed to individuals, the speakers should see a copy of what they said (or what the editor thinks they said), preferably in context. They should then be allowed or persuaded to correct their comments, clear up obscure points, and provide references as necessary.

If a conference includes a session towards the end of the meeting at which the topic as a whole is discussed, it can, be exciting for participants if this is transcribed, edited and presented for comment before everyone disperses. The mechanics are that the editor and assistants work extremely hard though most of the day or night (or both) after the general session, while the conference participants enjoy themselves sight-seeing, shopping, or relaxing in other ways. A final session is then held to correct misapprehensions, sharpen some conclusions and provide participants with tangible evidence that the conference has been worth-while. In published form, this kind of discussion section serves as a useful summary for the reader and nicely rounds off the book.

There are several other ways of handling discussions at large or medium-size meetings. At some conferences, speakers write down their comments and hand them in immediately. At others, tape recorded discussions are transcribed quickly and unedited transcripts are given to participants to correct before they escape from the conference room; at these meetings, if there is no stenographer present, the editor or an assistant should list the speakers' names and take down enough words for the transcriber to be able to attribute the right, statements to the right speakers. Another method is for each discussion session to be summarized by the editor or by a reporter appointed for the purpose-though summaries of this kind tend to lack the cut-and-thrust of the original debate.

For meetings of 15-25 people, if discussion is intended to play an important part in both the meeting and the eventual publication, the following procedure for dealing with tape-recorded discussions is recommended. The editor, who attends all the sessions and must quickly get to know each of the participants by sight, lists each person's name as he or she speaks in discussion. This allow's contributors to join in the discussions informally without giving their names each time they speak. As well as writing down the names, the editor makes long hand notes of what each person says, giving either the gist of the comment or a few verbatim phrases—especially any difficult technical words and comments obscured by coughing or other notices. Rough drawings or notes of anything drawn on the blackboard or shown on the screen are made, to help with editing the transcript later. The tape-recordings are transcribed (typed in treble spacing) by audio-typists who use the editor's notes to identify the speakers.

Later the editor, after re-reading the manuscripts under discussion, listens to the tape-recording and edits the transcripts fairly strictly, improving the grammar, structure and style but leaving in as many of the speakers' own words as possible. Irrelevant references to the temperature of the room and empty compliments on papers that are then verbally torn to shreds are deleted, as are any inessential introductory phrases addressed to or made by the chairman, and all comments that are recognizably repetitious. When 'audio-eating' is finished, the editor polishes each transcript into what sounds like an intelligent conversation amongst the participants, writes queries and requests for references or further information in the margins, and rearranges the comments in a more logical order whenever necessary. A list of the points made or topics covered sometimes helps to show which comments should go where-and the list may convince the editor that the order of some papers needs to be changed too, if the discussions show that they are closely related. It is more important to obtain a smooth progression of ideas in the published discussion than to present the comments in their original order in the supposed interests of historical accuracy.

The edited transcripts are next retyped, again in treble spacing, to given speakers enough room to make changes, and the queries and requests for documentation that were noted on the original transcript are transferred to the retyped version. Participants are sent copies of every page of edited transcript on which their own comments appear, plus the pages immediately before and after each of their comments, to remind them of the context. They are asked to correct and return the edited transcripts within two to three weeks, and are warned that they will not see any proofs of the discussions. When corrected transcripts come back, the editor makes sure that comments still flow logically and that editorial queries have been answered. Other points to check are whether participants' questions to one another have all been answered, deleted or reworded as statements instead of questions and whether all the necessary reference have been supplied. A final version of the discussion can then be typed for the printer.

This method may sound laborious, but tit works. Sending speakers either unedited transcripts of their own remarks isolation or transcripts of the whole meeting is a recipe for disaster, or at least for unrewarding reading.

A final point about discussions is that they should be indexed as careful as the papers, and speakers' names should be included in the index of contributors, with page numbers for each discussion comment.

Both discussions and papers at conferences are, like material for any other book, edited with the expected readership in mind. That is, the editor or copy editor expands specialist shorthand into more generally recognizable language, condenses rambling comments, spells out abbreviations or explains them at first mention, inserts cross-references, introductory passages or linking statements between papers as needed, reconciles contradictions, monitors the level of writing, arranges papers in the most logical order, and does all the other editorial work with proof-reading later on.

If commissioned or invited papers turn out to be unsuitable for publication, it is probably best to reject them at once. This course, however, can hardly be followed unless authors have been told, when invited to contribute, that their papers would be referred. If no warning of this kind was given, the editor has to exercise much tact in persuading authors to rewrite their papers or revise them drastically in time to meet the printing schedule. Alternatively the editor has to do the work and then ask the authors to approve what has been done.

(1) A conference that is worth holding is not necessarily worth publishing.

(2) A conference worth publishing is not necessarily worth publishing in full. Further, the papers need not always be collected in a book but might appear in a journal issue or supplement, or even be submitted separately to journals in the usual way.

(3) Published proceedings should consist either of original papers, preferably referred, and similar to journal articles, or of papers written specifically for the conference, especially for the kind of meeting that allows plenty of time for discussion; both lands of proceedings should be published as quickly as possible, and in a retrievable form.

(4) A firm timetable for receipt of synopses and manuscripts must be drawn up.

(5) Discussion should be carefully edited to make them useful, readable and retrievable.

be referred. If necessary [illegible] extent the [illegible] the [illegible] language [illegible] their papers [illegible] to meet the printing [illegible] the work and then ask the authors to [illegible] what has been done.

(1) A conference [illegible] necessarily worth publishing.

(2) A [illegible] not necessarily worth publishing [illegible] the papers need not always be collected in a book but might appear in a journal [illegible] be submitted separately to journals in the usual way.

(3) Published proceedings should consist either of [illegible] papers, preferably [illegible] and similar to journal articles, or [illegible] of proceedings [illegible] should be [illegible] as quickly as possible, and in a flexible form.

(4) A [illegible] and monographs [illegible]

(5) The [illegible] should be [illegible] to make them [illegible] and [illegible]

7

Scheduled Learning

Technological Revolution

Programmed learning is one of the important invocations of the 20th century in the teaching-learning process. It is a self-instructional technique for providing individualized instruction or learning experience to the learner. In programmed learning, the subject matter or learning experience is logically sequenced into small segments. The learning experience is self-corrective.

The English writers prefer to use the term programmed learning and the American authors prefer the use of programmed instruction.

It is held by some educators that 'Gita' is the first example of programmed learning. They hold that the text of the 'Gita' has several ingredients of programming: initial behaviour, small steps, active participation of the learner, terminal behaviour, immediate feedback and self-evaluation by the learner.

Several educators regard Socrates as the earliest programmer. Socrates used to guide his followers to gain knowledge by conducting them conversationally along a path from fact to fact and insight to insight.

Programmed learning emerged in the beginning of the 20th century from the efforts of American psychologists. E. L. Thorndike (1874-1949) was the first psychologist whose findings bear direct relevance to programming. Other important psychologists who have made significant contribution in the field are Sidney L. Pressy, Robert M. Gagne, Robert Mager and B. F. Skinner.

Programmed learning is related with the 'Law of Effect' as explained by Thorndike. Sidney L. Pressy, a psychologist of Ohio State University, is credited for developing in the middle 1920's practical machines which could teach as well as test. The teaching machines as developed by Pressy present a series of questions to a student and inform him immediately whether his response is right or wrong.

In 1943, Skinner and his two other colleagues started programming by teaching a pigeon to roll a small bowling ball by operant conditioning. By 1954, Skinner and James G. Holland devised the auto-instructional methods which have served the present generation as the basis for present work in programmed instruction. In Skinnerian programmed instruction, whether mechanised or otherwise, the learner is initially asked a question which he can easily answer correctly without any previous study of the particular lesson. The learner is taught by the sequence of questions. He is asked more and more as the lesson proceeds in very small steps.

In 1955, Norman A. Crowder developed what he calls "automatic tutoring by intrinsic programming" as against "extrinsic programming" developed by Skinner.

Robert Mager (1958) gave a new concept known as "Learner Controlled Instruction" which is a kind of Socratic dialogue in reverse, in which the learner led the instructor. The instructor remained silent until the learner himself stimulated the instructor with questions that suggested the needed illustrations, demonstrations, practice or some other help.

Stoluron, at Illionis, aimed at developing a process which should provide for greater individualization by measuring needs and developing programmes that require a computer to assist instruction.

In 1962, T. F. Gilbert gave formalized expression of his technology of education called Mathetics. Pennington and Slack expressed in 1962 further detailed methods of preparing lessons from mathetic principles.

Scope and Definition

Programmed learning is a process of arranging material to be learned in a series of small steps designed to lead a learner through self-instruction from what he knows to the unknown of new and more complex knowledge and principles. A programme takes the place of a tutor and leads the learner through a set of frames of specified behaviour designed and sequenced to make it more probable that he will behave in a given derived way.

In programmed learning, it is said that the most efficient, pleasant and permanent learning takes place when the student proceeds through a course by a large number of small, easy-to-take steps. Wilbur L. Schramm (1962) lists the essential elements of programmed instruction as:

(a) an ordered sequence of stimulus items,

(b) to each of which a student responds in some specific way,

(c) his responses being reinforced by immediate knowledge of results,

(d) so that he moves by small steps,

(e) therefore, making few errors and practicing mostly correct responses,

(f) from what he knows by a process of successively closer approximation, toward what he is supposed to learn from the programme.

Following definitions provide a comprehensive view of programmed instruction.

Dale, Edgar (1962) : Programmed learning is a systematic, step by step, self-instructional programme aimed to ensure the learning of stated behaviour.

Das, R. C (1993) : Programmed instruction is a method of individualised instruction where each individual learns by himself at his own rate. Programmed learning consists of elements of new knowledge called 'steps' which are arranged in a sequence in such a way that a student can easily learn by himself.

Espich, James E. and William B (1965) : Programmed instruction is a planned sequences of experiences, leading to proficiency in terms of stimulus response relationship.

Gulati and Gulati (1990) : Programmed learning as popularly understood is a method of giving individual instruction in which the student is active and proceeds at his own pace and is provided with immediate knowledge of results. The teacher is not physically present. The programmer, while developing programmed material has to follow the laws of behaviour and validate his strategy in terms of student learning.

Jacobs and Others (1966) : Self-instructional programmes are educational materials from which the students learn. These programmes can be used with many types of students and subject-matter either by themselves, hence the name "self-instruction" or its combination with instructional strategies.

Kampfer (1970) : Programmed learning is a device which presents an exercise or a problem to a student, inducing him to respond; and revealing to him whether or not his response is correct.

Leith, G. O. M (1966) : Programme is a sequence of small steps of instructional material (called frames), most of which require a response to be made by completing a blank space in a sentence. To ensure that expected responses are given, a system of cueing is applied, and each response is verified by the provision of immediate knowledge of results. Such a sequence is intended to be worked at the learner's own pace as individual self-instruction.

Luonsdaine Arthur, A (1964) : An instructional programme is a vehicle which generates an essentially reproducible sequence of instructional events and accepts responsibility for efficiently accomplishing a specified change from a given range of initial competencies or behavioural tendencies to a specified or terminal range of competencies or behavioural tendencies.

Marke, Susan (1969) : Programmed learning is a method of designing a reproducible sequence of instructional events to produce a measurable and consistent effect on the behaviours of each and every acceptable student.

Navi, N. S. (1984) : Programmed instruction is a technique of converting the live instructional process into self-learning or auto-instructional readable material in the form of micro-sequence (the segments of subject-matter) which the learners are required to read, make some right or wrong response, correct wrong responses or confirm right responses and attain the complete mastery of the concept explained in the micro-sequences.

May, K. O. (1965) : Educational programming is the scheduling and control of student behaviour in the learning process.

Smith and Moore (1962) : Programmed instruction is the process of arranging the material to be learned into a series of sequential steps. Usually it moves the student from a familiar background into a complex and new set of concepts, principles and understandings.

Stolurow (1966) : Programmed learning can be described as a process in which a teacher presents (i.e., communicates), a subject matter to a learner so that he responds to it (i.e. communicates to the teacher) the next item of information to be presented.

Major Aspects

From the above mentioned definitions of programmed learning, following characteristics may be derived:

1. It is a method of individualized instruction.
2. In this technique, instructional material is logically sequenced and broken into suitable small steps or segments of the subject matter called 'frames'.
3. For sequencing a particular unit of the instructional material, the programmer has to pay due consideration to the initial or entering behaviour of the learner.
4. In actual operation, the beginning is made by presenting a 'frame'. The learner is required to read or listen and then respond actively.
5. Programmed instruction system has an adequate provision for feedback.
6. The interaction between the learner and the learning material or programme is very important.
7. Programmed learning provides self-pacing to the learner.
8. Programmed learning provides for continuous evaluation.

Learning material : There are three basic types of programmed instructional material—The teaching machines, the programmed textbook and scrambled textbook.

The teaching machine : A teaching machine is intended to function as a private tutor. It is simply a mechanical devise or piece of apparatus designed to present to the student a sequential programme of learning activities comprising instructional items which requires the student to make an overt response and which provides the student with immediate knowledge of the accuracy of his response. It represents the practical application of laboratory technique of education.

Programmed textbook : Each page of the programmed textbook consists of usually four or five panels. The student begins with the top panel on page one, responds to it, turns to page two to get his answers confirmed on the top panel, goes to the top panel on page three, responds to it, confirms the answer by turning the page, and so on.

The scrambled textbook : In a scrambled textbook, branching or intrinsic technique is used.

Fundamental Principles

Principle of small steps : It is shown by experiments that even the dullest students can learn as effectively as the brightest students if the subject matter is presented to them in suitable small steps. When we divide the task to be learnt into very small steps, and ask the students to learn only one step at a time, then probably all the students will be able to learn one small step at a time and sequentially learn all the steps. It is a difficult task to climb a mountain but once steps are built even a child can climb the mountain very easily. This is known as the 'Principle of small steps'.

Principle of active responding : The second psychological principle is that the students learn better and faster when they are actively participating in the teaching-learning process. In our classroom teaching the teachers to ask a few questions and the students respond. But is not possible for the teachers to ask all the students to respond at each small step. A teaching machine text or a programmed text contains a large number of questions—one question at each small step and the students respond actively. The principle of active responding is used for the programmes. The teaching machines and programmes have proved to be superior because they provide opportunity to every learner to respond at every small step.

Principle of reinforcement : Every response even approximately correct must be reinforced immediately. Delayed reinforcement fails to work. This is possible only when a teacher has to teach only one student at a time. The most ideal situation is when the teacher can cater to the needs of his students individually. But in classroom teaching this is hardly possible. No teacher, however efficient and sincere he may be, can reinforce each correct response of each of his students as soon as it is made in a classroom situation where he has to teach abut 40/50 students. The teaching machines and the programmes do the job more efficiently.

Principle of self-pacing : The programmed instruction is based on the basic assumption that learning takes place effectively if the learner is allowed to learn at his own pace. Therefore, a good programme of the material always takes care of the principle of self-pacing. A learner moves from one frame to another according to his own speed of learning.

Principle of student-evaluation or student testing : Continuous evaluation of the student and the learning process leads to better teaching-learning. In the programmed instruction, the learner has to leave the record of his responses because he is required to write a response for each frame on response sheet. This detailed record helps in revising the programme.

Important stages in the Development of the Programmed Instruction.

Preparation : This is the first stage in the development of the programme. It includes:

(i) Selection of the topic.

(ii) Writing assumptions about learners.

(iii) Defining objective in behavioural terms.

(iv) Writing the entry behaviour (present status) of the learner.

(v) Developing specific outline of the content.

(vi) Preparing a criterion test.

Construction or writing of the programme : The programme is written under these heads :

(i) Writing draft frames in a sequence i.e. from simple to complex.

(ii) Editing the draft frames by a team of experts usually comprising a subject-matter expert, a skilled writer and the programmer.

Try out revision : It includes :

(i) Trying out the programme on a few individual learners and finding out their reactions and making necessary changes in the light of reactions,

(ii) Trying out the programme on a group of learners and making necessary changes on the basis of their reactions; and

(iii) Trying out the programme in the field.

Evaluation : This implies finding the success or the failure after implementing a programme.

Programmes based on Illustration

CIVICS-CLASS X

Introduction : This a programme meant for you for the study of salient features of the Constitution of India.

In this programme you will find paragraphs which are called frames. Study each frame carefully and write down what is required. Answers are given at the end. After stating you answers, check them. If your answer is wrong or you do not understand anything, you can again go back to the frame. It is not a test but instead it is a self-study programme.

Frame 1 : The Constituent Assembly of India was set up under the provisions of the Cabinet Mission Plan to frame the Constitution of India which was formally adopted on 26th Nov. 1949 and came into force on 26th January 1950. It took nearly three years to complete the work.

(i) What was the work assigned to Constituent Assembly?

(ii) Under whose provision was it formed?

(iii) When did our Constitution come into force?

(iv) When was it adopted?

(v) How much time did Constituent Assembly take to complete its work?

Frame 2 : The Preamble of the Constitution has a great significance but is not a part of the Constitution. The Constitution was framed by the people of India through their representations. It stresses the fact that the reign of the land lies with the people of India.

(a) Is the Preamble a part of the Constitution?

(b) By whom was the Constitution framed?

(c) In whose hands does the reign of law of India lie?

Frame 3 : The Preamble of our Constitution is as under:

We the people of India having solemnly resolved to constitute India into a Sovereign Socialist Secular Democratic Republic and to secure to all its citizens:

Justice, social, economic and political;

Liberty of thought, expression, belief, faith and worship

Equality of status and of opportunity; and to promote them all;

Fraternity assuring the dignity of the individual and the unity and integrity of the Nation.

In our Constituent Assembly this twenty-sixth day of November, 1949, do hereby adopt, enact and give to ourselves this Constitution.

Note—Three new terms—Socialist, Secular and Integrity were added to the original text of the Preamble when it was amended in 1976 with the 42nd Amendment.

The Preamble stresses the democratic basis of the Constitution by stating that the People of India gave to themselves this Constitution. It also states objectives like justice, liberty, equality and fraternity.

(i) Who has given the Constitution of India?

(ii) What kind of justice has been ensured by the Preamble?

(iii) What type of Republic is to be constituted?

(iv) What kind of equality has been given to its citizen?

(v) How many types of liberty can a citizen enjoy?

Frame 4 : Another important feature of the Preamble is that the people themselves adopted and enacted the Constitution. Thus, the representatives of the people frame the laws of the country and they have the power to change or amend the Constitution.

(a) Who frames the laws of the country?

(b) What has the power to amend the Constitution?

Frame 5 : The Constitution of India has many unique features which distinguish it from Constitutions of other countries. The framers of the Constitution freely borrowed ideas but took care to adapt these to the needs of the country.

The Constitution makes India a Sovereign, Socialist Secular, Democratic Republic. The word Sovereign means that India is completely free from external control. No outside power has the right to interfere either in her internal administration or direct her in the conduct of her foreign policy.

This was emphasised to ensure that India was no longer 'dependent' on the British Empire as she had been before Indian Independence Act 1947 or 'dominion' as she had been from 15th August, 1947 to 26th January 1950.

(a) What kind of status did India enjoy during 15th August 1947 to 26th January 1950?

(b) Was India sovereign between 15th August 1947 to 26th January 1950?

(c) What is the meaning of the word 'sovereign'?

(d) Does the Constitution of India have unique features?

(e) Did the framers of the Constitution borrow ideas?

ANSWERS

1. (i) To frame the Constitution of India.
   (ii) Provision of the Cabinet Mission Plan.
   (iii) 26th January 1950.
   (iv) 26th November 1949.
   (v) Nearly 3 years.
2. (a) No.
   (b) People of India through their representatives.
   (c) People of India.
3. (i) People of India.
   (ii) Social, economic and political.
   (iii) Sovereign Socialist Secular Democratic.
   (iv) Equality of status.
   (v) Five.

4. (a) Representatives of the people.
   (b) Representatives of the people.
5. (a) Dominion.
   (b) No.
   (c) India is completely free from external control.
   (d) Yes.
   (e) Yes.

Evaluative Exercise

Merits of programmed instruction

1. A well-programmed instruction is a great thrust in the direction of individualised instruction, as it is tailored to the needs of the individual learner in the class.
2. It permits individual learner to progress at his own speed. An intelligent learner needs no longer to be bored or allowed to lose interest on account of his slow progress of other learners of the class. He can make progress as he is capable of.
3. Since a programme requires continuous response from the learner, it overcomes the inertia and passivity on the part of the learner.
4. The teacher can give explanation in the classroom if the error is common or he may arrange individual conferences on specific points.
5. Learning material in a programmed instruction is presented in such a way that learning becomes an interesting game and the learner is motivated to meet the challenges set by his own capabilities.
6. Programmes are developed by experts. They are empirically tested and modified till they are standarised. A number of learners can use a single good programme and thus evade textbooks.

7. In programmed instruction the learner is immediately reinforced to correct his response and this reinforcement sustains the motivation of the learner.
8. The self-instructional technique presents material in which its complexity is simplified through the analysis of the subject-matter into small and more easily assimilated segments of information.
9. The introduction of programmed instruction is of great significance for developing countries which are set on the path of educating millions of learners and are short of teachers.
10. Good teachers are freed from the boredom of routine classroom teaching and they are in a position to devote more time to more creative activities.
11. The programmed instruction has been used more successfully in teaching the discernment of the logic of various disciplines and inspiring students to creative thinking and judgement.
12. Certain motor skills and intellectual abilities normally taught by frequent drills and rote memorisation can be very efficiently taught by self-instructional devices.
13. Self-instructional materials have been found to be very useful in the West in revolutionising the social setting of the classroom. Problems of discipline have been solved and a new hope for eliminating emotional and social problems has been generated.
14. Programmed instruction enables the teacher to diagnose the problems of the individual learner.
15. The introduction of programmed instruction is very helpful in certain situations where human instructors are not easily available in the required number, for instance small schools in the isolated or hill areas.

Programmed materials have been severely criticised as a threat to replacing the teacher.

It is also argued that there is too much emphasis in learning facts and very little emphasis on the mastery of principles and concepts.

Some critics of programmed instruction maintain that the user of a programme does not now where he is headed to.

They also point out that the learners are not aware of the organisation and programmed instruction is unrelated to other aspects of instruction.

It is also argued that the programmed instruction material is very costly and only rich nations can afford it.

It is also stated that the development and use of programmed instructional material require expert knowledge and training. An average teacher finds it very difficult to make use of this device.

Varied Kinds : As a result of experimental studies and research, following types of programmed instruction have emerged.

1. Linear or Extrinsic Programming
2. Branching or Intrinsic Programming
3. Mathetics Programming
4. Rules System of Programming
5. Computer Assisted Instruction (CAS)
6. Learner Controlled Instruction. (LCS)

The first three styles—linear, branching and mathetics are the basic formats. The rules system represents the deductive and inductive approach to teaching. The other two types, Computer Assisted Instruction (CAI) and Learner Controlled Instruction (LCI) are not the basic format of Programming.

They are, infect, the ways and means of providing instruction. Here we have taken up only the basic type of programming.

Linear Programming

B. F. Skinner is the originator of linear programming. It is also called a single tract programme. According to Skinner, a creature, a bird or a human being can be led to a desired behaviour by means of a carefully constructed programme consisting of small steps leading logically through the subject-matter from topic to topic, provided each step is reinforced by some kind of favourable experience or reward. The increments in information which the learner is expected to absorb are small. The favourable experience or response increases the probability of the same response to occur again in the future. The process of rewarding the correct response to a stimulus increases the general tendency to give a response.

The sequence of frames and path of learning in programmed learning is systematic and linear. That is why, this type of programming is referred to as linear programming. Hence all the learners have to proceed through the same frames and in the same order.

In a linear programme, learner's responses are controlled externally by the programmer sitting at a distant place. Hence linear programming is also termed as extrinsic programming. In branching programming, learner's response is controlled by the learner himself internally. It is, therefore, also called intrinsic programming.

Merits

1. Immediate knowledge of results acts as a great motivator and releases anxiety and tension.
2. The smallness of the frames brings the sub-goals within the reach of the learner and thereby facilitates secondary reinforcement.

3. Repetition strengthens the responses and ensures learning.
4. Easy nature of the programme provides 'success experience' to the learner.

Limitations

1. In linear programming, the learning process becomes quite dull on account of the following reasons (a) Subject matter is broken into very small pieces, (b) Responding is quite mechanical and restrictive, and (c) The learning process is quite slow.
2. The use of linear programming is limited to some subjects and topics.
3. Linear programming cramps the imagination of the learner and initiative for creative, integrative and judgement learning.
4. Linear programming encourages guessing.
5. Linear programming does not develop the discriminating power of the students.

Intrinsic Programming

Branching or intrinsic programming was developed by Norman A. Crowder (1954) an American technician. According to Crowder, branching or intrinsic programme is one which adopts to the needs of the learners without the medium of any extrinsic device such as a computer. It is not controlled extrinsically by the programmer.

Norman A. Crowder was a technician who was working in the United States Air Force. He was faced with the problem of efficiency of vocational training. His programme is based on intuition. His approach at the most is practical. This type of programme employs multiple choice response patterns. The learner is required to select one right answer out of several responses presented to him.

Merits

1. Big size of a frame as well as the branching minimises unnecessary repetitions and responding, thus reducing the amount of learning time and fatigue.
2. The pitfalls and consequences of erroneous logic are usually explained in the remedial frames so that the learner not only gets the correct responses but also understands why some other response is not correct.
3. Instead of simple response it provides alternatives in the form of multiple choice.
4. Through its broad frames, branching programme provides for more freedom to respond and scope of choosing one's path of learning according to one's need. Thus, it helps in maintaining the interest and initiative of the teacher.
5. Branching programme is helpful in the development of the power of discrimination of the learner.
6. Branching programme helps in the development of creativity and problem-solving ability.
7. Branching is most useful in the areas beyond facts, definitions and basic skills. 8. The frames being of a large size contain a good deal of information and this may enable the programmer to enrich the style and expand his ideas.

Programmed Instruction	*Traditional Method*
1. It is an individualised technique of instruction.	1. It is a group technique.
2. It is based on the teaching principles that have been known for years.	2. It becomes difficult to apply teaching principles in crowded classrooms.
3. It presents the instructional matter step by step in logical order.	3. It presents the instructional matter as a whole.

Contd...

Programmed Instruction	*Traditional Method*
4. The size of the unit of information presented to the pupils is a small bit of information.	4. The unit is a lengthy one. There is very little provision for response from the students in the form of answers to questions.
5. Immediate feedback is given to the learner.	5. The learner does not get immediate feedback.
6. Objectives are defined very clearly in operational terms.	6. Objectives are not well-defined and are usually vague.
7. The programmer prepares his programme with care and precision.	7. Very little preparation is made.
8. Programme is prepared in such a way that the student automatically participates actively by making responses continually.	8. The student usually remains a passive listener and the teacher himself does the summarising and reviewing.
9. A programme is developed empirically through a series of tryouts and refined gradually. Effective sequences students reaction of frames are retained and ineffective ones discarded.	9. It is usually found to be very difficult to modify traditional instruction.

Limitations

1. The multiple choice questions provided in this programming may lead to guess work on the part of the learner and he may not understand the subject matter of the frame.

2. The setting of appropriate multiple choice questions suiting to the entire material of the frames proves a difficult task.
3. No branching method can provide infinite branching to take care of all possible needs of every individual student.
4. The cost of branching programme is very high when compared with traditional teaching approaches.
5. The branching programme is not suitable for small children as they are unable to express symbolisation.
6. The programme needs revision after every five years.
7. It is difficult to cover the entire subject matter of the curriculum in the stipulated time.
8. The diagnostic questions framed by the programmer may or may not suit the needs of the individual learner.
9. The programme cannot shape the behaviour of the learner.

Teaching Instruction and Programmed Instruction. According to Edger Dale, "Teaching' is a broad, vague, ill-defined term and instruction' is a purposeful, orderly, controlled sequencing of experience to reach a specified goal. 'Programmed instruction' is a sub-head under instruction and represents a more rigorous attempt to develop a mastery, over specified goals to secure 'insured' learning."

Role of Teacher

Programme learning cannot replace the teacher. Any innovation in the school programmes and practices must remain in the hands of the teachers. The radio and T V did not displace the teacher. Similar is the case with programmed instruction. It is upto the enlightened teachers to take up the challenging task of preparing programmes. We have got a wide market. The programmes can be sold all over the country. A student who is convinced that he can learn better, achieve more with the help of this programme, will definitely prefer instead of buying this programme to buying a text book. By taking up this challenging task we will not only help the cause of education, help our fellow teachers by setting them free from the routine task of information, giving help to the students to achieve more, but we will be helping ourselves also.

It may also be remembered that these gadgets can be used mainly in the cognitive field and possibly in the psychomotor field to develop certain abilities and skills of the students as an individual. A teacher is something more than all these gadgets put together. He has to bring about socialization of the individual; he has to promote socially desirable attitudes and interests and mould the personality of the students.

The effective domain is almost reserved for his care. At present the teacher is not able to devote his energy and time to this important task as most of his time and energy is consumed by his routine job as an information giver. We always talk of education for three 'H's'—the head, the hand and the heart. But it has almost remained a mere slogan. Programmed learning, teaching machines and other gadgets will set teacher free from routine work. These are labour-saving devices for the teacher so that he may function more effectively in a field of his own choice.

Technique involved in programmed instruction can be used in teaching different subjects. Teaching of mathematics, science, social studies and elements of Indian languages can be done effectively with the help of this new technique. The teacher has to formulate objectives of teaching a particular subject, undertake content analysis of the subject matter in the light of objectives, frame a chain of questions which will lead the pupils in the direction of the objective and present the questions to his pupils who are expected to try their hand at answering the questions independently.

The teacher will have to play the role of a friend, guide and philosopher in the class when the pupils are engaged in solving the riddle and at the same time acquiring knowledge or skill. The question of class discipline may not arise as the pupils will be found busy doing the task assigned to them by the teacher. The teacher will have to do remedial or corrective teaching as the weakness of his pupils will be located in the very act of learning. The pupil will also undergo a process of self-evaluation as he completes his work.

Role of the teacher in the changed context of Programmed Learning may be stated as under :

1. Teacher as an advisor in helping students in the selection of programme learning material.
2. Teacher as a discussion leader for focussing the attention of the learners on important points.
3. Teacher as a guide to clarify doubts and elaborate on various points asked by the learner.
4. Teacher as an evaluator of the learning outcomes.
5. Teacher as a consultant to the various agencies engaged in production of programmed material.

Attitude in Classroom Teaching

The programmed learning approach can be adopted in normal classroom teaching in the following ways:

1. A teacher can make use of the principles of programmed learning such as active responding, minimal errors and confirmation while teaching various subjects in the conventional manner.

2. A teacher can define behavioural objectives in advance of teaching.
3. A teacher can validate the instructional systems of a class in terms of the performance of learners immediately after teaching is over.
4. A teacher can regulate questions and answers. The answer of a learner can be immediately reinforced by informing or telling whether it is correct or incorrect.
5. A teacher can plan the entire instructional programme of a classroom and can treat the terminal behaviour, the prerequisite skills and content analysis in advance.

Komoski (1960) an expert has observed "Two thousand years ago the world's first public administrator, a gentleman by the name Quintilian wrote what might be called a handbook for teachers." In it he has one bit of advice which will serve as an excellent starting point for a discussion of programmed learning and its potential uses. His advice is: "Do not neglect the individual student. He should be questioned and praised."

Instruction-based Programme

Programmed instruction is still in its infancy in India. Programmed instruction as an optional or elective paper has been included at the B. Ed./M.Ed. level in a few universities in India. It also forms a part of the paper of Educational Technology/Educational Innovation. However, as regards its classroom use, it may be observed that it is almost nil. As far back in 1966, the Kothari Commission suggested to develop programmed material in different subjects to test the suitability of the technique in Indian conditions. An Association of Programmed Instruction has been formed to coordinate the research being done at different centres in the country.

The association also disseminates the information on new studies through its journal issued from time to time. The National Council of Educational Research and Technology has also done some work in the field. In spite of all these efforts, it may be stated that the application of programmed instruction has not yet made an appreciable impact on our classroom teaching. Our methods of teaching still remain traditional, by and large.

Following are the important factors which stand in the way of introducing programmed instruction in Indian schools:

1. Resistance to change.
2. Lack of good programmes.
3. Lack of facilities.

8

Role of Media

The main function of the press is to communicate news along-with the editorial opinion. As a media of information, we can even call the press as an important adjunct to the school as an educational institution. In fact, now more and more opinion is veering round to the point that journalism should be considered as a medium of education and mass communication.

Every newspaper has a point of view which is reflected both in its news columns, on the editorial page and, to some extent, in the columns of its syndicated writers. Although, the fiercely partisan press of the past has more or less disappeared, it is still difficult to discover a newspaper which is completely neutral. Every newspaper as a free medium should have a point of view and should interpret the news in depth. There is no doubt that it must maintain a balance and an integrity in which the news is not slanted or tilted completely.

The Status

Similarly, the editorial while taking a position should not be false or misleading. Some degree of partisanship is always there, but it should not be done at the cost of dissemination of truth. There is always a point where espousal should stop, so that accuracy of information can be maintained. A newspaper which becomes too much involved in the advocacy of its partisan views, loses its audience, because it compromises its main function of the communication of information. In fact, just like other professions there should be a code of ethics or code of conduct even for the journalists.

In every country, the press has to function within the framework of the laws of that country. Generally, under a democratic government a newspaper is not prohibited from printing any information, provided it is not libellous, slanderous or obscene. No doubt, in times of war or during some national emergency the newspapers should impose some self-censorship, because the press is also responsible for what it prints. It is also susceptible to the laws of libel. The press as an institution suffers from the same limitations and restrictions as any other media or social institution.

Freedom of the press is also subject to a continuing struggle, a continuing appraisal and a constant effort by pressure groups to erode it.

Freedom of the press does not imply a license to print anything and everything. It is always subject to legal review as well as to the pressure of public opinion. Generally, the rule of reason prevails over the press and it stops short of engaging in activities which are contrary both to the laws and public interest.

In fact, it is not the democratic society alone which has made freedom possible for the press. The press and other media are also equally responsible for the successful functioning of democracy. The press and other mass media are the most powerful sources in the society for creating an informed public opinion. There is no doubt that the relations between the press and the government have always been delicate and full of troubles. It is due to the lack of trust between the government and the press that the 'credibility gap' comes into existence between the government and the people.

It is necessary for the government that it should allow free access to the reporters to perform their functions regarding the collection of news. The newspapers have always argued vigorously to preserve their right to receive and report the news freely. Sometimes, the newspapers and other media are accused of misreporting the news. Certain reporters of newspapers have also been accused of giving a tilt to their stories in favour of certain parties or certain personalities. Sometimes, the owners of the newspapers have been criticised for harassing certain reporters for their objective and true reports criticising a particular point of view. Fortunately, these cases are not very many and public opinion is always against such misdemeanour either on the part of the journalist or the press.

Encountering all Odds

There is no doubt that conscientious journalists would always resist the pressure either from the editors or the owners to slant their news. Even the self-respecting editors would not like to use any pressure on their reporters to give coloured news. But sometimes, the owners of the press who have certain other industrial interests also, use certain pressures on the reporters to safeguard their own selfish interests.

It is also sometimes alleged that the government exerts pressures on the press overtly or covertly which is a big danger to the existence of a free press. The attitude of the government of the day is very important for the existence of a free press.

Every government must remember that the more the difficulties it places in the path of the reporter in gaining access to the news, the greater will be the credibility gap between it and the press. It is the duty of the press to make all efforts to get the news and report it to the public impartially. Maintenance of a healthy interaction between the press and the society and between the newspaper and its readers is the basis of a truly democratic society.

Honours of Professional Nature

There has been a great change in the newspapers as mass medium over the past thirty years. The press has now become a vast institution and a medium of mass communication. Advertising has become an essential part of newspaper publishing and large circulation has become necessary for attracting the advertisers successfully. The press today has become not only a national institution but it has been completely institutionalized. Newspapers have become a part of large business enterprises. Of course, journalism has now also become more newsworthy and more informative. Now-a-days editorials are written more cogently and objectively rather than out of sheer partiality. The twentieth century has seen the appearance of journalistic empires.

Concerns in Entirety

Journalism has not only been institutionalized but concentration and consolidation of journalism has taken place all over the world. There has been a trend towards the merger of newspapers in order to survive. Modern journalism is an impersonal corporate type enterprise. Many newspapers depend on wire copies from newspaper agencies. Printing of pictures by tele-photo has also speeded up both the transmission and printing enormously. Now-a-days, newspapers are circulating with dispatch due to the development of the linotype machine which has replaced setting of type by hand.

This change has also brought about stereotype and standardisation in journalism, which has resulted in loss of independence and enterprise to some extent. The big news agencies have tended to standardize the news printed in the press. These agencies have also made it possible to print national and international news quickly. In this manner, these news agencies supply the news to their client papers quickly and accurately. Of course, there are still newspapers having their own sources of news, especially the weekly and the small town newspapers.

Efforts in Collective Way

So many news agencies and syndicates have come into existence which supply news, readymade features, serials etc. to their clients all over the world. Today, journalism depends heavily on advertising and circulation to keep it viable financially. Although the press is an institution, yet it is also a business. Therefore, it must function with economic success, if it has to remain in business. There is no doubt that the costs of producing and distributing newspapers have risen too much during the recent years. Still the owners of the newspapers are also entitled to expect a fair return on their investment.

In many advanced countries of the world, most mass media are corporately owned. They are also financed by the sale of stock in the market. No newspaper can be run in the present day only on the profit of circulation. Hence, there is heavy reliance on the source of advertising. Due to economic problems many big newspapers in the world had either to go out of business or merge with others in the recent past. Even in advanced countries, a lot of caution is observed in newspaper journalism. Newspapers that do not function with economic success, are frequently absorbed in mergers where success prevails.

Sometimes, this continued merger of newspapers has

resulted in the monopolistic ownership. The press today, as a medium of mass communication, has become a huge and powerful institution with an enormously delicate and complex involvement on national and international scale. In the present times, newspapers do not suffer from a lack of news but from an overflow of news. In this way, by reporting and interpreting the news the press has become a very important source of education and information.

On the one side, being a private enterprise, the press is an institution, but on the other side it is also clearly a public service. The news is selected on the basis of a certain value judgement. With the widening scope of newspapers and other media, this media must assume a greater degree of social responsibility. These medias are accountable not only to the public but also to other social institutions for their behaviour as means of communication. Because of its vast readership and the consequent influence, the press needs to maintain a high standard of moral responsibility. Good journalism should not only give the public what the public wants, but it should also give them what it thinks is good for the public. In this way, the press should enjoy its freedom with responsibility and balanced reporting of news and views.

Liberty of Expression

Freedom of the press is very essential if the press has to play a significant and constructive role in the life of a nation, especially in a democratic society. Unless the press itself enjoys freedom, how can it become the defender and protector of the rights and liberties of the citizens ? A free press signifies an open society where decisions are made according to democratic traditions and not according to the dictates of one person. The press can only perform its sacred duties of the fourth estate if it is free and independent in reporting its views and news.

But like all other freedoms, freedom of the press should

also not be used as a licence. It should not be misused to create a situation of the law of the jungle. The press should observe certain self imposed limitations on itself, so that instead of publishing views detrimental to the interests of the nation, it strengthens the national unity, upholds the laws of the land and contributes towards the emotional integration of the country. For example, howsoever free the press may be, it cannot be allowed the freedom to call in question the integrity of the judges of the High Courts and the Supreme Court or to defame them. It cannot be allowed the licence to incite communal riots in the country. No state can grant such unlimited freedom to the press by which law and order in the country is endangered.

On the other hand, the press should also not be afraid of upholding and supporting a just and righteous cause, because it may antagonise the governmental machinery or some influential interests. The press has to be eternally vigilant to protect the rights, of the workers, backward people and the suppressed sections of the society. It should also give a balanced view of the things and happenings, so that the people can be helped in the formation of a healthy public opinion and correct perspective of the events. The press can play havocs by suppressing a news, or giving it an importance out of all proportions. Our constitution under Article 19, has recognised the freedom of expression and speech of the citizens, which is the basis of the freedom of the press.

In India, since our independence the press has been enjoying more or less complete freedom in its working. The press in India has on many occasions crossed swords with the government and has done a good service in protecting the democratic traditions. But during the nineteen months following the imposition of internal emergency, which was declared on 25th June, 1975, the freedom of the press in India was curtailed by the government. Strict censorship was imposed upon the press and it was not at all allowed to publish any report against the government. This censorship was removed only after the sixth General Election in March 1977, when the above emergency was revoked.

In reality, freedom of the press is very essential for the free flow of information and success of democracy everywhere. There has been a demand in our country that an appropriate amendment should be made in the Constitution, so that in future no government is able to clamp censorship on the press. Even there has been a demand that the freedom of the press should be included in the Chapter on Fundamental Rights and made an essential feature of the Constitution, subject to reasonable restrictions.

There is no doubt that censorship on the press violates the freedom of speech and expression of the citizens. It also violates the citizens' right to free flow of information. Censorship cannot be justified except in times of war or internal insurrection. Freedom of the press is, in fact, the symbol of dignity and freedom of man. However, as already stated, like other freedoms, freedom of the Press should also not be used as a licence.

Sense of Authority

The press plays a very important role in the modern age. Inspite of the heavy impact of television news coverage on the public, newspapers still continue to serve as the basic news medium for a majority of the population. Although the newspapers lack the speed and visual quality of television news, yet they provide greater depth and variety in reporting. People today depend greatly on the press for local, national, and international news. They cannot be kept well informed about these in the absence of newspapers. A newspaper reader can obtain a lot of information regarding local, national and international affairs from a single issue of a newspaper. A newspaper caters to the needs of different readers by publishing various types of news such as political, economic, social, scientific, developmental etc.

Although there is more mental effort in reading a newspaper than watching a television news programme, yet the effort is worthwhile. In a way, we can say that the newspapers are the written record of our contemporary civilization. The increasing literacy in the developing countries and the suburban spread of cosmopolitan cities have led to the creation of many new daily newspapers. There are different sizes of newspapers, some are small and some are big. A small newspaper may be employing only a few persons, whereas a big newspaper may be employing hundreds of persons with a daily circulation of several lakh copies.

Whether newspapers are large sized or small sized, all of them are printed by type and ink on newsprint. The main purpose of the press is to inform and influence the people who read it. Into the pages of every newspaper goes an essential but intangible extra ingredient, the minds and the spirits of the men who produce it. Journalism work is like an adventure which is full of fresh experiences and unexpected developments take place everday. No doubt, there is a firm discipline involved in the bringing out of a newspaper, because every issue of a newspaper should be printed in time so that it can reach its subscribers and the news stands at the fixed time. The regularity and punctuality in printing a newspaper or a journal can only be maintained if a definite work pattern is followed in all departments.

There are innumerable exciting things that can happen in the production of a newspaper. The reporters feel the stimulation of being on the inside of big developments, of watching history being made. They also have the thrill of meeting important and interesting persons. Similarly in those persons who work on the advertising and circulation side, there is the satisfaction that in conceiving and executing ideas they bring in money and influence the people through their skill with the word. By working in a newspaper a person has a lot of opportunities to create ideas and put them to work. The successful newspapermen handle the necessary routine connected with the production of a newspaper meticulously. These people always try to bring to their jobs an extra element of creative thinking. Such persons cannot remain in the newspaper business for a long period, for whom there is no excitement in the atmosphere of journalistic activities.

The press performs a very important role as a means of mass communication media in the modern world. The press tries to inform its readers objectively about what is happening in their community, country, and the world at large. To bring certain developments into focus, editorial comments on the news are also given. Now-a-days the newspapers also provide the means whereby persons with goods and services can sell and advertise their goods. The newspapers also play a very important role in eliminating the undesirable conditions prevailing in the society. Sometimes the newspapers carry on campaigns for some highly desirable civic projects for the service of the society.

For the entertainment of their readers the newspapers publish comic strips, special features, interesting columns written by famous columnists etc. Sometimes, certain newspapers also act as friendly counsellors for their readers. And they give them information regarding specific matters through question and answer columns. The newspapers also act as the champions of the rights of the citizens. Whenever the rights of the individuals are infringed they come to their rescue. Sometimes the newspapers also expose the corruption prevailing in the ruling circle or the high society. For example, the Watergate scandal was brought to light by two young reporters of Washington Post, Bob Woodward and Carl Bernstein.

Major Works

When the press plays such an important role, in the society, it becomes integral part of it. The newspaper has become so much a part and parcel of our life that we cannot do without it. A strike in the daily newspapers creates an all round confusion in the economic, social and political activities of the community. A regular subscriber of a newspaper feels very lonely if he does not receive his, newspaper even for a single day. Without his daily newspaper a person feels as if he has missed something or lost something. There is no doubt that the printed word has a permanent and lasting impression whereas a spoken word or a visual image has only a transitory effect. In the case of a printed world a reader can refer to it time and again. Newspaper clippings of important news, comments, stories and happenings can be preserved in a reference file for future consultation. In this way, we see that newspapers play a very important role in the modern society.

Future Challenges

In the past, the press mainly concentrated on two important functions, that is information and influence. But now-a-days, it performs four major functions. In addition to the above two functions the press now also performs the functions of entertainment and paid advertising.

Information : This function includes all reports, news and happenings concerning the daily life. It does not include any information involving or concerning the pursuit of leisure. But it does cover all news, regarding government, politics, foreign affairs, weather, accident, business, labour, education etc. This function consists of most of the matter which is given in news-broadcast on the radio and T.V. as well as the news-columns of the newspapers and magazines. It does not include information regarding sports, hobby columns, theatre reviews, films, short stories etc.

Influence : It means influencing the opinion of the readers through editorials, articles, or certain special features. It also includes editorials, cartoons and comments made on the news and events by the journalists or the editors. But it does not include the slanted news or any other form of indirect influence, accidental or otherwise. In this, we should include only attempts which are made directly to influence the readers and listeners. It also excludes the space which is sold to the advertisers.

Entertainment : The next important function of the press is entertainment of the readers. Under this function can be included all types of fiction like comic strips, stories etc. It also includes the factual material, sports news, theatre reviews and hobby columns which deal with leisure. The entertainment function of the press is very important. This function not only competes for space and time with other functions, but it can also exert indirect influence and impart information incidentally.

Advertising : This function of the press can very easily be recognised, because it is commercially oriented. Sometimes, the advertisements also have some public service messages under the prestige advertisements regarding family planning, driving safely, child care, health care etc. The commercially oriented advertising seeks to promote the sale of their goods.

Generally, people have to depend upon the press for the major share of their total news information, because even television newscasts cannot carry that much bulk, nor could the television viewers assimilate it, if they did. Of course, information can be written and edited in such a slanted fashion that it exerts more influence than the printed editorial. Entertainment is the most important function of journalism, because it is like a magnet which attracts and holds large audiences. It plays a vital role in selling newspapers and magazines by the millions. The sports pages, comic strips, astrology columns, advice to the lovelorn and cross-words are essential to the average newspaper's survival as a mass media.

The entertainment function's greatest threat to good journalism is its competition against information and influence for media space and time and consumer attention. Addition of an extra page of comic strips may add to circulation and accompanying advertising revenues, thus enabling the newspaper to add editorial material, or it may simply oust a few columns of news and commentary. Similarly, a second lovelorn column not only steals space from significant offerings, but also tempts more readers away from the remaining substance.

The Ability

There is no doubt that information and influence play a very important role in the success of the largest general interest magazines. For example, much space of Reader's Digest is devoted to articles and opinion pieces, about government, foreign affairs, current morality issues, and education-Advertising also plays a very important role in the success of running a mass media. Advertising provides the largest part of the revenue to finance the most elaborate technically sophisticated press system. In fact all sorts of daily newspapers, magazines, publications depend on advertising revenue. Advertising also supplies essential marketing information to the public and helps inform the businessmen of changes within their fields.

9

Computer Learning

New Communication Technologies are those which are of recent origin. Interactivity is their distinguishing feature. The use of computers in one form or the other, as an integral part of their system, is what enables them to be interactive.

Computer's Role

The idea of interlinking and communicating with the aid of computers was as old as the mainframe computers of the 1970s. But the mainframes could be owned only by mega-establishments, individuals could not afford them for personal use. The networking of computers, it was found, allowed simultaneous access to a single mainframe by any number of users. This development suited owners and users alike. In the decades that followed, computer technology advanced by leaps and bounds. This resulted in the invention of much smaller computer.

In our own country, computer networking are widely used by public sector organizations. On a global scale, Internet is the largest computer network which permeated almost all parts of the world. Internet can offer any immense range of information services such as electronic mail, file transfer, data bases and multi-media. It also provides connectivity to mobile receivers. Computer network thus has several advantages over interpersonal communication.

Teleconferencing : It is a means by which individuals or groups located at different places can exchange data, speech, visual materials like graphs or diagrams and other relevant informations. Teleconferencing is made possible by the integration of computers and communications in such a manner as to form a hostile system which can work in real-time.

It is gaining popularity due to the minimal physical travel demanded of its participants. The time-saving involved in this process is also a significant factor. Teleconferencing can be classified under the following types:

(a) Computer Conferencing

(b) Audio Conferencing

(c) Audio-Graphic conferencing

(d) Video Conferencing

Teletext : It is a form of broadcast technology by means of which several 'pages' of textual information can be transmitted on an already existing television channel. The teletext information is encoded in the so called 'Vertical blanking internal' of the TV screen which is invisible in the normal course of television viewing. Facilities exist in teletext to enable viewers to choose a particular page of teletext containing relevant information.

Teletext is a simple technology which can be used to advantage for public communication.

Radiotext : Better known by the term 'Radiodata systems' (RDS), Radiotext is a technology similar to teletext but with a difference that it works in conjunction with FM Radio while teletext works on television. Radiotext is to be seen as a value-added service on FM Radio. This technology essentially consists of transmitting data and other textual material on the FM carrier so that the listeners/ viewers who are equipped with a Radiotext 'decode' can extract this signal from an ongoing FM transmission and watch the same on a computer screen which forms a part of the Radiotext receiving system.

Videotex : It is another form of interactive communication technology which is in wide usage in several advanced countries. This works with the help of the public telephone network. The integral components of this system are-home computer, telephone connection and domestic TV set. It is essentially interactive and has much more to offer than teletext or Radiotext, which provide only selective information exchange and retrieval.

Interactive Cable Distribution Systems : Dissemination of television programmes via cable to a community of households started in the 1950s. The cable distribution was seen as improving the reception conditions of television in isolated mountainous regions. Later, TV signals received via satellite were put out on cable distribution systems. The spread, of cable distribution system grew dramatically. Advancement in digital technology and fibre optics have resulted in further improved versions of cable distribution.

Communication Satellites : Transmission of television programmes from one country to another, became a reality with the development of communication satellites. These satellites are stationed in an orbit above the earth's equator at a height of about 36,000 km called the geostationary orbit.

Communication Satellites are owned by various individual nations as well as collectively by groups of nations to cater to several applications like broadcasting, television and telecommunications. INTELSAT (International Telecommunications Satellite Consortium) is an international body consisting of more than 90 member countries of which India is one. Our country has also developed its own satellite system called, INSAT (Indian National Satellite System). It is a multi-purpose satellite service catering to telecommunications, radio and TV transmission and weather forecasting.

Mushrooming of satellite-based transnational television in recent years is a cause for concern as well as hope. Many national newspapers which are published simultaneously from multiple locations take advantage of satellite communications for instant transmission of their pages from one publishing centre to another.

Most-modern Devices

Every technology has its distinct attributes, advantages and disadvantages, because of which an optimal technology selection is possible for any given application.

A relative assessment of the various technologies has been discussed below on the basis of interactivity, asynchronicity and demassification.

Interactivity : It is a property in which the new communication technologies excel over the traditional ones. Teleconferencing and video-teleconferencing can be cited as the most interactive while, teletext or radiotext can be placed at the other end of the interactivity scale.

Asynchronicity : This term refers to that property of the medium whereby the simultaneous presence of all the participants in a communication exercise is not compulsory. The degrees of asynchronicity, however, varies from one technology to the other. It is highest in teleconferencing where all computers are required to interact without live human intervention, but least in a two-way video teleconferencing.

Demassification : Traditional media like press, radio or television are instances of 'one-to-many' kind of communications. Therefore, they are unsuitable where the communication needs are more individualised. Demassification refers to the extent to which a given technology can lead itself to such individualised communication. The normal telephone system is an ideal example of a technology endowed with a high degree of demassification. Teleconferencing or computer communication are high in their demassification while teletext is at the lower end of the demassification ladder.

Societal Characteristics

The new communication technologies have not yet penetrated sufficiently in Third World countries like ours. Therefore it is not able to determine their likely impact on our society with any degree of certainty. Communication scholar, Everett Rogers says that the new communication technologies have a marked social impact in the following respects, especially during their adaptability stages:

(a) As the new technologies are relatively costlier and knowledge-intensive, they will be adopted only by the higher strata of the society at first, who can afford them.

(b) Advanced countries which are already information-rich tend to become richer, thus, widening the information gap between countries. This may lead to unfavourable situation for the 3rd World countries.

(c) Information overload is likely to happen, which in turn poses problems of coping with selective retrieval of required information, from heaps of randomly accumulated information. Here again new technologies help us.

(d) Unemployment may abound in certain sectors as the new technologies would eliminate or render surplus certain traditional jobs and occupations. Some new jobs and occupations may be created in their place, but not in numbers sufficient enough to compensate the loss of traditional jobs.

(e) The universal presence of computers and easy access to them is likely to raise problems concerning privacy and security of communications. Use of special passwords and the like are of course an obvious protection, but they too have their limitations. Clever use of special software may also enable computer miscreants to break the secret passwords and get the information.

(f) Greater use of the new technologies may enable the organizations concerned to become more decentralized in their decision making and other functions. But again, an exact opposite may be possible as the new technologies permit much tighter monitoring on the movements and performances of subordinate staff.

10

Medium for Learning

The Nomenclature

Audio-Visual aids, Audio-visual material, audio-visual media, communication technology, educational or instructional media and learning resources — all these terms, broadly speaking, mean the same thing. Earlier the term used was audio-visual aids in education. With the advancement in the means of communication and that of technology, educators coined new terms, More specifically media refers to films, filmstrips, recordings, etc. The use of newer terms Educational Technology or Instructional Technology is primarily due to the dynamic expansion of programmed learning, computer assisted instruction and education T.V. This revolution in the field of audio-visual education is the outcome of the development in electronics, notably those involving the radio, tape recorder and computer.

Brief history of the use of audio-visual aids : A Dutch humanist, theologian and writer Desiderious Erasmus (1466-1536) discouraged memorization as a technique of learning and advocated that children should learn through the aid of pictures or other visuals. John Amos Comenius (1592-1670) prepared a book known as *Orbis Sensulium Pictus.* (The world of Sense Objects) which contained about 150 pictures on aspects of everyday life. The book is considered to be the first illustrated textbook for childhood education. This book gained wide publicity and was used in childhood education centres all over the world. Jean Jacques Rousseau (1712-1778) and other educators stressed the need of pictures and other play materials. Rousseau condemned the use of words by teachers and he stressed 'things'. He pleaded that the teaching process must be directed to the learner's natural curiosity. Pestalozzi (1756-1827) put Rousseau's theory into action in his 'object method'. He based instruction on sense perception.

The term 'Visual education' was used as early as 1926 by Lelson.I.Green.

Eric Ashby (1967) identified four revolutions in education: education from home to school, written words as tool of education, invention of printing and use of books and lastly the fourth revolution in the use of electronic media i.e., radio, television, tape recorder and computer in education.

Scope and Definition

Burton : Audio-visual aids are those sensory objects or images which initiate or stimulate and reinforce learning.

Carter V. Good : Audio-visual aids are those aids which help in completing the triangular process of learning i.e., motivation, classification and stimulation.

Edgar Dale : Audio-visual are those devices by the use of which communication of ideas between persons and groups in various teaching and training situations is helped. These are also termed as multi-sensory materials.

Good's dictionary of education : Audio-visual aids are anything by means of which learning process may be encouraged or carried on through the sense of hearing or sense of sight.

Kinder, S. James : Audio-visual aids are any device which can be used to make the learning experience more concrete, more realistic and more dynamic.

Mckown and Roberts: Audio-visual aids are supplementary devices by which the teacher, through the utilization of more than one sensory channels is able to clarify, establish and correlate concepts, interpretations and appreciations.

Importance and Benefits

Audio-visual aids or devices or technological media or learning devices are added devices that help the teacher to clarify, establish, co-relate and co-ordinate accurate concepts, interpretations and appreciations and enable him to make learning more concrete, effective, interesting, inspirational, meaningful and vivid. They help in completing the triangular process of learning viz., motivation-clarification-stimulation. The aim of teaching with technological media is 'clearing the channel between the learner and the things that are worth learning'. The basic assumption underlying Audio-visual Aids is that learning—clear understanding—stems from sense experience. The teacher must 'show' as well as 'tell'. Audio-visual aids provide significant gains in informational learning, retention and recall, thinking and reasoning, activity, interest, imagination, better assimilation and personal growth and development. The aids are the stimuli for learning 'why', 'how', 'when' and 'where'. The 'hard to understand principles' are usually made clear by the intelligent use of skilfully designed instructional aids.

According to Gandhi Ji, "True education of the intellect can only come through a proper exercise and training of bodily organs—hands, feet, eyes, ears and nose."

Commenting on the use of audio-visual aids, the Kothari Commission 1964-66 observed that it should indeed bring about an 'educational revolution' in the country. It further stated that the supply of teaching aids to every school was essential for the improvement of the quality of teaching.

The National Policy of Education, 1986 and as modified in 1992 has laid a great stress on the use of teaching aids, especially improvised aids, to make teaching-learning more effective and realistic.

In the words of Edgar Dale, "Because audio-visual materials supply concrete basis for conceptual thinking, they give rise to meaningful concepts enriched by meaningful association, hence they offer the best antidote for the disease of verbalism."

Some of the important values of the proper use of audio-visual aids are given below:

Antidote to the disease of verbal instruction **:** They help to reduce verbalism. They help in giving clear concepts and thus help to bring accuracy in learning. As observed by Raymound Wyman (1957) "We (teacher) tell students, and we provide them with written material so much of the time. Words are wonderful. They are easily produced, reproduced, stored and transported. But the overuse or excessive use of words can result in serious problem, chiefly, the problem of verbalism (using or adopting words or phrases without considering what they mean) and forgetting."

Best motivation **:** They are the best motivators. The students work with more interest and zeal. They are more attentive.

Clear images **:** Clear images are formed when we see, hear, touch, taste and smell as our experiences are direct, concrete and more or less permanent. Learning through the senses becomes the most natural and consequently the easiest.

Vicarious experience **:** It is beyond doubt that the first-hand experience is the best type of educative experience. But it is neither practicable nor desirable to provide such experience to pupils. Substituted experiences may be provided under such conditions. There are many inaccessible objects and phenomena. For example, it is not possible for the pupils living in India to see the Eskimos. Similarly, it is not possible for an average man to climb the Mount Everest. There are innumerable such things to which it is not possible to have direct access. So, in all such cases, these aids help us.

Variety : 'Mere chalk and talk' do not help. Audio-visual aids give variety and provide different tools in the hands of the teacher.

Freedom : When audio-visual aids are employed, there is great scope for children to move about, talk, laugh and comment upon. Under such an atmosphere the students work because they want to work and not because the teacher wants them to work.

Opportunities to handle and manipulate : Many visual aids offer opportunities to students to handle and manipulate things.

Retentivity : Audio-visual aids contribute to increased retentivity as they stimulate response of the whole organism to the situation in which learning takes place.

Based on maxims of teaching : The use of audio-visual aids enables the teacher to follow the maxims of teaching like 'concrete to abstract', 'known to unknown' and 'learning by doing.'

Helpful in attracting attention : Attention is the true factor in any process of teaching and learning. Audio-visual aids help the teacher in providing proper environment for capturing as well as sustaining the attention and interest of the students in the classroom work.

Helpful in fixing up new learning : 'What is gained in terms of learning, needs to be fixed up in the minds of students. Audiovisual aids help in achieving this objective by providing several activities, experiences and stimuli to the learners'.

Saving of energy and time : A good deal of energy and time of both the teachers and students can be saved on account of the use of audio-visual aids as most of the concepts and phenomena may be easily clarified, understood and assimilated through their use.

Realism : The use of audio-visual aids provides a touch of reality to the learning situation. By seeing a film show exhibiting the life of the people of the Tundra region, students learn it more effectively in about 2 hours than by spending weeks by reading.

Vividness : Audio-visual aids give vividness to the learning situation. A film on Buddha provides a vivid picture of his life and teachings.

Meeting individual differences : There are wide individual differences among learners. Some are ear-oriented, some can be helped through visual demonstrations, while others learn better by doing. The use of a variety of audio-visual aids helps in meeting the needs of different types of students.

Encouragement to healthy classroom interaction : Audio-visual aids, through their wide variety of stimuli, provision of active participation of the students, and vicarious experiences encourage healthy classroom interaction for the effective realization of teaching-learning objectives.

Spread of education on a mass scale : Audio-visual aids like radio and television help in providing opportunities for education to people living in remote areas. They also help in promoting adult education.

Promotion of scientific temper : In place of listening to facts, students observe demonstrations and phenomena and thus cultivate scientific temper.

Development of higher faculties : Verbalism promotes memorisation. Use of audio-visual aids stirs the imagination, thinking process and reasoning power of the students, and calls for creativity, and inventiveness and other higher mental activities on the parts of students and thus helps the development of higher faculties among the students.

Reinforcement to learners : Audio-visual aids prove effective reinforcers by increasing the probability of re-occurrence of the response associated with them and thus render valuable help in the teaching-learning process.

Positive transfer of learning and training : Use of audio-visual aids helps in the learning of other concepts, principles and solving the real problems of life by making possible the appropriate positive transfer of learning and training received in the classroom.

Positive environment for creative discipline : A balanced, rational and scientific use of audio-visual aids develops motivation, attracts the attention and interests of the students and provides a variety of creative outlets for the utilisation of their tremendous energy and thus keeps them busy in the classroom work. In this way, the overall classroom environment becomes conducive to creative discipline.

Using teaching aids : psychological elements : In addition to reading, vicarious experience can be gained from still pictures, films, filmstrips, resource persons, simulations, mock-ups, television, and the like. The more concrete and realistic the vicarious experience, the more nearly it approaches the learning effectiveness of the first level. Of course, unless the learner realizes that he is dealing with a substitute, his learning may not be comparable to that of real-life learning.

Interest in the role of the senses in learning was already

there in educational circles when instructional media began their ascendancy. It has long been recognized that the various senses condition the reception of messages in the communications act. Research done by Cobun (1968) indicated that:

1 per cent of what is learned is from the sense of TASTE.

1.5 per cent of what is learned is from the sense of TOUCH.

3.5 per cent of what is learned is from the sense of SMELL.

11 per cent of what is learned is from the sense of HEARING.

83 per cent of what is learned is from the sense of SIGHT.

Retention of what is learned is likewise related to sense experience.

Observation and research by Cobun tended to show, holding time as nearly constant as possible, that people generally remember:

10 per cent of what they READ.

20 per cent of what they HEAR.

30 Per cent of what they SEE.

50 per cent of what they HEAR AND SEE.

70 per cent of what they SAY.

90 per cent of what they SAY as they do a thing.

Popular sayings

I hear, I forget.

I see, I remember.

I do, I understand.

Characteristics

1. They should be meaningful and purposeful.
2. They should be accurate in every respect.

3. They should be simple.
4. They should be cheap.
5. As far as possible, they should be improvised.
6. They should be large enough to be properly seen by the students for whom they are meant.
7. They should be up-to date.
8. They should be easily portable.
9. They should be according to the mental level of the students.
10. They should motivate the learners.

Principles of important nature

Principle of selection : Teaching aids prove effective only when they suit the teaching objectives and unique characteristics of the special group of learners. Following points may be kept in view in this regard :

(i) They should suit the age-level, grade-level and other characteristics of the learners.

(ii) They should have specific educational value besides being interesting and motivating.

(iii) They should be the true representatives of the real things.

(iv) They should help in the realization of desired learning objectives.

Principle of preparation : This principle requires that following points should be attended to:

(a) As far as possible, locally available material should be used in the preparation of an aid.

(b) The teachers should receive some training in the preparation of aids.

(c) The teachers themselves should prepare some of the aids.

(d) Students may be associated in the preparation of aids.

Preparation of physical control : This principle related to the arrangement of keeping aids safely and also to facilitate their lending to the teachers for use.

Principle of proper presentation : This principle implies the following points :

(i) Teachers should carefully visualise the use of teaching aids before their actual presentation.

(ii) They should fully acquaint themselves with the use and manipulation of the aids to be shown in the classroom.

(iii) Adequate care should be taken to handle an aid in such a way as no damage is done to it.

(iv) The aid should be displayed properly so that all the students are able to see it, observe it and derive maximum benefit out of it.

(v) As far as possible, distraction of all kinds to be eliminated so that full attention may be paid to the aid.

Principle of response : This principle demands that the teachers guide the students to respond actively to the audio-visual stimuli so that they derive the maximum benefit in learning.

Principle of evaluation : This principle stipulates that there should be continuous evaluation of both the audio-visual material and accompanying techniques in the light of the realisation of the desired objectives.

Problems of Grave Nature

While all these aids are becoming more and more popular day by day, there are still some problems to be faced and solved. These are :

Apathy of the teachers : Teachers in general are yet to be convinced that teaching with words alone is very tedious, wasteful and ineffective.

Indifference of students : The judicious use of aids arouses interest but when used without a definite purpose they lose their significance and importance.

Ineffectiveness of the aids : Due to the absence of proper planning and the lethargy of the teacher and without proper preparation, correct presentation, application and discussion and the essential follow-up work, the aids do not prove their full usefulness. A film like a good lesson has various steps—Preparation, Presentation, Application and Discussion.

Financial hurdles : The Central and State Governments have set up Boards of Audio-Visual Education and have chalked out interesting programmes for the popularization of teaching aids but the lack of finances is not enabling them to do their best.

Absence of electricity : Most of the Projectors, Radio and TV cannot work without the electric current which is not available in a large number of schools.

Lack of facilities for training : Training colleges or specialised agencies should make special provision to train teachers and workers in the use of these aids.

Co-ordination between centre and states : Good film libraries, museums of audio-visual provision to train teachers and workers in the use of these aids.

Language difficulty : Most educational films are in English. We should have these in Hindi and other important Indian languages.

Not catering to local needs : Little attention is paid in the production of audio-visual aids to the local sociological, psychological and pedagogical factors.

Improper selection of films : Films are not selected according to the classroom needs.

Today, the problem is not whether visual aids should have a place in education. Their place has been recognised long ago. The problem, now, is that of extending the benefits of these aids to all teachers and all children. The future can be bright if there is proper planning on the part of the Government and co-ordination between producers, teachers and students. Useful and effective aids can be produced after getting the reaction of the audience and doing research work in the field. A great deal is being done already but a lot more still remains to be done.

Categorising Teaching Aids

Classification Number 1: Projected and Non-Projected Aids

Projected Aids	*Graphic Aids*	*Display Boards*	*3-Dimensional Aids*	*Audio Aids*	*Activity Aids*
1. Films	1. Cartoons	Blackboard	Diagrams	Radio	1. Computer-Assisted Instruction
2. Filmstrips	2. Charts	Bulletin	Models	Recordings	2. Demonstrations
3. Opaque Projector	3. Comics	Flannel Board	Mockups	Television	3. Dramatics
4. Overhead Projector	4. Diagrams	Magnetic Board	Objects		4. Experimentation
5. Slides	5. Flash Cards	Peg Board	Puppets		5. Field Trips
	6. Graphs		Specimens		6. Programmed Instruction
	7. Maps				7. Teaching Machines
	8. Photographs				
	9. Pictures				
	10. Posters				

Classification Number 2: Audio Materials, Visual Materials and Audio-Visual Materials

Audio Materials	*Visual Materials*	*Audio-visual Materials*
(1) Language Laboratories	(1) Bulletin boards	(1) Demonstrations
(2) Radio	(2) Chalk boards	(2) Films
(3) Sound distribution system sets	(3) Charts	(3) Printed materials with recorded sound
(4) Tape and disco recordings	(4) Drawings etc.	(4) Sound filmstrips
	(5) Exhibits	(5) Study trips
	(6) Film strips	(6) Television
	(7) Flash cards	(7) Videotapes
	(8) Flannel boards	
	(9) Flip books	
	(10) Illustrated books	
	(11) Magnetic boards	
	(12) Maps	
	(13) Models	
	(14) Pictures	
	(15) Posters	
	(16) Photographs	
	(17) Self-instructional	
	(18) Silent films	
	(19) Slides	

Big media and little media : Big media include computer, VCR and TV. Little media include radio, films strips, graphic, audio cassettes and various visuals.

Three dimensional aids

(i) Models

(ii) Mock-ups

(iii) Specimens.

Three dimensional aids are the replicas or substitutes of real objects.

All the learning experiences which can be utilised for classroom teaching are shown by Edgar Dale in a pictorial device—'pinnacle form'—which he called the 'cone of experience'. If we go up the pinnacle from its base, we find that every aid has been arranged in the order of increasing abstractness or decreasing directness. In a simple language, it may be stated that the 'cone' classifies the audiovisual aids according to their effectiveness in communication—aid at the base of the cone as 'most effective'—relative effect gradually decreases.

At the pinnacle of the 'Cone', the direct, purposeful experiences are represented. At the pinnacle of the 'Cone', the verbal symbols are represented.

The experiences included in the cone are as indicated below:

Direct, purposeful experience : The experiences gained through the senses are direct and purposeful. It has been amply observed, "An ounce of experience is better than a tonne of theory, simply because it is only as an experience that any theory has vital and verifiable significance." This, direct experience is gained through the aids mentioned at the base of the cone.

Contrived experience : When the real thing cannot be perceived directly, its simplification becomes necessary. Contrived experience is like a working model which is an editing of reality and differs from the original either in size or in complexity. The real object may be too small or too big, may be confused or concealed. In such a situation imitation is preferred for better and easier understanding.

Dramatic participation : In dramatics, certain real events are presented through the play, the pageant (kind of community drama, usually based on local history), pantomine (actors do not speak, make movements), tablean (pictureline scene in which the characteristics stand still, silently), and the puppets.

Explaining Various Aids

Actual objects : Actual objects and specimens are indispensable in science and other subjects. They are very vivid and impressive. They make a direct appeal to the senses of children. It is not possible for a child to have a clear picture of a river, a factory or a mountain unless he has seen these. The teaching of history and geography can never be effective without visiting places of importance, valleys, lakes, old forts, monuments, etc. The students get a correct idea of various minerals when they are shown these objects. In framing the multiplication table, counting of beads and sticks prove to be very useful at the earlier stages.

Blackboard : Blackboard and a piece of chalk prove very helpful in illustrating concepts and ideas to the students. These can be used for drawing diagrams and sketches, etc. Blackboard is a simple and unique device which, in spite of new devices and techniques in teaching, is irreplacable as well as indispensable. It is the oldest and the best friend of a teacher. It is the mirror through which students visualise all about the teacher's mind regarding the lesson in hand, his way of explaining, illustrating and teaching as a whole. It is the cheapest teaching device and continues to be the *'sine quo non'* of our educational system. It is the most universally used aid. Writing on clay and sand was the ancient form of blackboard writing. It helps 'crystallizing' the main points, 'summarising' and 'reviewing'.

Blackboard use

1. The teacher can illustrate the main points of the lesson on the blackboard.
2. Abstract statements can be clarified in the exposition

stage and a summary containing the salient features can be given at the recapitulatory stage.

3. Questions and problems can be listed on the blackboard.
4. Pupils' interest in classwork can be stimulated by blackboard writings and drawings.
5. A teacher can use the blackboard for graphs, graphics, sketches, maps and statistics, etc.
6. A blackboard provides a lot of scope for creative and decorative work.
7. The teacher can erase writings and drawings and start afresh.
8. It helps the teacher to focus the attention of his students on the lesson. It takes heed of varying capacities and rates of grasp of the students.
9. A teacher can review the whole lesson for the benefit of the class with the help of the blackboard.

Types of blackboards

Fixed blackboard : Fixed in the wall facing the class and normally made of wood or concrete cement.

Blackboard on easel : A portable and adjustable blackboard put on a wooden easel can be taken out of the classroom while taking classes in the open.

Roller blackboard : Made of thick canvas wrapped on a roller mostly used for teaching higher classes.

Graphic board : It has graphic lines and is used for teaching mathematics, science and statistics.

Magna board : A board which enables teachers to make three-dimensional demonstrations with objects on a vertical surface. Small magnets are used to hold suitable objects fixed wherever they are put on this vertical surface.

Chalk boards of different types of surfaces

1. Paint-coated pressed wood.
2. Dull finished plastic surface.
3. Vitreous-coated steel surface.
4. Ground glass board.

Use of chalks

Colour of the blackboard	*Colour of the chalk*
1. Green chalk board	White or Yellow chalk
2. Grey board	Yellow
3. Red chalk board	Green, Yellow
4. Orange chalk board	Blue or light Green
5. Yellow chalk board	Blue
6. Rose chalk board	Purple, dark Blue
7. Black chalk board	Any colour

Effective use of blackboard

Following points may be kept in view while using the blackboard :

1. Blackboard should be kept clean so-that writing on it could be easily read by the students from all parts of the room.
2. Writing on the blackboard should be legible.
3. Letters and drawings should be large enough to be seen from all parts of the room.
4. Writing should be started from the top left corner.
5. Writing should be in straight rows.
6. Extreme lower corner of the blackboard should not be made use of as writing on it cannot be seen easily.

7. Material on the blackboard should not be covered by standing.
8. Only salient points of the subject-matter should be written on the blackboard.
9. Diagrammatic visual presentation involving many processes should be prepared before the beginning of the lesson.
10. It should be ensured that blackboard is well lighted by natural or artificial means.
11. Everything needed for the blackboard should be got together before the class begins i.e., collection of chalk, rulers, T. Square, Compass, Projector, etc.
12. While writing on the blackboard, the teacher should ensure that the class is attentive.
13. Duster and not hand or handkerchief should be used in cleaning the blackboard.
14. Occasionally students may be asked to write or draw diagram on the blackboard.
15. Teachers should develop the ability to draw freely on the blackboard. The map or chart or diagram that grows before the very eyes of the students is much more useful and valuable than a well finished map, chart or diagram.
16. It should be ensured that the blackboard is periodically serviced.

Usage of charts : A chart is a combination of pictorial, graphic, numerical or vertical material which presents a clear visual summary. The most commonly used types of charts include outline charts, tabular charts, flow charts and organisation charts. Other types of charts are technical diagrams and process diagrams. Flip charts and flow charts are also being used. Ready made charts are available for use in teaching in almost all areas in all subjects. But charts prepared by a teacher himself incorporating his own ideas and lines of approach of the specific topic are more useful.

Purposes of charts : Charts serve the following purposes:

1. For showing relationship by means of facts, figures and statistics.
2. For presenting materials symbolically.
3. For summarising information.
4. For showing continuity in process.
5. For presenting abstract ideas in visual form.
6. For showing development of structure.
7. For creating problems and stimulating thinking.
8. For encouraging utilisation of other media of communication.
9. For motivating the students.

How to use charts effectively?

1. Teacher-made charts should be preferred.
2. Students should be involved in the preparation of charts.
3. Charts should be so large that every detail depicted should be visible to every pupil in the class wherever he is sitting.
4. Charts should display information only about one specific area in a subject.
5. A chart should not contain too much written material.
6. A chart should not contain too many details.
7. A chart should give a neat appearance.
8. When a chart is to be used in the classroom, the teacher should make sure that there is provision for hanging the chart at a vantage point.

9. The teacher should have a pointer to point out specific factors in the chart.
10. Straight pins, staples, pegboard lips, gummed hangers, paper-clips, folded making tapes may all be used for fastening charts without damaging them.
11. Charts should be carefully stored and preserved for use in future.

Types of charts : The following is a list of basic types of charts in terms of arrangements and the kinds of ideas which they may express :

1. The narrative chart, an extended left-to-right arrangement of facts and ideas for expressing: (a) The events in a process such as shoe making, oil cracking, or the like, (b) The events in the development of a significant issue to its point of resolution or to present status (sometimes a time limit). Example: the events leading to the separation of the Bangladesh from Pakistan, the events leading to the establishment of the idea that an individual should be free and that he should have a voice in his own government and the events leading to increased regulation of business by government, (c) Technological improvement over a period of years such as improvement in transportation, communication, manufacturing etc.
2. The tabulation chart, a left-to-right, top-to-bottom arrangement of facts and ideas for expression: (a) Numerical data for making comparisons, (b) Lists products, mountains, rivers, or the like in selected areas.
3. The cause and effect chart, usually a limited left-to-right arrangement of facts and ideas for expressing: (a) Relationship between standard of living and such factors as economic system, availability of natural resources, level of technological advancement,

(b) Relationship between a culture and neighbouring cultures, (c) Relationship between rights and responsibilities, (d) Relationship between a complex of conditions and change or conflict, (e) Relationship - between the elected and the electors, (f) Relationship between community workers and the community which supports them.

4. The chain charts, a circular or semi-circular arrangement of facts and ideas for expressing: (a) Transitions, such as the transition from raw materials to useful products, (b) Cycles, such as the water cycle.

5. The evolution chart, a left-to right arrangement of facts and ideas for expressing: (a) Changes in specific item from beginning to date, perhaps with projections into the future. Example: origin of the automobile and its subsequent development, early basic homes and changes in basic homes to date, (b) Change in standard in food consumption, length of work, weak purchasing power of a rupee, or the like.

Diagrams : Diagrams are very helpful in supplementing vertical illustrations in teaching. Difficult operations may be explained with the help of diagrams. The parts of a flower or leaf can be suitably explained by means of sketches drawn by the teacher in front of the class on the blackboard: Simple diagrams can be used to explain different phenomena in geography and science. The diagrams of battle plans and forts can be drawn on the blackboard. The area and volume, etc., in mathematics can be illustrated through diagrams. A teacher is expected to possess the skill of drawing diagrams easily, neatly, rapidly and readily on the blackboard.

Epidiascope : The epidiascope is an instrument which can project images or printed matter or small opaque objects on a screen, or it can project images of a 4" × 4" slide. With the help of any epidiascope, any chart, diagram, map, photograph and picture can be projected on the screen without tearing it off from the book. No slide is needed for this purpose. An epidiascope serves two purposes. It works as epidiascope when it is used to project an opaque object. It works as epidiascope when it is used to project slides (by operating a lever). It works on the principle of horizontal straight line projection with a lamp, plane mirror and projection lens. A strong light from the lamp falls on the opaque object. A plane mirror placed at an angle of 45° over the project, reflects the light so that it passes through the projection lens forming a magnified image on the screen.

Film strip : A film strip is 35 mm wide and has a series of 12 to 48 picture frames arranged in a sequence so that they develop a theme. A film strip can be prepared by taking a series of photographs using a 35 mm camera and then by taking a positive print of the negative film on another 35 mm film.

Globe : Knowledge of map is unreal without the knowledge of globe-the true map. It is the true representative of earth's physical personality. A globe gives a true idea of the total environment at a glance in a classroom situation. It is through globe that a child can understand the concepts of time, space, wind's planetary relations and proportion. Hence, every school shall have globes. Four types of globes may be kept in every school.

(1) Political globes,

(2) Physical globes,

(3) Washable projection globes,

(4) Celestial globes.

Graphs : Graphs are flat pictures which employ dots, lines or pictures to visualise numerical and statistical data to show relationships or statistics.

Several types of graphs

Line graph : In a line graph, data is represented with the help of simple lines horizontally or vertically drawn. For increasing the interest and readability of concepts, pictorial illustrations and cartoons are occasionally used on the line graph.

Bar graph : A bar graph consists of bars arranged, horizontally or vertically from a 'zero' base. The colour, length and size of the bars represent different values.

Circle graph : Data may be presented in a circle graph.

Magic lantern : Magic lantern is the earliest invention in the history of audio-visual aids used for projecting pictures from a transparency (slide) on a wall or screen. When the figure or illustration is very small and it is required to be shown to the entire class, a transparent slide of the small figure is prepared. Then, this slide is placed into the slide carrier part of the magic lantern. This magic lantern device projects it on the screen by enlarging its dimension and making the vision more clear and sharp.

Map study

Significance of map study : In several subjects, especially social studies, the learning of many geographical, historical and economic concepts remains unreal, inadequate and incomplete without map media. A resourceful teacher by motivating the pupils will turn the fear of map into the genuine love for them. This, however, presupposes the invariable uses of maps at every possible opportunity by the teacher in the classroom, and the possession of individual atlases by the pupils. Every student should also know certain elementary aspects of map preparation such as copying, enlarging and reducing, symbolizing, colouring, and preparation of key. Most of the students develop an aversion to maps because they do not know skills relating to map preparation.

Meaning of map : A map is an accurate representation of plain surface in the form of a diagram drawn to scale, the details of boundaries of continents, countries, of etc. Geographical details like location of mountains, rivers, altitude of a place, contours of the earth surface and important' locations can also be represented accurately with reference to a convenient scale with suitable colour scheme.

Identification of various aspects of maps

1. Understanding and interpreting the key of index.
2. Understanding the lines-boundary lines, lines of communication, lines indicating the rivers, contours, meridians and parallels.
3. Understanding the colours, tints, shadows, symbols in a map or globe.
4. The top of every map is not north, but the direction of northern pole is north.
5. Distinction between the various types of maps such as relief, political, distribution maps, etc.
6. Understanding of the position of earth in the universe. Many students suffer from a notion that the earth leans in June towards the Sun northwards and in December southwards and thus the seasons are formed. Earth never dances that way. The student shall understand that the inclination of earth is constant and the learning effect changes due to its rotation around the sun.

Various types of maps

Relief maps (regional and the world) : This requires the knowledge of colours, contours, symbols and the other connected ethics of map making.

Historical maps : Maps in history reveal the changing times and the growth and decline of various kingdoms.

Knowledge of lines of boundaries and other symbols is necessary.

Distribution maps : Generally, the student shall associate with the following types of distribution maps: (1) Vegetation maps, (2) Population maps, (3) Economic maps, (4) Statistical maps, (5) Dot maps, (6) Pictorial maps, (7) Language, race and other human division maps, etc.

Geographical maps : Contour maps, weather maps, seismological maps, archaeological maps, rainfall maps, geological maps, etc.

Microfilm : The microfilm and microfiche are used widely for storage and retrieval of information. Microfilms contain photographed reading material on 35 mm film, each frame being the reduced photograph of a printed page. Thus, printed matter of a book can be stored in a small loop of 35 mm film. When the microfilm is passed through a microfilm reader, an enlarged image approximately of the size of the printed page is formed on a ground glass (rear-view) screen and the observer can read the matter. By moving the film through the microfilm reader, images of different pages can be obtained and read.

Models : Models are substitutes for real things. A model is a three-dimensional representation of a real thing. Models are concrete objects to explain clearly the structure or functions of real things. A model is a replica of the original. Models enable students to have a correct concept of the object. Being three dimensional, models evoke great interest and simplify matters. Models enable us to reduce or enlarge objects to an observable size. It may not be possible or even practicable to make students see the whole of a large industrial unit or even a large machine unit, but a model will give the correct perspective. Preparation of models could, form a topic for project work. It is essential to create interest in creative activity in students. Models are working as well as static. A working model will secure immediate attention and serve as motivation to learn. Model can be prepared with several kinds of materials like cardboard, plastic, plaster of paris, wood, clay, and thermocol etc. (See also under three Demential Aids)

Museum's Importance

The Secondary Education Commission, on the role of school museums observed, "Museums playa great part in the education of school children as they bring home to them much more vividly than any prosaic lectures, the discoveries of the past and the various developments that have taken place in many fields of science and technology." Again the Commission observes, "We believe it is necessary from the educational point of view to establish such museums in important centres at least wherein both ancient and modern collections will be exhibited and in some cases even demonstrations given of the actual process of development of various scientific discoveries. Nothing can impress students in the formative age so much as the actual visualising of these experiments in a graphic manner,"

Museums are made up of materials used in classroom teaching which, in many cases, are collected, classified and exhibited by students, with or without the help of a teacher. The museum activities may be an extracurricular function of the class or the school or they may be incorporated into a scientific-experimental method of teaching. The objectives of this type of museum are:

(a) to form within the school or the classroom an embryonic community dedicated to the usual occupations reflected in the school life of adults;

(b) to permit visual instruction and experimentation with actual museum specimens;

(c) to stimulate enthusiasm for study and research among both teachers and students;

(d) to stimulate interest, co-operation and participation in the cultural activities and scientific research conducted by the larger museums;

(e) to instruct students in proper scientific methods of laboratory, research and museum conservation and exhibition techniques;

(f) to form, in the absence of larger museums in the community, a nucleus from which the classroom museum can grow beyond the limits of the school to serve ultimately the community and the region as a whole.

Exhibit programmes, interpretation, visual communication: What then are some of the ways in which museums as cultural and educational centres of the community can communicate successfully with their transitory visitors of heterogeneous composition? Based on various audience-testing experiments the following media can be used to heighten the effectiveness of visual communication.

Dramatic labels : Usually they are far too short in the museums or far too long. They actually frighten away rather than entice the average museum visitor. Experiments suggest that large letters placed at the focal point of the case or exhibit area will successfully headline the exhibit and catch the visitor's attention. Like a newspaper headline, the main label tends to direct the eye to smaller, less conspicuous letters that outline the most important points of the exhibit.

Dramatic lighting : Light is a means of visual communication as well as an attention getter. Coloured lights that change, fade or highlight an exhibit can be used with great dramatic effect. Light can also be used to tell a story and to convey a sense of passing time. Light is particularly important in art museums.

Dramatic utilization : Again experiments suggest that museum visitors should be given a chance to touch exhibits as well as to see them. Of course, much depends on the nature and expendability of the object involved but certain types of material-objects of wood, stone and metal and special "touch me" samples of animal skins and fabrics-can be used with great success to satisfy the visitor's urge to which while permitting a minimum of danger.

Dramatic sound effects : Sound, like light, can be used to heighten the dramatic effect of visual communication. For example, an Amazon rain forest exhibition can be made vastly more effective by adding the sound of tropical rain, the croaking of frogs, the chattering of monkeys, and the beat of drums. An exhibit of mediaeval art can be made more meaningful if it is accompanied by music of the same period:

Effective use of space : Special concepts are also important in planning visitor traffic patterns within the exhibit areas.

Using pictures : Pictures are very much liked by children and especially of lower classes, pictures provide an environment of 'reality'. A lesson in history can be made interesting and stimulating by showing the pictures of kings and queens, costumes and dresses, forts and weapons, monuments and tombs, etc. Similarly in a geography lesson, we can show the pictures of animals, deserts, lakes, mountains and rivers, etc., and also the various aspects of lives of people of other lands with great effect.

Following points need to be kept in view while showing pictures to the students:

1. Child's point of view should be the main criterion in the selection of pictures.
2. Pictures should be relevant to the topic.
3. As far as possible, pictures may be coloured.
4. Pictures should be accurate and of a suitable size.
5. It is desirable if the teacher himself prepares the pictures and takes help from the students.

6. Pictures should be shown in such a way that all students in the class can easily watch.
7. Too many pictures should not be displayed in one lesson.
8. After showing the picture, it should be removed from the view of the students.
9. Sufficient time should be given to see the picture.
10. Students who are good at drawing should be encouraged to draw pictures.

Using projector

Micro projector : The combination of a microscope and a slide projector is an instrument called micro-projector. The microscope is used to see very minute parts of objects by magnifying the same hundreds of times. The minute part usually of a plant or an animal is put on a glass slide and a magnified image formed by a combination of leuses in a microscope which can be seen by an individual through the naked eye. The micro-projector attachment consists of a projection lens; a plane mirror fixed at 45 degrees to the vertical plane and a vertical ground glass screen. It is very useful in teaching science.

Overhead projector (OHP) : Over head projector is a device that can project a chart, a diagram, a map, a table or for that matter, anything written on transparent plates, upon a screen or the white wall before students in a class. This makes teaching illuminative, illustrative and impressive. It also saves a great deal of the teacher's time used in drawing or writing. These transparencies can also be preserved by the teacher for future display while taking up the same topic. It is very simple to prepare such transparencies. All that a teacher has to do is to draw or write, as the case may be, upon transparent plates with any dark ink with a fibre tipped pen. Any material meant for display before the class while teaching can also be typed on such transparencies using a good carbon paper. In case transparencies are to be washed out for use, washable water colour can also be used for writing on the transparencies.

Slide projector : With a slide projector, photographic slides can be projected on the screen or the wall before the class. Photographs of relevant matter meant for teaching in the class can be developed on celluloid slides and displayed with the help of such a projector. The teacher's lesson can also be recorded on an audio cassette and played with a tape recorder suitably synchronising with the slides by manipulating a remote control switch.

Such an arrangement is called a tape-slide sequence. In case there are several slides to be shown in quick succession, the tape-slide sequence can bring as interesting an effect on the viewers as do the movie films. An ordinary slide projector has a frame containing two slits into which slides are put for focusing. They are manually and continuously replaced by other slides one after another. An improved type of a slide projector consists of a circular disc with more slits where even a hundred or more slides can be inserted in a sequential order which can be projected on the screen with the help of a remote control switch to be suitably manipulated by the teacher as he delivers the lesson.

Puppets : Puppetry is one of the old and popular arts in India. The use of puppets has been very popular in China, Egypt, Greece and Japan. Puppets can serve as an effective aid to learning. They can be made to illustrate lessons in civics, geography, history and hygiene. Puppets throw a lot of light in an interesting way on the life of historical personages if they are accompanied by effective narration. There should be plenty of dancing and music in the display of puppetry. While presenting puppet programmes, the age and tastes of the pupils should be duly considered. A short puppet play is always preferable to a long play. Puppets are of three types:

(i) Hand puppets which fit in the hand like a glove and are operated from below by fingers.

(ii) Rod puppets which are operated from below the stage by a combination of rods and springs,

(iii) Marionettes or string puppets which are figures with moving limbs. These are operated from the above by means of strings.

Use of reprographic equipments : Reprographic is a branch of technology dealing with methods of duplication or reproduction. Duplication involves making a number of identical copies of the original. Reproduction enables preparation of one or more identical copies of the original, same size or of different size in monochrome or colour. Equipment and processes, included are: duplicators, reflex printing and photography.

Using record player : Record players are a means of audio playback. They are older types of hardware using records of discs for the needed playback. Four sizes of records 7", 10", 12" and 16" are in common use. There are also high speed record player with standard stylus. The record players now in use are equipped with speed changer mechanisms permitting the playing of the slower long-playing 45, 33⅓ and 16⅔ r.p.m. records played by microgroove stylus.

The use of recorded pieces in education has great value in language learning, appreciation of poetry and literature and presentation of brief dramatised episodes from history, from development of musical knowledge and discrimination. Long-playing records with 20 minutes of recorded information per side provide several diverse selections inscribed on each side and are very suitable for classroom instructional purposes.

The needed selection for a particular learning situation can be easily identified by the specific microgroovering it occupies on the record. 'Talking books' for the blind also consists of recordings of essential literature for the visually handicapped.

The older, manually wound spring powered gramophone's place now has been taken up by electrically powered multi-speed record players and changers with built-in amplifying unit or linked to separate amplifying units and speakers. Likewise, the older mechanical recording has given place to electrical imprinting involving greater clarity and fidelity.

Tape-recorder : A tape-recorder in its own can be very effective for classroom instruction. Pre-recorded tapes consisting of lessons by eminent teachers on any subject can be played in the class. Such instructions become impressive not only because of the novelty but also because of their being well-thought out and planned. The tape-recorder has proved to be a boon in teaching foreign languages like English. Pre-recorded tapes on English lessons can be played in the classroom to teach not only the contents of the lesson but also proper accent, pronunciation and intonation which an average English teacher very much lacks.

Video tapes played through TV : Pre-recorded video tapes can be played through TV in the classroom. Video films on educational topics shown through TV in the classroom have the same effect on the students as the ordinary cinematic educational films do. Video films have the added advantage over ordinary films in that the arrangement is compact and requires little space and time for manipulation. It is the most convenient of all audio-visual teaching-learning materials.

Video Cassettes' Use : The potential advantage of video cassette lies in the fact that control of the equipment and the learning process is placed in the hands of the learner through control over the mechanics of the machine, i.e. stopping, starting, timing, reviewing and previewing and consequently the capacity to order the sequence of events, controls the rate of learning, and facilitates practice sequences.

The potential exists for providing the basis for learning a

wide range of motor, intellectual and cognitive and interpersonal skills, as well as affective aspects. These are important aspects which printed materials cannot deal with adequately.

This facility could be particularly useful where distance education programmes are involved with updating skills and techniques of workers in the field. For example, new horticulture techniques can be transmitted to field workers to improve farming techniques. Mid-career retraining can also be catered for.

In some countries as a way of regionalizing a centrally produced programme, video cassette programmes are being built round the study centre concept, a location where several video machines are available to which students bring their study notes. The students run the programmes as individuals. Sometimes study centres provide for group sessions during which video cassettes are played. Unless some supplementary teaching is provided, this technique can become another version of broadcast technology.

In other countries some institutions assume that students can gain access to such equipment and make programmes which will be used on an individual basis as either supplementary learning material or integral to the teaching programme.

The problems associated with video cassettes are of two kinds: (i) cost; and (ii) production of programmes.

(i) Equipment costs cannot always be kept down by using lower quality equipment. Cheaper equipment formats do not enable technical material such as animal or plant tissue to be represented adequately or tapes to be reproduced in quantity without loss of fidelity.

(ii) Video production for educational purposes calls for

new techniques different from the entertainment modes. Producers, directors, scriptwriters need to be knowledgeable about teaching and learning. Many of the old techniques of film and television will no longer be of use. For example, the very basic concept that programmes must have a beginning, a middle, and an end will no longer apply as a cassette could just as easily consist of a series of short video events which sets a problem, teaches a technique, or brings together a range of visual material to make concepts or principles clear.

Employing Three-dimensional Aids

Three dimensional aids serve as good substitutes for the real objects. There is no doubt that an encounter with real objects serves as an unmatchable source of learning. But on account of several reasons it may not be possible to bring the real objects in the classroom. The real objects may be too large to move or store in the classroom. It may be too small to be seen for a group of students. It can be too complicated in real form to be understood. Its movements may be too slow to be studied completely. It can be too expensive to be purchased by an, educational institution. Being handicapped in such situations, a teacher has to search for some good substitute for the real objects.

Models diagrams, mock-ups and specimens are the important three dimensional aids.

Models : Models are the replicas or copies of the real objects. Models are usually of three types: solid, cross-sectional and working. Models are concrete objects, some considerably larger than the real object. Sectional models explain clearly the structure or functions of the original. In some cases working models of the original are used where the specific function of the original is duplicated and could be explained easily.

Following are the important functions of models:

1. Models simplify reality.
2. Models concretise abstract concepts.
3. Models enable us to reduce or enlarge objects to an observable size.
4. A model provides the correct concept of an industrial unit or a bridge or a dam like, the Bhakra Dam etc.
5. A working model explains the various processes of objects and machines.
6. Preparation of models could form a topic for project work. This is very helpful to create interest in creative activity in pupils.

Cardboard, plastic, plaster of paris, wood thermocol' and metal, etc., can be used in the preparation of a model.

Mock-ups : A mock-up refers to a specialised model or working replica of the object being depicted. In a mock-up, a certain element of the original reality is emphasised or highlighted to make it more meaningful for the purpose of instruction. While a model is a recognizable limitation of an object (though larger or smaller than the original one), a mock-up may or may not be similar in appearance. Mock-ups of aeroplanes, automobile engines, bridges, ships and tunnels, etc., may be demonstrated for explaining their structure and actual working. Mock-ups are often used in technical institutions for training purposes.

Dioramas : A diorama is a three dimensional scene in depth incorporating a group of modelled objects and figures in a natural setting. The diorama scene is set up on a small stage with a group of modelled objects kept on the foreground which is blended into a painted realistic background. Dioramas are very effective in the teaching of biological and social sciences.

11

New Educational Pattern

Recommendations of the Education Commission 1964-66 were considered by various educational organisations and institutions. These were also discussed by educators all over the country. Many educational conferences were held to think over these recommendations. Meetings of Vice-chancellors, State Education Secretaries, Directors of Education were convened. All these discussions and debates resulted in the adoption of a resolution on the national policy on Education in 1968. The Resolution was adopted in the Parliament. A major decision in the field of education was taken by the Central Advisory of Education in November 1974 when it recommended the introduction of a New Pattern of Education which is popularly known as 10 + 2 + 3 pattern of education. Four other important documents that greatly affected the implementation of the recommendations are:

1. Curriculum for the Ten Year School—A Frame Work, published by the NCERT 1975.
2. Higher Secondary Education and Its Vocationalisation—published by the NCERT 1976.

3. Report of the Review Committee (Ishar Bhai Patel) Committee 1970-71.
4. Plus 2 Committee Report—Adiseshiah Report 1978. Following is a brief description of the recommendations which have been partly or wholly implemented in the country and which deserve special consideration.

Introducing the New Method of Education

On the recommendations of the Education Commission and in accordance with the National Policy on Education (adopted by Parliament in 1968), Central Advisory of Education adopted a resolution in its meeting held in November 1974 recommending the introduction of the 10+2+3 pattern of Education all over India during the Fifth Plan period. The resolution followed widespread consultations with several educational bodies and other concerned agencies throughout the country. By the end of the year 1980-81 this pattern had been introduced in 19 States/Union Territories, Assam, Andhra Pradesh, Gujarat, Jammu & Kashmir, Karnataka, Kerala, Maharashtra, Sikkim, Tamil Nadu, Tripura, West Bengal, Andaman and Nicobar Islands, Arunachal Pradesh, Chandigarh. Dadra and Nagar Haveli, Delhi, Goa, Daman and Diu, Lakshadweep and Pondicherry.

Vocationalising of higher secondary education : A centrally sponsored scheme for vocationalisation was initiated in 1976-77. Under it the State Governments were provided with central assistance during the Fifth Five Year Plan period and thereafter the programme would be run on a regular basis as a State scheme.

It is proposed to conduct vocational surveys of 130 districts in a phased manner during the current plan period. Out of the districts so surveyed, 40 districts will be selected for the introduction of vocational courses at an average of 16 courses per district. On the basis of the recommendations of a National

Conference organised by N.C.E.R.T. on June 5-6, 1976, a document entitled 'Higher Secondary Education and its Vocationalisation has been brought out by the N.C.E.R.T. The Central Board of Secondary Education, Delhi, introduçed a large number of vocations at the higher secondary stage from the academic session 1977-78.

Experience in the work : As recommended by the Education Commission, work experience has been made an integral part of the new scheme of studies under the pattern 10 + 2 + 3.

Banks of book : About one lakh book banks have been established in educational institutions which provide books to the students belonging to the weaker sections of the society.

Dual-level courses : Under the new pattern of education, provision has been made for the students to select courses in some subjects at two levels i.e. ordinary and advanced depending upon their capacity to work and comprehend.

Teachers' revised pay scale : The pay scale of teachers working in schools were revised almost in all the States as a result of the recommendation of the Education Commission.

Introducing national institution : The working party on Educational Planning Administration and Evaluation in the Fourth Five Year Plan set up by the Planning Commission reiterated the recommendation of the Kothari Commission and accepted this recommendation and accordingly initiated at the Asian Institute as Indian Programme in Educational Planning and Administration as a precursor to the National Staff College. The National Staff College for Educational Planners and Administrators began to function on 1st January, 1971 after it was registered under the Indian Society Registration Act, 1860, on 31st December, 1970. With the expiry of agreement with UNESCO, under which the Asian Institute of Educational Planning and Administration was functioning, the staff and activities of the Asian Institute were taken over by the staff college from 1st March, 1973. The staff college is located at the premises of the NCERT. Its main function is to provide pre-service and in-service training and professional guidance to the senior educational officers of the Central and State Governments and Union Territories. Now this college is known as a National Institute.

Commission's Recommendations

Following areas have remained ignored by and large. They have not received the due attention they deserved:

1. Development of a 'Streak and Quality' programme.
2. Creation of school complexes.
3. Development of 'neighbourhood' concept of educational institutions.
4. Establishments of suitable organisations for assessing manpower needs and or employment opportunities at the national and state levels.
5. Evolving integrated plans of development.
6. Development of a large programme of scholarship at all stages and in all sectors.
7. Creation of Indian Education Service.
8. Creation of District School Boards.
9. Strengthening of the offices of the District Education Officers.
10. National Education Act.
11. Creation of a National Board of School Education.
12. Establishment of a Farm University in each state.
13. Recognition of autonomous educational institutions.
14. Freedom to Headmasters.
15. Making Institutional Plans as an integral part of district, State and National Plan of Education.

16. Developing partnership between educational authorities and industry.
17. Discouragement to Public Schools.

Whatever the difficulties, the Government must make genuine efforts to implement as much report of the Education Commission as it can. The country's highest asset is its human resources and the more it invests in them the richer will be returns in terms of general well-being. It must be remembered that no development plan can succeed in the long run if it fails to relate educational system to the larger social and economic goals. We stand at a critical cross road of history where we must choose between good education and disaster.

A vigorous and sustained implementation of such great programmes demands three things—Conviction, Sacrifice and Passion. In the past we have failed on each of these counts. It is hoped we would meet the challenge effectively. The task is supremely urgent, not merely for national growth or progress but for mere survival.

It is envisaged that the country will refuse to be content with apologetic, half-hearted educational policy but will awaken to the nature of the new challenge and realise the intimate relationship between education and total national reconstruction.

12

Aims and Goals

The Commission observed "The most important and urgent reform needed in education is to transform it to endeavour to relate it to the life, needs and aspirations of the people and thereby make it a powerful instrument of social, economic and cultural transformation necessary for realisation of the national goals." For this purpose the Commission suggested a five fold programme:

1. Relating education to productivity.
2. Strengthening social and national integration through educational programmes.
3. Consolidation of democracy through education.
4. Development of social, moral and spiritual values.
5. Modernisation of society through awakening of curiosity, development of attitudes and values and building up certain essential skills.

Objectives of Education and Productivity

Following programme has been suggested:

(a) Science education to become an integral part of school education and ultimately a part of courses at university stage.

(b) Work experience to become an integral part of all education.

(c) Orientation work experiences to technology and industrialisation.

(d) Application of science to productive processes, including agriculture.

(e) Vocationalisation of secondary education.

(f) Agricultural and technical education to be emphasised.

Objectives of Social and National Integration : Following steps have been suggested to strengthen national consciousness and unity:

1. Adoption of a common school system of public education as the national goal and its effective implementation in a phased programme spread over 20 years.
2. Organisation of social and national service programmes concurrently with academic studies in schools and colleges and to make them obligatory for all students at all stages.
3. Development of community life in every educational institution.
4. Getting much of the work needed in the educational institutions and hostels done by the students.
5. Participation of the students in programme of community development and national reconstruction at all stages of education.

6. Continuation of NCC on its present basis till the end of the Fourth Five Year Plan.
7. Exploration of the possibility of providing NCC training on a whole time basis, in a continuous programme of about 60 days at the undergraduate stage.
8. Development of alternate programme of social service.
9. Formulation of an appropriate language policy.
10. Adoption of regional language as the medium of instruction.
11. Adoption of this programme within ten years.
12. Energetic action for the production of the text books and technical books in regional languages and the special responsibility of the universities assisted by UGC.
13. Continuation of the use of English as the medium of instruction at the All Indian institutions.
14. The eventual adoption of Hindi to be considered in due course subject to certain safeguards.
15. Regional languages to be made the language of administration for the regions concerned at the earliest possible time.
16. Continuation of the proportion of the teaching and study of English right from the school stage.
17. Encouragement to be given to the study of other languages of international communication.
18. Special attention to be given to the study of Russian.
19. English language to serve as a link language in higher education for academic work and intellectual inter-communication.
20. Hindi to serve as the link language of the majority of our people.

21. Adoption of all measures for the spread of Hindi in the non-Hindi areas.
22. Provision of multiple channels of inter-State communication in all modern Indian languages.
23. Establishment of strong departments in some of the modern Indian languages in every university.
24. Combining two modern Indian languages at the B.A. and M.A. levels.
25. Promotion of national consciousness through the promotion of understanding and revaluation of our cultural heritage and the creation of a strong driving faith in the future towards which we aspire.

Relevance of Education and Consolidation of Democracy: The Commission has suggested the following steps:

(i) Provision of free and compulsory education of good quality for all children upto the age of 14 years as envisaged in Article 45 of the Constitution.

(ii) Organisation of programme of adult education aiming not only at the liquidation of illiteracy but also at raising the civic and national efficiency and general cultural level of the citizen.

(iii) Training of efficient leadership at all levels by expanding secondary and higher education.

(iv) Provision of equal opportunities to all children of merit and promise irrespective of economic status, caste, religion, sex or place of residence.

(v) Development of a scientific mind and outlook, tolerance, concern for public interest and public service, self-discipline, self-reliance, initiative and a positive attitude to work.

Education vs Modernisation

(i) Awakening of curiosity, the development of proper interests, attitude, values and the building up of such essential skills as independent study and capacity to think and judge for oneself.

(ii) Creation of an intelligentsia of adequate size and competence.

Developing of Social, Moral and Spiritual Values : The Commission suggested the following:

(a) Adoption of measures by the Central and State Governments to introduce education in moral, social and spiritual values in all institutions under their (or local authority) control on the lines recommended by the University Education Commission and the Committee on Religious and Moral Instruction. Same steps to be taken by the privately managed institutions.

(b) Setting apart of some periods in the timetable for this purpose apart from education in such values being made an integral part of school programmes generally.

(c) Such instructions to be given by general teachers, preferably from the different communities, considered suitable for the purpose.

(d) Special concern of the University Departments in Comparative Religion with the ways in which these values can be taught wisely and effectively.

(e) Undertaking preparation of special literature for use by students and teachers by these departments.

(f) Promotion of tolerant study of all religions so that citizens can understand each other better and live amicably together and the inclusion of syllabus giving well chosen information about each of the major religions as a part of the course is citizenship or as part of general education to be introduced in schools and colleges upto the first degree.

(g) Highlighting the fundamental similarities in the great religions of the world and the emphasis they place on the cultivation of certain broadly comparable moral and spiritual values.

(h) A common course on this subject in all parts of the country and the preparation of common text books at the national level by the competent and suitable experts available on each religion.

General View

To sustain the claim of being 'revolutionary', it should have provided a philosophy of education suited to the needs and aspirations of the Indian people and their future advancement.

There is no evidence of any such broad vision. Mahatma Gandhi had conceived a system of national education that would develop in the child his hands, his brain and his soul. He went on to say; 'The hands have been atrophied. The soul has been altogether ignored'.

'Basic Education' evolved by Dr. Zakir Hussain and others, was an attempt to implement Gandhian concepts. During a session of the Rajya Sabha, our gentle President sadly confessed that 'he was the father of a still born child'. The Commission's report is that child's official death certificate.

The emphasis generally is on education as a social instrument rather than as an intellectual discipline; this may be a proper response to the needs of the times, but it tends to ignore the fact that only adequate intellectual development can sustain and guide the desired social and economic effort. The report has much to say about instruction in democratic values, development of a national consciousness and creation of a strong driving faith in the future. These are unexceptionable aims, but they can only permeate education when life reinforces their validity. There is certainly no harm in their pursuit in education but excessive talk of lofty ideals, with little regard to the reality of the country's social and economic conditions may only increase the prevailing cynicism among students, teachers and the general public.

The Commission was required to apply its mind to the entire field of education ranging from the primary stage to post-graduate research and to examine a host of educational problems in their social and economic context. These tasks have been fulfilled most admirably by Dr. Kothari and his colleagues who apparently did not allow themselves to be deterred by the formidable nature of the assignment. Though there has been considerable progress in education in quantitative terms during the past 15 years or so, this has been generally accompanied by a visible and startling fall in educational standards. The only exception is technological education which has expanded and also improved in quality. For the rest is a dismal picture. In such a situation the remedies have to be radical if they are to be effective. Yet, it is equally essential to ensure that the remedies are not beyond the capacity and the resources of the country. Else there is the danger that the recommendations might be dismissed as visionary and impractical proposals. The Commission was fully aware of this and it has made a serious effort to be realistic and bold at the same time.

The Commission's proposals are on the whole eminently sensible and certainly deserve to be accepted by the Government.

This is particularly true of the proposals which are designed to make primary education more effective; to introduce work experience as an integral element of general education; to vocationalise secondary education; to improve the quality of teachers at all levels and to provide teachers in sufficient strength, to strengthen centres of advanced studies and strive to obtain higher international standards in at least some of the universities; to lay special emphasis on the combination of teaching and research; and, to pay particular attention to education and research in agricultural and allied sciences. The teaching of science needs to be introduced at an early stage in the student's curriculum and it also needs to be strengthened at the secondary and higher levels both through the use of improved pedagogic methods and the provision of laboratory facilities. Additionally, there is an obvious case for linking it to agriculture in rural areas.

Fresh Scheme for Education

The Education Commission has attempted to strike a balance between permitting the gradual deterioration in standards to continue and introducing the radical changes necessary to make the system fit the requirements of a forward looking society and to enable the nation to take its rightful place among the more advanced. It has also struck a balance between crying needs and scanty resources.

There is no doubt that it has pinpointed the weaknesses of the existing system and indicated the direction of future development.

Comprised Form

The following points may be stated in brief:

1. It is perhaps for the first time that national objectives of education have been defined clearly by the Kothari Commission. Not only this the Commission has made valuable suggestions for the realisation of these objectives. The Commission has very rightly outlined the role of education as under:

(i) Education for increasing productivity. This is proposed to be achieved through vocationalisation of education and making Work Experience as an integral part of education.

(ii) Education for achieving social and national integration.

(iii) Education for strengthening democracy.

(iv) Education for accelerating the process of modernisation.

(v) Education for cultivating social, moral and spiritual values.

2. The Education Commission has struck a balance between materialism and spiritualism. The Commission has aptly remarked. "If science and 'Ahimsa' join together in creative synthesis of belief and action, mankind will attain to a new level of purposefulness, prosperity and spiritual insight." The Kothari Commission has further supplemented this statement by quoting Jawaharlal Nehru, 'can we combine the progress of science and technology with this progress of the mind and spirit also? We cannot be untrue to science because that represents the basic fact of life today. Still less can we be untrue to those essential principles for which India has stood in the past throughout the ages. Let us then pursue our path to industrial progress with all our strength and vigour and at the same time remember that material riches without toleration and compassion and wisdom may well turn to dust and ashes."

3. Prem Kripal has summed up the merits of these recommendations in his book entitled 'A Decade of Education in India' in these words. "The Commission has recommended that education should be related to the productivity by emphasising science education,

research, vocationalisation and by including work experience as an integral part of all education at all stages. It has also suggested a programme for the development of common school system of public education, a compulsory social and national service for young people and the development of Hindi and modern Indian languages to achieve social and national integration and to promote national consciousness as well as international understanding. It has also emphasised the cultivation of social and moral values and inculcation of a sense of social responsibility in the rising generation."

4. Recommendations of the Commission for national development may be envisaged as a spark which may lead to the bright light. The aim is an inspiration to make progress in every sphere of life.

13

Global Media

There is now an enormous amount of communication about communication-a literature which relates *inter alia* to cybernetics, neurology, linguistics, psychology, social anthropology, physics, group dynamics, semantics and the sociology of culture. We must also add library studies and documentation. The librarian is indirectly concerned with communication because his collections of material need to be organised for use, and until they are so organised an important agency in the communication process breaks down. The information role of the librarian involves him in the world of communications, and that is why students should study methods and types of communication. What follows is an outline of some communication problems, but I have been particularly concerned to make clear that the sphere of information is a limited one, whereas communication is basic to our culture in a different and more fundamental sense.

Global Journalism

The ability to communicate is a key element in culture, and most living things have developed rudimentary methods of communication which include sound as well as visual display. The communications of animals include cries, gestures and thumps which express simple responses to stimuli such as the mating call, or the alarm signal, or the warning display. The purpose has apparently gone beyond this stage of development and uses a language which linguists are trying to decipher. Claims are even made for the domestic fowl, which according to one authority, possesses an international 'language' made up of thirty basic sentences. The social insects such as the ants have communications systems, and the bees do their 'dance' to indicate the locations of a new source of nectar.

But non-human creatures have not evolved a formal language in the true sense, and it is this which in this context distinguishes them from humanity- In the beginning was the word. Apes possess several characteristics which are necessary for culture, such as the ability to walk and to use thumbs and vocal cords. In addition, their children mature slowly and they share with man the dubious blessing of a continuous sex urge. Indeed, sexual activity may well be the most basic of all forms of communication. The vast literature of sex probably owes its origins to the fact that sex relations represent an attempt at total communication, and an escape from isolation. Further more, sexual union exhibits one important characteristic of true communication insofar as it is, or should be, a two way process: to use the current jargon, feed-back occurs.

Hence the only valid objection to solitary masturbation as a practice is presumably that it excludes communication with others. McLuhan's otherwise dubious dictum that the medium is the massage is perhaps most applicable in this sphere. But to return to the animals, they cannot be said to possess true culture because they cannot symbolise, and the essence of human culture is accumulation-the retention and passing on of cultural manifestations from one generation to another. The extraordinary cries of birds, for example, can be recorded and even preserved in libraries, but this, of course, is for our benefit, not theirs.

Medium's Significance

It is established, then, that when homosapiens uttered his first words human culture really began, just as the child enters the cultural heritage when it begins to speak. But the original cause of spoken language is not known. Conflicting theories have been advanced and they are commonly and seriously known by fanciful names. The 'bow-wow' theory claims that men learnt speech by imitating animal cries. The 'pooh-Pooh' adherents believe that language developed as a result of involuntary noises provoked by violent stimuli, in contrast to the 'ding dong' people who propose that men must have imitated all kinds of noises in an onomatopoeic fashion. The 'yo-ho-ho' explanation is that men acquired speech to assist in co-operative labour, just as songs are used in the same manner today. Finally, other linguists have suggested that the first words were used to accompany gestures which must have long preceded speech.

Whatever the origins, we know that the languages of the world can be classified into families which were produced by the wandering of tribes and peoples. The resultant babble of tongues is one of the most obvious barriers to communication, when our earliest fore-fathers built the city and the tower of Babel, the people had one language and were therefore building a true community wherein 'nothing will be restrained from them which they have imagined to do'. But in developing their isolated city culture they were neglecting their global responsibilities as laid down, which required that they should be scattered abroad upon the face of all the earth. Accordingly, the Lord said "Go to, let us go down and there confound their language that they may not understand one another's speech." So the Lord scattered them abroad.

That was long ago, yet we are still confounded and are likely to remain so. The proposals for an international language (such as Esperanto) ignore cultural realities, particularly the fact that languages are not artificial creations but reflections of a way of life in time and place. The foreign language barrier is, of course, a great obstacle to all forms of international communication, and is felt so particularly in the field of scientific research where speed of communication is important.

There is in consequence a bibilographical problem with which we are not concerned here. What is more-relevant to our theme is the fact that obvious foreign language barriers may be less dangerous than the other divisive elements in culture mentioned elsewhere. In most countries people officially speak to write the same language as each other, but the use of language may vary so much that communication fails. Groups in one country often have more in common with groups in another country than with their own compatriots, in spite of the language complications.

After the invention of language the next step was the development of the ability to produce pictures to correspond with a thing described in words. Those symbols which literally represented things pictorially are called pictograms, whereas what is called ideogrammatic writing used symbols which indicate by association. The ancient Egyptian hieroglyphic contained both forms, and the Chinese language to this day is based on the dual principle. Such methods of writing have the advantage that they are 'international', in the sense that algebra or chemical formulae or musical scores are, but the corresponding disadvantage is that there is no link with words. It is an entirely visual medium-and those who used it had to learn two 'languages' which were not at all related. Modern scholars can decipher early pictorial languages, but they do not knew what they sounded like when 'read' aloud. If visual communication had remained pictorial, written languages would have remained separate from spoken languages and the latter would have succumbed to a proliferation of dialect and jargon. That is what happened in China.

The Egyptians hieroglyphics included some signs which represented sounds, but they did not develop a phonetic linear alphabet. This was the achievement of the Phoenicians, who produced a practical alphabet, the main limitation of which was that it contained no vowels. Modern sematic languages such as Hebrew also have this characteristic. The final development-that of providing vowels-was carried out by the 'Greeks, and the alphabet had by that time become substantially what it is now. Usage in the Western world was fixed by the Romans, who wrote horizontally from left to right in descending lines and used the letters which we still use,

Aspects of Technology

The fourth stage in the evolution of media was the invention in the fifteenth century of printing from movable type. It has remained the main medium of visual communication for the last 500 years. Its significance is too well known to warrant description. It is because of printing that the repository role of the library became so important, since libraries were able thus to accumulate culture. The role of the librarian is to make communication possible. In our time the mass media of communication are to some extent modifying the role of print.

So far we have been discussing what is mainly rational communication involving the conscious levels of the mind. There remain those regions where people communicate by means which involve other faculties and other types of perception. Some of these are still a matter for conjecture and dispute, so that I shall omit telepathic communication or psychic phenomena such as messages from beyond the grave or from supernatural beings. In any event, these are not normally considered to be part of a librarian's responsibility. It is however impossible to ignore the fact that, even though language or print may be used, messages are sometimes conveyed by indirect means, often in order to try to express the inexpressible. Thus the literary artist will use words to reflect a multiplicity of human experiences which has many levels and many meanings. This incorporates both the aesthetic sphere and the technique of suggestion used by the advertiser and the propagandist.

State of Affairs at Societal Level : Pre-literate communications were oral, and when human memory is the cultural connecting link we invariably find it impossible to distinguish between history and legend. Indeed history without written records it myth (unless it can be substantiated by precise archaeological research); who knows whether King Arthur ever did ride to Camelot? Having noted this it should be added that many myths have been explained in other ways without reference to history; they have been variously described as parables, allegories and early scientific theories. Fraud, basing his theory on the remarkable similarity of content in the myths and folk tales of the world, and on his analysis of individuals, claimed that myths are thinly disguised representations of unconscious fantasies common to all mankind, Lung carried this theory further with his concept of the collective or racial unconscious, which lies below the personal unconscious, and beyond this yet again the deepest levels common to all humanity. For him the collective unconscious is the deposit of ancestral experience for millions of years, and he calls certain themes which recur in dreams and in mythology 'archetypes'. The postulation of a collective unconscious seems to suggest that certain 'ideas' may be inherited, and it is not one which scientists will normally accept, but Lung's work has been influential and much of his terminology has passed into our culture.

The Preacher, then, apparently overstated his case when he asserted that 'There is no remembrance of the former generations, neither shall there be any remembrance of the latter generations that are to come, among those that shall come after'. But his words serve to remind us that those, who invented the alphabet also invented Time, which eventually became fully mechanised with the arrival of printing and with the invention of the clock. When this happened the old organic cycle of generation, birth, development and death lost its full meaning. Non -literate cultures do not have this impatient sense of time as duration. As soon as we consider language as a medium of communication it becomes apparent that language and reality are not the samething. Language is not a mirror of experience, not even a destroying mirror, because it exists in its own right, and interacts with other social realities. A word is in fact a thing-in addition to being a symbol of some other thing. As Jesse Shera says (in Documentation, p. 66) 'We do not know the effect of the symbolic structure that is language upon the behaviour patterns of society'.

We do know, however, that language can be used consciously or unconsciously to conceal objective truth. This is obvious enough in the case of detectable untruths, and psycho-analysis has made us all familiar with the processes of rationalisation by which individuals deceive others and, make particularly, themselves. If people are unable to communicate with one another, it emerges at once that language (or the thinking based upon it) serves many other purposes than external communication, and many of these purposes are either evil or supersitions. The word itself, as Ogden and Richards emphasised in 'The meaning of meaning, may gather round itself occult powers and the aura of taboos.' There have been many deities whose names are held to be unmentionable, and so on. As a thing the word is inevitably a conservative force, and produces a kind of cultural lags, because it reflects (insofar as it reflects at all) a reality which no longer exists. In a time-of rapid change, such as the present, this is one reason why the middle aged (i.e., anyone over thirty) cannot understand the young-and why the young try to invent a new language.

It follows, therefore, that words are not labels but social tools, whose use and meaning depend on conventions which differ according to the class and group affiliations of individuals. If this relates to education at all it only does so insofar as the education structure may reflect (or modify) diverse social backgrounds. In fragmented societies there are various partially separate groups or subcultures who use language in a way which may not be comprehensible to other groups. For complete understanding, a community of experience and thought is required, and when this is absent we state literally that people 'are not speaking the same language', even though their vocabularies may be identical. It is the understanding which is lacking, and this is nothing to do with language as such. This is commonly appreciated with regard to conversation: many people, particularly those past middle age, either do not talk at all, or else rarely finish their sentences, because they have lost faith in language as a means of communication. The other groups have gone beyond the pale-and one group, or one individual (the 'outsider') or one class becomes culturally alienated. This overworked term (alienated) expresses a variety of meanings, but the common factor in all of them is a psychological condition produced by social isolation. Where no real community exists there can be (by definition) no communication, and alienation is therefore very relevant to communication problems.

The concept of cultural alienation as originally used by Marx, and before him by Hegel, Schiller and other German philosophical idealists, is worth a further note, since it is a part of Marxism which has become relevant at the present time and one which has brought about an attempt by some European Christian thinkers to continue a 'dialogue' with Marxism. According to Marx, man has become self-estranged, or dehumanised, or alienated, because what he produces becomes objectified-turned into a 'thing' or 'reified' as something separate from him which he can no longer control. Marx, at least in his early work, blamed Christianity for this process, because of its 'other worldly' nature and because of the emphasis on the individual which meant that collective social life was ignored. But ultimately and more particularly in his later work he regarded alienation as fundamentally economic in nature, "So that it could only be healed by political revolution. These ideas have been developed and modified in Sartre's influential Critique of dialectical reason, 1960, and, like many American writers also, Sartre automatically supports the 'anti-social' alienated individual (such as Genet), which the English tradition, as exemplified in Leavis, does not Raymond Williams, for example, has always stressed social values and his belief that alienation need not occur even now, and will be overcome in a return to a true socialist community.

It will be seen that the term 'alienation' as commonly used at present means something much less precise than this, and may simply refer to cultural or social fragmentation which results in separate sub-cultures, such as those of the teenagers, or the black Americans, or the very-poor-or, in another sense, that of the intellectuals. The use of language, then, rests on assumptions which are shared these are present in all of the members of a particular group. Since everyone belongs to some types of in-group, how can the influence of closed groups be modified or destroyed? Aranguren, in Human communication, p 140, suggests that this is the special social function of the intellectual: 'A intellectual is someone who is capable either of emerging from the social group to which he belongs or else of criticising it from within', This is way intellectuals are usually only partially dntegrated in society. At a further extreme, this is why, in Aldous Huxley's words in Literature and science, p 13. The elements of experience which are unique, aberrant, other than average remain outside the pale of common language.

It remains to note that in open or pluralistic, societies these groups are partly an abstraction, since individuals may belong to several different ones. But the result in cultural terms is the same, and from the point of view of the individual, conflicts between groups will naturally be reflected in his mind-which is not necessarily a bad thing, since it helps to ensure social progress.

Promoting Science

Meredith, in Instruments of communication, stresses the social elements in scientific information work: 'Social communication among scientists is an essential condition of their work'. He claims further that because of the limitations of the printed word, it is more important in science to talk to people than to read books. Noting the traditional classical concept of oratorical argument where, because uncertainty prevails, emotive techniques can be used, he points out that there are not only depths of emotion which traditional rhetoric recognised, but also depths understanding which it failed to distinguish. It follows that communication problems are rooted in social and technical changes which go far beyond the realm of language studies. From the more narrow point of view of librarianship, the implications have been recognised by many of those engaged in the retrieval of scientific imformation. A number of investigations have indicated that scientists use information retrieval systems and library information service far less than might be expected, and that social factors are largely responsible.

There are, therefore, or there should be, as many types of spoken and written language as there are types of readers, and bad writing is simply that which is inappropriate for its purpose, and which fails in the full sharing of understanding. When one considers that the most effective means of communication in modern physics, for example, is often the use of mathematical symbols alone, but that the results of its researches must also be presented to the understanding of the layman; the extent of the problem becomes apparent. Kapp, in 'The presentation of technical information' has indicated the main difference between functional and other kinds of writing, by noting that a good functional style maintains receptivity in the reader: it should not be 'creative', since receptivity cannot be stored. But as far as scientific research or discovery is concerned, there is obviously a 'creative' element, which means that scientific activity is by no means as wholly objective as sometimes alleged. The creative aspect in science includes subjective insights, and in consequence there are often accidental features in research and discovery. The information scientists have also had to recognise this element, hence the increasing attention which has been paid to 'serendipity', or random selection.

Apart from these factors, language in itself often fails as an instrument of communication because of the rapidity of change. There is in fact a language crisis now, because the old association been words and the things they represent becomes impossible. The older use of language was much more rhetorical, in the sense of the word used above: this rhetoric may now hinder contact with 'reality', which, at least as far as the material world is concerned, is increasingly scientific.

Within the field of linguistics itself, a number of authorities have studied the fact that our thinking is determined by the structure of particular languages. This work has been particularly associated with the theories of B L Whorf, who, in Language, thought and reality, claims that language actually organises reality. According to Whorf, the world is presented in a kaleidoscope flux of impressions which has to be mentally organised-and this is done not by classification systems, but largely by the linguistic structures in our minds. The pattern of our language imposes an obligatory codification.

Negative Aspect : Increasing concern has been expressed in many quarters that an outstanding defect in modern cultures is a failure in communication. The proliferating literature on communication studies exhibits the same use of specialists' jargon, incomprehensible to the layman, which characterizes other specialist topics: the communicators are talking to themselves. Seligman's Encyclopedia of the social sciences defines communication as a 'network of partial or complete understandings' one might equally well substitute the word 'misunderstandings'. What follow is a discussion of some of the possible reasons for this relative failure.

Information Power

The increase in the quantity of information (and the speed with which it appears) is the factor which most librarians think of which considering how to control the flood of publications by bibliographical and library means. The first problem is to ensure that relevant information gets to users at the right time. As is indicated in my book 'Bibliography and the provision of books,' these matters are fundamental to library and bibliographic organisation. The same figures are constantly repeated for the quantity of publications, with particular reference to science and its exponential rate of growth. One authority (Professor Price of Yale University) has pointed out there if the present rate continues, there will soon be more scientists than people; another has calculated that there are more scientists alive today than in the sum total of the past.

The answers to the explosion lie in the field of social and bibliographic organisation. Yet even if solutions on this level were to be found, there is no evidence that real communication would be achieved. The fact that information is emitted or disseminated, and even received, is no guarantee that communication occurs. The transmission in itself has no meaning, and the informatiom has to be deciphered and interpreted, and as a result it is frequently not understood. There are, in fact, more fundamental barriers to communication, some of which we have already noted in relation to language.

Within the field of information flow as a social process it

is evident that a modern society requires a far-ranging network of communications in order to function at all. It is only to be expected, therefore, that information often fails to circulate. The apparatus of the welfare state, for example, is so complex that many citizens (particularly those who need the services most) are not aware what actual benefits they might receive. State agencies, and all organisations within the state, organise information services, and this is an essential element in management technique. As a social process the free flow of information is wholly dependent on the existence of free democratic (*i.e.,* politically unrestricted) institutions at all levels, and on the absence of censorship or authoritarian suppressions. It is possible to have a free flow of some types of information within particular organisations and still not have a free society, because there is some overall control. The growth in size of modern organisations, particularly those engaged in scientific research, may also produce, and indeed is producing, a situation where individuals work on a specialised job without knowing for what purpose their particular operation is intended, or what the complete venture is. This is a further example of the dehumanisation which can occur. It follows that a man may be working, could be working on some totally anti-human form of research without even being aware of the fact.

One response to this and similar problems is the current demand for 'participation' in all forms of social, political and economic life. This amounts to a claim that information itself is not enough and a consideration of it would take us beyond information as such, and into politics.

It was suggested above that the use of language is often inadequate because it no longer describes reality. This seems to be part of a trend which has many facets. In Kafka's nightmares, the main protagonists never discover what is happening or why. The 'theatre of the absurd' is truly absurd on one level at least, because nobody can communicate at all, and Becket's clowns and tramps are primarily studies in the manners of non communication. The key factor in modern developed society, as Herbert Marcuse constantly proclaims, is that social structures seem to be wholly rational but rebellious individuals instinctively feel that this rationality does not satisfy human needs. As Daniel Bell states in Technology and social change, edited by Eli Ginzberg, p 59, 'The whole breakdown of the rational cosmology is imminent and will ultimately create the most serious problems for society because of an alienation of the modes of perception about the world'. Society is unable to find cultural terms for expressing what is happening and twentieth country thought lacks confidence in the rational solution of social and cultural problems.

The implication can only be that the 'rational solutions' are inadequate. Many radical critics would dispose of the matter in the traditional Marxist manner by pointing out that capitalist ideology inevitably obscures the real nature of society. (It should not be forgotten that the word 'ideology' means, or originally meant, a system of beliefs which does not explain, but explains away reality, just as rationalisation obscures reality for the individual.) If this is the case, as it certainly is in the USA, it is probably true in the USSR also, where the official ideology corresponds even less with life as it is experienced and furthermore any attempts to modify radically this discrepancy cannot appear above ground.

There is therefore a blockage in the communication of ideas. Traditional political or religious faiths provided an analysis of social reality which *inter alia* explained how society (and the universe) was believed to work. At one time the Christians, and the Marxists, explained everything to the satisfaction of millions of adherents. Up to the end of the country even the scientists provided answers whose implications could be understood by everybody. The gods have failed now because their analysis is irrelevant, and in consequence their panaceas do not help. As McLuhan has claimed, the overworked concept that God is dead really refers to the

Newtonian universe that has passed away, and the ground rule upon which so much of the Western World is built is dissolved. Because of this we cannot control events, and 'nobody knows what is happening.' (Harrington deals with this at length and that is why he calls his book on our times the accidental century.) In many spheres where ideas are important, few people have anything valid to say, and for this and other reasons we stop listening to the message and there is a widespread growth of disbelief, scepticism and negative criticism but leaders seem to be more in the dark than anybody else, illustrating in a new guise Acton's dictum that power corrupts. A Bob Dylan has it, 'Something is happening but you don't know what it is-do you Mr. Jones?'

It is most noticeable in the case of the revolting young that they tend to use terminology-for example anti-capitalist slogans-which does not really express what they are trying to say. They are grouping towards a new language-a true communication-but, meanwhile, in adequate slogans from the past must serve. The millions of young people who stick a poster of the Guevera on their wall do not share either his beliefs or his language. Most of them are aware of this circumstance: they are also very conscious that there is this need for true communication, and the leaders of the pop world like the Beatles have frequently said so. This is why the trends in clothes and long hair are to them so important: they are fundamentally methods of communication. There is a Beatles song called 'All you need is love', which on the face of it is a banal and puerile statement, but they are not simply referring to the usual commercial concept at all. Sex as a basic form of communication was discussed above. On another level it is beyond doubt that without love, in the sense used by most of the great religious leaders, true human communication is impossible. If society as it exists does not allow for this act of communication, either because the structure is wrong or because of social injustice or because there is no freedom to express opinions, then the social consequences will be revolutionary.

The trumpet calls for human solidarity are based on a recognition of this, but what usually happens in practice is that the kind of solidarity which is based on human love only occurs temporarily within small groups (opposed to other groups), or where societies are at war or in times of revolution and crisis. Or else these human needs are perverted and rendered evil by false prophets like Hitler, who must base their movements on error. This brings us back to those radical opposition movements which fundamentally reject modern societies, since what they are fighting is hypocrisy in all its forms: where untruth prevails, communication breaks down. That is why this chapter is not about technical processes such as 'positive and negative feedback loops'. All the loops in the world cannot obliterate fabrication.

Case Study : The history of the press is at the same time a reflection of political history. Journalists are the chroniclers of their age and the results of their labours, the newspapers, reveal what problems confronted the different epochs in a nation's history.

Germany is the mother country of the modern press. It is true that other countries made attempts to provide information for the' population by means of periodic announcements on the part of the state or the state authorities. This was the case for instance in ancient China, where an official journal was published, being printed by the woodcut method. The official journal appeared from the ninth century onwards under the name of King-Po, and in the course of centuries, with a succession of titles, it developed into the precursor of the later official imperial gazette in the Celestial Empire. Before the Chinese however the Romans had also found ways and means of providing the population with information on the affairs of state in a kind of prejournalistic publication. This was the daily gazette which was published by Caesar under the title of Acta Diurna making public the decrees of the Roman authorities around about the middle of the first century before Christ.

Press in Germany

The modern press, which originated in Germany, could not really have been created anywhere else than in the land of Gutenberg.

Gutenberg was the first person in Europe to invent movable type and is thus the father of the modern art of printing, the black art, the art which is concerned with the colour black which has become the symbol not only of journalism but of the entire modern age. Gutenberg might however also justifiably be called the father of journalism. His efforts to create an instrument for circulating news rapidly and simultaneously in many areas corresponded even in those days to the journalistic flair which in Gutenberg was combined with the boldness of the inventor and the precision of the scientist. Gutenberg's name is closely connected with the German city of Mainz. "Golden Mainz" (the name which the first arcbbishopric of the Holy Roman Empire bore for centuries, just as Cologne for instance was known as "Holy Cologne" was Gutenberg's birthplace.

Gutenberg's real name was Henne Gausfleisc zu Laden, but he became more well-known under the name of Johannes Gutenberg. In the year 1854 his 42-line Bible appeard for the first time. Many copies of the Holy Scriptures, previously written out laboriously by hand on parchment by the monks, could now be circulated among the people. The art of printing with movable type, invented and perfected by Gutenberg in the space of about a decade, began its triumphant progress throughout the world.

The man whose invention of printing gave the entire 'population access to learning and knowledge, which bad hitherto been confined to the privileged wealthy few, did not however get any thanks for his invention. In order to perfect his printing machine he was forced to borrow money from a wealthy citizen of Mainz, Fust by name. Round about 1447 appeard the first Gutenberg publication, period at his parents' house, the name of which was "zum Gutenberg", and it was by this name that Henne or Johanes Gansfleisch was later known. This publication was a minor epic work by some contemporary, known as the Weltgerichts-gedicht (The poem of the universal court). A year later appeared the "Calender for 1448". But people did not yet display much interest for the new technique.

This did not happen until the printer came out with the idea of publishing the Bible. Now people in Mainz began to prick up their ears. The above-mentioned Fust lent Gutenberg so much money that after the publication of the work, on which Gutenberg had laboured for two years or so, that entire inventory of the Gutenberg printing works belonged to him. Fust later went into partnership with another wealthy burgher and created the Fust-Schoffersche Press. The inventor of printing however lived a hand-to-mouth existence. Relatives supported him and enabled him later to bring out smaller publications now and again. Thus the Catholicon which appeared in 1465, was probably printed in his workshop. Today no one knows where this was situated. The Bible was printed in living quarters where Gutenberg had some time before established a workshop, in the house "zum Humbrecht", a building which today in Number 18/20 in the "Schustergasse".

The Archbishop Adolf von completely impoverished inventor gave Gutenberg a place in his him by means of this board death. Nassau took pity on the in his old age. In 1465 he household, thus preserving and lodging from certain.

Later generations desired to make good the neglect which Gutenberg suffered at the hands of his contemporaries in Mainz. In 1837 Maim; erected a fine Gutenberg Memorial, designed by Thorwaldsen. The inscription-on the memorial reads:

Artem quae Graecos latuit latuitque Latinos Germani sollers extudit ingenium. Nunc quidquid veteres sapiunt sapiuntque recentes, Non sibi, sed populis omnibus id sapiunt. (The art which remained concealed from the Greeks and Romans Was brought to light by the inventive genius of a German. Now the knowledge of ancients and moderns is not confined to Them alone, but known to all the nations of the world.)

The Gutenberg Museum established at Mainz in 1900 and the Gutenberg Society set up in 1901 have kept alive the memory of one of the greatest inventors of all time.

The man who received such honour at the hand; of later generations died in 1467 or 1468; the exact date is not known. He was buried in the Franciscan Church, which was demolished in 1742. There is nothing to recall the last resting place of this great citizen of Mainz. With his invention he heralded the dawn of a modern age, and set in motion the mechanism that was to cause an intellectual awakening. In the same period, by some strange whim of fate an unknown man in far-away Korea was using movable copper type for making reproductions. In the Far East no one took any notice of this invention. Within a century however it altered the entire social and intellectual face of Europe, making education and culture the common property of all men.

One of the historians of the German press, Robertrot who published his Geschichte des deutschen Journalismus (History of German Journalism) in 1845, rapturously described journalism as the highest form of Gutenberg's art Journalism is the most perfect use to which Gutenberg's invention could be put; it is, so to speak, the press in its, most concentrated form the energetic quintessence and embodiment of all the effects produced by the art of printing.

The newspaper which appears regularly every day with the daily news have various names in different languages, which point to its characteristic features. In German the daily paper is called "Zeitung". In the fourteenth century this word was written as "Zitunge", a form which originated in Central and South Germany. The word "Zeitung" originally meant nothing else than "news". Thus the first journals, flysheets and pamphlets, which were only produced in connection with some specific event, were called "Neue Zeitungen" (or "Newe Zytungen" in the spelling of that period), meaning the "Latest news". The oldest printed work still in existence is a Newe-Zytung von orient und auff gange (Latest News from the Orient and the East), from the year 1502. Pamphlets of this kind were however already appearing in Germany in the last decades of the fifteenth century.

In time there also appeared what were known as serial issues of newspapers, dealing with a major political event il1 two or three issues. This scheme was also frequently employed for announcing some military event or other, an imperial proclamation or an event of religious and political significance.

As well as these serial issues there were also the so-called Messrelationen, published quarterly or monthly at the time of the Spring and Autumn Trade Fairs in Frankfurt-on-Main by the historian Michael von Aitzing at Cologne. These Messrelationen, journals which gave information about the trade fairs, may be described as the precursors of economic periodicals and also of political journals. Experts on the history of the press are not absolutely certain of the publication date of the first newspaper to conform more or less with the modern definition of "mass medium". Some take the view that it was the Historische Relation, printed by Samuel Dilbaum of Augsburg, and published by Leonhard Straub at Rorschach. A complete annual volume of this monthly journal from the year 1597 is still in existence. At that time, however, several journals must already have been appearing regularly. In 1587 for instance there was already a periodical with the following title: Newe Zeittung/Warhafftiger Bericht aus Nurnberg an einen guten Freundt geschrieben/was sich im Monat April dieses 1587. Jahrs zugetragen und begeben (Latest news/ Accurate report from Nuremberg, written to a good friend of the events and happenings in the month of April in this year of 1587.) Some German researchers cautiously describe these monthly journals as the forerunners of the weekly periodicals. The newspaper expert Professor Hans A Munster for instance has the following to say in an article entitled "The oldest Periodical Newspaper and Review" (Die alteste periodische Zeitung and Schrift), which appeared in the monthly Die Deutsche Zeitung, Bielefeld, July 1953:

> 'There is thus nothing new in describing the old monthly reviews as the "oldest periodicals", and certainly there are good grounds for this assumption. For the longer gap between dates of publication in the case of monthlies as compared with weeklies is after all not a fundamental difference but only a relative one. The step forward from the "Newe Zytungen", which did not appear regularly, to the periodicals was taken by the publication of either the monthly reviews (in 1587 and 1597 respectively, or the "Messrelationen" (in 1588).

Most historians of press history however hold the opinion ,that the year 1609 is of special significance for the development of the press and that it was in this year that really modern newspapers came into existence. In 1609, for the first time, there appeared two weekly papers, and the complete annual volumes of them both are still in existence. These two papers were called Relation and Aviso respectively.

It is likely that the Relation was published at Strassbourg. It is a rather more Protestant journal, which made available information on political and economic affairs to readers in the former German imperial city. The full title of the journal was as follows: Aller Furnemmen und gedenckwurdigen Historien/ so sich hin und wider in Hoch und Nieder Teutschland/auch in Franckreich/ftalian/Scbott and England/Hispanien/ Hungern/Polen/Siebenburgen/Wallachey/Moldaw/

Turckeyetc. Inn diesem 1609. Jahr verlauffen und zugetragen mochte. Alles auf das trewlichs wie ich solche bekommen und zu wegen bringen magjln Truck verfertigen will. (An account of all undertakings and noteworthy events/occurring in Upper and Lower Germany/as well as France/Italy/Scotland and England/Spain/Hungary/Poland Transylvania/Wallachia/ Moldavia/Turkey/etc., in the year 1609. Everything having been edited and printed exactly in accordance with the news items as they came in.)

The geograpbical origin of the news items printed in the second newspaper, the Aviso, already reveals a bias towards American and Asiatic countries. The name of this periodical with the characteristic heading and long-winded title corresponding to the fashion of the time reveal the still close relationship of the periodical with the book. The full title was as follows: Relation oder Zeitung. Was sich begeben and zugetragen hat/in Deutsch: und Welschland/Spanien/Nieder landtjEngelland/Franckreich, Ungern, Oesterreich, Schweden, Polen und in allen Provintzen/in Ost: und West Indian etc. So aIlhie den... angelangt. Gedruckt im Jahre 1609. (Journal or newspaper. The events and happenings in Germany and Italy/ Spain/The Neitherlands/England/France/Hungary/Austria/ Sweden/Poland/and in all the provinces/in the East and West Indies etc. All items printed as they arrived, in the year 1609).

It has still not been definitely established where the journal was printed. It might have been Augsburg, but Nuremberg is also a possibility, while there are various reasons that would appear to suggest Wolfenbuttel as its source.

The significant thing about these newspapers was not that they attracted a large circle of readers but that were read by a small class of politically and economically important persons who now suddenly received regular information from a news paper. This then was the birth of the political press, i.e. the press of modern times.

Between 1618 and 1648 there appeared various new pamphlets, which for the next few years proved something of an obstacle to the development of periodicals. All the same, it was precisely in this early period that well-known publishers such as Andreas Aperger of Augsburg developed into prominent newspaper publishers.

Newspaper history reveals that the towns where there newspapers originated were not the political centres but the' famous merchants cities of the Holy Roman Empire. Thus an important weekly paper was published at Frankfurt-on-Main as early as 1615, while by 1617 this city already had two weekly competitors.

During the Thirty Years War a forerunner of the press in our own century appeared at Magdeburg; it was published in, 1664 by what afterwards became the Muller-Faber publishing house, later developing into the Magdeburger Zeitung which is published in the Federal Republic of Germany today; this newspaper is read in exile by the citizens of Magdeburg who have fled from the Soviet Zone.

During the sixteenth century a number of German book printers emigrated to other countries and, just as they had already been doing in isolated places for a century, disseminated the art of Gutenberg to an ever growing extent beyond the boundaries of the Holy Roman Empire. The first forerunners of the French newspapers developed as early as 163 Land some time later the first papers were also published in England. From the very beginning the English papers differed considerably from the continental ones in that they revealed differences of opinion, whereas the French government had some control over newspaper policy right from the start. The German press however reflected the attitude of the various German princedoms.

One of the old trade centres was Leipzig, the city where the traditional Leipzig Trade Fair is held. This citv can claim to have published the first daily newspaper of modern times. The Leipzig daily newspaper appeared on I January 1660 with the following title: Neu einlauffende Nachbricht van Kriegsund Welt-Handeln, (The latest news of events from the military and commercial sphers.)

A feature of the seventeenth century is the establishment of various prominent newspapers and journals, for instance the Frankische Kurier in 1673, or the Jenaische zeitung in 1674. The first German learned periodical appeared in 1682, entitled Acta Eruditorum. Six years later there also appeared the first learned periodical printed in German: Schertz-und ernsthaffter Gedanken uber allerband nutzliche Bucher und Fragen... (Humorous and serious thoughts on diverse books and questions, both amusing and instructive).

In 1693 we find a monthly journal appearing in Jena with the following title: Monatlich mutzspielende Lustfragen zu Gelehrter und Ungelehrter sonderbarer Ergetzung. (A monthly review of useful humorous matters for the amusement of scholars and others. This journal is a forerunner of the type known as "moralist weeklies", established for the political and moral instruction and enlightenment of society, which originated in Germany in the year 1713. The first genuine moralist weekly to appear in Germany was Der Vernunfller (The Sophist) in Hamburg. In 1725, with the publication of the weekly journal Die vernunfligen Tadlerinnen (The judicious-Faultfinders) which appeared in various places, such as Halle Leipzig and finally Humburg, the writer Gottsched bestowed a certain measure of fame on these moralist weeklies in Germany and the rest of the world. The journals themselves are based on English models, Defoe, Steele and Addison having. become models for German journalists. Already the press was growing aware of its international significance.

The beginning of the eighteenth century also saw the birth of the intellectual reviews which were to have such a stimulating effect on intellectual life in Germany. In the year 1703 the famous Wiennerische Diarium appeared, a review which still appears today under the same title, and is the doyen of all publications of this nature in the German-speaking world.

Another new type of publication were the so-called' "privileged journals". In 1740 the Koniglich privilegierte Nachrichten von Staats und Gelehrtensachen (Journal of affairs of state and scholarship, under royal patronage) appeared in Prussia. The King himself, Frederick the Great, was responsible for its publication. Later, as the Haude Spenersche Zeitung, this newspaper was to represent the old middle classes of Berlin. There was however an even earlier forerunner of these "privileged journals". A weekly periodical published in Berlin from 1691 onwards, called Allergnadigst privilegierte Curiosen Natur-, Kunst-, Staats und Sittenprasenten erster Jahrgang durch R. Oelven zum Nutzen und Ergotzen. (The first and annual volume of curious events from the realms of science, art, politics, and morals, published by R. Oelpen for the instruction and amusement of all).

In this period Frederick the Great, who was rebelling against the Empress Maria Theresia, founded the forerunner of what was later called the Schlesische Zeitung; it appeared in 1741 in the German city of Breslau, entitled Schlesisch privillegierte Staats-, Kriegs- und Friendenszeitung (Silesia, journal of state, war and peace, under royal patronage). Today the Schlesische Zeitung is read by all the German Silesians who were expelled from their homeland and do not forget Breslau or other towns in the territory of Eastern Germany.

One could compile a long chronological table giving the most important dates of foundation for German newspapers.

The most significant names to appear are the forerunners of the Bremer Nachrichten (1743), the Braunschweigische Zeitung (1744), the Saarbrucker Zeitung (1761), the Anhalter Anzeiger (1763), the Kolnische Zeitung (1763), the Elbinger

Zeitung (1789), the Vogtlandische Anzeiger and Tagesblatt (1789) and the Geraer Zeitung (1795).

The seventeenth and eighteenth centuries thus displayed a welcome degree of initiative in the sphere of the press. At the same time however the newspapers were not without their critics. At Leipzig, as for back as 1672, Professor Otto Mencke had introduced a kind of historical and political study of the press into the university syllabus. Some years later Ahasver Fritsch published the first learned work on the press: Discursus de Novellarum quas vacant Neue Zeitunge Hodierno usu et abusu (Discourse on the Present Day Uses and Abuses of the Publications Known as Newspapers), which appeared at Jena in 1676. In the same year Christian Weise followed with a similar work. In 1679 Johann Ludwig Hartmann had a book published under the title of Unzeitige Neue Zeitungssucht. (Untimely Passion for Newspapers). This look is the first learned work on the press published in German.

Leipzig was also to be the place where the first treatise of the press was published. It was written by Tobias Beucer in 1698 and entitled De Relationibus Novellis (On Newspapers). Hamburg followed in 1695 with Kasper Stieler's Zeitungs Lust und Nutz (Amusement and Instruction from Newspapers), while in the same year the first treatise on press law, entitled Jus Novellarum was published by Friedrich Hagen at the University of Kiel. Thus the outlines for newspaper and press research were marked out. When Johnn Peter von Leipzig began to lecture on "The uses and abuses of newspapers" at the newly founded University of Halle in the year 1698, the study of the press bad already become a field of research taken for granted at the universities. It is astonishing bow the world of learning subjected the mass media to critical scrutiny during the seventeenth century revealing an admirable and instinctive awareness of the danger and advantages of the press.

During the reign of Frederick the Great, the government

of Prussia as it was then was liberal and tolerant in its treatment of the press. This factor also had a decisive influence on neighbouring regions. Until the seventeenth and eighteenth centuries German journalism, that is to say the press in German speaking countries, had been the province of anonymous writers. Of course, as has already been mentioned there were a number of prominent writers contributing to journals of a high standard. But the type of journalist able to achieve a certain amount of power and consequently exercise a considerable influence on public opinion does not appear until later on in the eighteenth century.

Mention should be made here in particular of the statesman and writer Justus Moser (1720-1794), who published a journal called the Wochentlicbe Osnabruckische Anzeigen (1766-1782), which represented a note-worthy achievement in the field of journalism. Another scholar who combined a statesman like insight with a flair for journalism was August Ludwig von Schlozer (1735-1809), who was active in the field of journalism as Gottingen, his more important publication being the Staats-anzeigen (1783-1794), which provided information on events in Europe at that time and the rest of the world. The journalist Friedrich Karl Freiherr von Moser (I723-1798) was active during the same period. In annual volumes entitled Patriotisches Archiv fur Deutschland, published from 1784 to 1790 and from 1792 to 1794, he created a unique documentation worthy to rank alongside the periodical documentary works of our time.

Similar to the link with politics, journalism was also even more intimately connected with art. The great writer Gottfried Ephraim Lessing, the German herald of tolerance, was for a period .of hour years literary editor of the Vossische Zeitung (1751-1755). During this time he created a critical journal that betrays the pen of the gifted writer that he was. Another writer Matthias Claudius (1740-1745), the editor of the Wandsbecker Boten (from 1751 to 1755), published a critical journal whose attractive style and responsible tone earned it a reputation that extended far beyond the local region and gained it subscribers all over Germany. Another of these prominent journalists was Wieland (1733-1813), who published a journal chiefly devoted to literary matters, whose political significance however cannot be overestimated; this was the Teutsche Merkur (1773-1810). The gifted but ill-starred Heinrich von Kleist (1777-1811) was publisher and editor of the Berliner Abendblatter (1810-1811). At the moment when Napoleon was taking steps to crush the press, Kleist was bold enough to show the nation, cautiously and cleverly, that national dignity and national aims were still possible. He was one of the German who fought against dictatorship and oppression. The Swabian Christian Friedrich Daniel Schubart (1739-1791) founded the Deutsche Chcronik (which appeared in Augsburg in 1794, in Vim from 1774 to 1777 and in Stuttgart from 1787 to 1791). In these journals we find over and over again a harmonious blend of revolutionary poetic enthusiasm and the prudence of journalists with a critical turn of mind. Other great journalists of the period were Ludwig Weckherlin (1739 to 1792), Moritz Flavius Trenck von Tonder 1746-1810) and Arnold M allinckrodt (1767-1825). It was the latter's dream, even in those days, that one day there might be a united Europe.

Apart from art, the book trade too now tried to establish - closer links with press. Particular mention should be made ,here of Johann Friedrich Cotta (1764-1832) and Friedrich Perthes (1772-1843). During the period of Napoleon's despotism Johann Josef Gones (1776-1848) was the most prominent ;figure in German journalism to join in the national struggle, with his outstanding periodical the Rheinischer Merkur (1814-1816). The Rheinischer Merkur's contribution to the resistance against Napoleon and to the efforts at reviving the Empire was so substantial that the mighty despot regarded it as a kind of fifth columnist movement.

After Napoleon, Europe was the realm of experiment for journalists who either on a national or a European basis proclaimed their desire for one great state of Europe united in the brotherhood of nations. Here one should note the journalistic efforts of Johann Georg August Wirth (I798-1898), the publisher of the Deutsche Tribune (1 July-18 December, 1831 at Munich, and until 18 March, 1832 at Homburg).

In the struggle against Napoleon and in the post Napoleonic era there appeared a new phenomenon in the world of journalism: the party press. Journals advocating a particular idea or policy were founded in that period, and the birth of the party press represents at the same time the birth of public opinion in the party political sense. The newspapers claimed to be liberal, but had a general moral, Catholic or Protestant bias, so that their readers were always groups linked by denominational or political connections. These newspapers in the first half of the nineteenth century are regarded by the German political press of today as their legitimate predecessors.

The nineteenth century however also witnessed another phenomenon in the sphere of journalism the birth of the popular press. Even in those days the popular press employed telegraphic communications, receiving news from the telegrafic agencies and news services. In the year 1849 the Wolff Telegraphic Agency was established in Berlin. This is the oldest modern news agency in the world.

It was in Germany, the traditional home of the "Relationen" and trade fair journals, that one of the largest and most important news agencies in the world commenced its activities: Reuter's was set up two years after the establishment of the Wolff Telegraphic Agency. We know the exact dates of its foundation On 22 April 1850 the newspaper correspondent Julius Reuter arrived at Aachen, where he was met by the brewery and distillery owner Heinrich Geller. This Heinrich Geller owned one of the largest earlier-pigeon lofts in the old imperial city of Aachen. The two men diliberated for two days, and then, on the 24 April, they signed a contract providing for

Reuter to establish a carrier-pigeon post for the conveyance of all kinds of news. This contract of 24 April represents the birth of a world enterprise which became a by word in the field of journalism.

The first carrier-pigeons were dispatched on 27 April. Important items of news-particularly stock exchange quotations were often reported in other places one or two days quicker than by conventional methods. A year later the great firm of Reuter's as Aachen, with its first branch at Verviers and connections with of the chief cities of Europe, had achieved such a reputation that it transferred its headquarters to London, the capital of the British Empire. There is 1865, Reuter's Institute, which had meanwhile expanded into an international undertaking, was converted into a limited company. Paul Julius Reuter, born at Kassel in 1821, died at Nice in 1899, having been created a baron by the Duke of Coburg-Gotha in the year 1871. Possessing German and British nationality, and at home too in France and Italy Reuter represented a considerable section of European thinking in the nineteenth century.

The nineteenth century was equally mindful of technical progress as well as intellectual activity. Thus in the year 1811 Friedrich Konig patented his invention of the mecbanical press. In 1814 this mechanical press was employed for the first time in the printing of a newspaper: The Times of London. The first newspaper on the European continuant to introduce the new invention in its printing house was the Haude-Spenersche Zeitung in Berlin, but this was not until 1823.

The result was that in 1824 the Haude-Spenersche Zeitung and the Vossische Zeitung in Berlin began to appear daily. Stereotype offset was invented in the year 1829, and this invention acquired particular significance in 1872 with the construction of the first German rotary press at Augsburg. Then, in 1852, the German teacher Philipp Reis demonstrated the first telephone, an invention which was just as important as that of Daguerre, who invented the process of photography in the years 1837-38.

The circulation of the popular press received a further impetus through the reduction in price that resulted from a new paper manufacturing process. Then, in 1880, Georg Meisenbach made it possible for photographs to be reproduced on newspapers with the aid of autotype. In 1884 the type-setting machine was invented by Ottmar Mergenthaler, who how had just emigrated to America, but such machines were not constructed and employed in Germany until 1896.

The 1920's saw the development of radio as a rival to the press. The first German radio company was established in 1923. A few years later Herman Tolle broadcast from Cologne the first spoken radio commentary and the first leading article on German radio. The first radio pictures appeared in 1927.

The popular press is noncommittal in tone. It does not represent any definite polical point of view, but is for the most part only interested in increasing its readership by pandering to the popular taste. A typical example of a nonpolitical newspaper of this kind was the Tagliche Rundschau in Berlin. This publication was strictly non-party. It made its first appearance on September 1881, presenting itself as a "newspaper for nonpoliticians, as well as a supplement to the political organs of all the parties." In the year 1884 it described its functions as being a "newspaper for non-political politics". Its slogan, as declared in leading articles and other publications, was to provide happiness and harmonious griety for all.

To some extent it was a newspaper apart, for unlike other papers it claimed to be political without supporting any particular policy. Later however it modified its point of view a little, tending more in the direction of the National Liberal Party.

It is interesting for historians of the press to know that the first official organ published by the Sovier military authorities in the occupied zone of Central Germany bore the name Tagliche Rundschau. However the former non-political Tagliche Rundschau was published in the early years of the Bismarck state at a time when even a harmless family gossip magazine like the Gartenlaube could appear; whereas the Tagliche Rundschau published by the Soviet authorities commenced an extreme policy of communist indoctrination.

Here we may be permitted to look back for a moment. In the era of the popular press the "General an zeiger" also played a prominent part. This type of newspaper claimed to be more serious than the average popular paper, but still tried rather to gained the non-political section of the population as its readers. The leading promoter of this type of newspaper was Josef La Rouelle, who experimented with publications at Aachen in 1871 and Cologne in 1875, before publishing his Billigste Zeitung fur Arm und Reich (Cheapest newspaper for rich and poor) in 1882, thus producing a genuine type of "Generalanzeiger". Hermann Minjon was active in Frankfurt, while the name of August Scherl is eternally linked with the history of the Berlin press. Other men prominent in the general advertiser press were W. Girardet and August Huck.

German newspapers were particularly active in the political sphere, whatever their political tendencies. Shortly before the First World War there were around 532 Conservative and Free Conservative newspapers, 509 National Liberal and Radical Democratic papers, 419 newspapers supporting the party of the Catholic Centre and 85 Socialist newspapers, plus 61 publications representing the Polish, Danish and other minorities. As opposed to this number there were a total of 1,621 non-party newspapers.

In 1932 the numbers were approximately as follows:

596 newspapers supporting the Centre and Bavarian People's Party,

197 supporting the German Social Democrat Party,
121 supporting the National Socialist German Worker's Party,
81 supporting the German National People's Party,
50 supporting the Communist Party,
14 supporting the People's Party,
11 supporting the Economic Party,
8 supporting the German State Party.

Another analysis presents the following picture: 562 newspapers advocating more conservative views, 363 with progressive middle-class views, 64 with more liberal views, 58 with liberal-democratic views, 19 with progressive republican views, and 9 with general socialist views, while 1,814 papers claimed to be independent; 123 newspapers advocated varying policies, and 337 made no declaration of their views at all.

The long list of newspapers existing at that time, many of which were what was known as "Kopfzeitungen", i.e., the political section on the first two pages was often taken over on matrices from a larger newspaper) presents a colourful and varied mixture a new and decisive event however was soon to compel the German press to take on a more gloomy and monotonous appearance.

On 30 January 1933 Hitler book office as Chancellor, and it did not take long before he usurped sole power in his position as Fuhrer and Chancellor, brusquely ignoring the promises he had given to the nation about allowing it the opportunity to criticise his policies at regular intervals. Dictatorship and dictators always proceed in accordance with a similar scheme. This period when the German press was in fetters has recently been the subject of particular study in quite a number of publications. General surveys have appeared of the process of concentration, throwing light on the National Socialists' control of the press. By the end of the Third Reich this process had led to 80 per cent of the newspapers and journals which appeared in Germany being in the possession of the party-owed Eranz Eher-Verlag at Munich. Today it requires considerable effort to get a clear picture of the mass of legislative and other measures taken by the National Socialists against the independent press in Germany. The result however was plain: the elimination of serious criticism. Apart from the Minister of Propaganda, Goebbels, the leading figure in the compaign to bring the press into line was Max Amann, director of the Eber- Verlag; in his capacity as representative of his party he brutally expropriated leading publishing firms and brought them under the control of his own giant publishing house. The press policy commenced in 1934, when the Ullstein house was transferred into the hands of the National Socialists, and continued until 1944, when Hugenberg's Scherlverlag was taken over. The National Socialists' Pravda was the Volkischer Beobachter. This newspaper had its origin in the Munchener Beobachter, founded in I887, appearing for the first time under its title Volkischer Beobachter on 9 August 1919. This was the beginning of a troubled period of German history.

This period of German history has however been consistently continued in one part of Germany which is not yet free. This is the case in the Soviet-occupied Zone of Germany, which with a conscious debasement of political terminology has given itself the title of "German Democratic Republic". The Communist and National Socialist ideologies, based on the same intellectual source, viz., a false interpretation of Hegelian philosophy, pursued the same policy in regard to the press, just as they also seized power in the same way. Their newspaper often bear epithets such as "free" or "national", or have tities like "die Wahrheit" ("The Truth"). But their newspapers are not intended to serve any human values, but simply and solely the aims of one party, a despotism represented by a minority in control of the state. The press in the Soviet Zone following Lenin's oft-quoted dictum, which applies today as much as it ever did, gave itself the task of "being not only a collective propagandist and a collective agitator, but also a collective organizer." True to this formula the Soviet Zone press has agitated, organized and spread party propaganda in accordance with the example of the Soviet press. It praised Stalin extravagantly. And the same men and the same pens were just as indignant in their criticism of Stalin when the Party came out wita its condemnation of the men without whom three decades of Communist history would be unthinkable. It also criticized Krushchev in exactly the same way, in accordance with its instructions.

The only criticism against measures taken by the authorities and the Party in a communist state is found in "readers" letters'. The situation is exactly the same in the Soviet Zone as in other communist countries, as the London Times wrote of Isvestia on 24 February 1965 in a series of articles entitled "Newspapers of the World":

> "In a communist country a letter to the editor is one of the few channels open to the individual to appeal against injustice and bureaucracy."

In the postwar period the press has experienced a great change in what is today the Federal Republic of Germany. After the end of the Second World War the press, which until then had been controlled by the National Socialists, virtually ceased to exist. At first the occupying powers published their own newspapers, and later gave certain persons licenses to publish newspapers and magazines. In the American and French Zones members of the different parties combined to publish independent newspapers, whereas in the British Zone the preference was given to a definite party press system. In the same way the Soviets favoured a party press system in their zone of occupation-the communist press and the so-called "middle-class press", which is subject to communist pressure. The existence of the latter is intended to lead the rest of the world to believe that the press supports different political parties in the Sovietoccupied Zone.

The licensed press continued until 1 September 1949; after which it was no longer necessary to hold a licence in order to publish a newspaper. As from this date, a large number of newspapers again began to appear under their former titles. In some cases there was a struggle, even carried out in public (for instance in the case of the newspaper Die-Welt), between these old papers, which called themselves local German papers ("Hdmatzeitungen") and the licensed press. Many of the old publishers' newspapers, which reappeared after 1 September 1940 suddenly failed to arouse the echo which they had hoped for, or they were unable to adapt themselves to changed conditions. The flood of expellers from the eastern territories of Germany, now under Polish and Russian Administration, and the flight of inhabitants of the Soviet occupied Zone to the Federal Republic of Germany also had a particular effect in that they wrought a considerable change in the composition (If the population. This change did not however make any difference for some of the other old newspapers which boldly took up the struggle against the licensed press and today, with an imposing body of regular readers, are again, playing a leading part in the sphere of the German press.

The monotony of a twelve year long totalitarian regime had thus given way to a press which again reflected public opinion, in accordance with the tradition of the press in the mother country of the press. In addition there are of course also news-, papers, which take no definite political line, adapting them selves to please tastes, or rather the alleged tastes of their readers. In the modern industrial state the popular press plays a prominent part in every field. As in every state which believes in free competition, there is rivalry among the publishers, who compete for the favour of regular subscribers. By and large the press in the Federal Republic is still supported by regular subscribers, the newspaper being delivered to the reader's house every morning. There are however also a few large popular tabloids which are sold at newspaper stalls and in the streets these are holding their own. With the popular tabloids there also came the illustrated magazines, of which a variety of types are available.

A gratifying large section of the press was concerned with publications for young people, ranging from school magazines to the younger readers' section in the weekend magazines. Many of these publications had a particular political bias, or follow a cultural or religious line. Unlike the totalitarian systems in the Third Reich of the National Socialist and in the communist Soviet Zone there were also a number of denominational newspapers and magazines in the Federal Republic, which commented and criticized as they please and meet with a positive response from their readers. It is true that there were newspapers which call themselves religious in totalitarian states too, but their influence is confined to the affairs of the parish, while the majority of the other papers, on the other hand, were free to attack religion and religious institutions with political means.

Journalists in Germany, have their own local associations and their German Press Association. In some cases they cooperate with the International Journalists' Federation, which endeavours to arrange a regular exchange of ideas on certain matters affecting the journalists' profession; it also investigates the position of journalists in all the countries of the world, considers salaries and wages, examines the development of radio and television and their effect on the printed press, organises international conferences on the subjects of vocational training and measures for the protection of journalists in the exercise of their profession, and generally deals with all matters connected with journalistic activity and the relationship among one another of journalists from different nations. It is also fosters good relations among journalists' and journalists organisations, and among the newspapers and publishers of different countries, as well as devoting itself to the struggle for the geniun internal freedom of the press. In the early days of printing Gutenberg's new invention rapidly conquered the world. The most imaginative offspring of his invention was the regular periodical, the newspaper or magazine, .read by millions every day. Millions of people who arc prevented from reading themselves, by reason of their age or their youth or other adverse circumstances, get others to read aloud to them. The newspaper is the link between events all over the world and the individual, and for this reason its task is considerable.

The most essential function of all newspapers however should be the eternal theme-to ensure that the nations of the world live in peace and harmony, to try to educate people in freedom and respect for other people's views, though rejecting totalitarian and ideological one-sidedness; the press should help to build such a world along the path of peace. The newspaper serves the printed world. In the Holy Scriptures of the civilized nations and the great religions, both Christian and non-Christian, in the Bible and in the ancient Veda scriptures of the Indians, the World has become a concept of a divine power which can reach the height of perfection. Christians speak of the World, the logos, which brought the world salvation. Christians and non-Christians understand the power of the Word: "And the World was made flesh..." The true Word is wedded to true reality, not the slogan or the political phrase. Let us repeat once again the Christian Word, the truth librates, and the words from the Upanished, which became the motto of the Republic of India-and there is no finer motto imaginable Satyameva jayate "Truth will conquer".

Journalists and pressmen from every era who have defended the nations right to freedom ought not to forget that every form of freedom begins with the freedom of the Word, the honourable Word uttered without haste or taint of propaganda.

Bibliography

Angharad, N. Valdivia : *A Companion to Media Studies,* Blackwell, New Delhi, 2004.

Bard, F. Eraser : *An Introduction to Journalism,* MacMillan Co., New York, 1958.

Chaturvedi, J.F. : *The Indian Press at Crossroads,* Media Research Foundation, New Delhi, 1992.

Chauhan, S.S. : *Principles and Techniques of Journalism,* Vikas Publishing House, New Delhi, 1982.

Critchfield, Richard : *The Indian Reporter's Guide,* Allied Pacific Pvt. Ltd., Bombay, 1962.

Davison, W. Phillips : *Mass Communication Research : Major Issues and Future Directions,* Praeger, New York, 1974.

Defleur, M. L. and Others : *Fundamentals of Human Communication,* Mayfield, London, 1993.

Emest, C. Hynds : *American Newspaper in* 1980s, Hastings House, New York, 1980.

Gandhi, M.K. : *Young India* (1919-27), Tagore & Co., Madras, 1922.

George, A.L. : *Propaganda Analysis,* Peterson & Company, Illinois, 1959.

Georgia, A Persons : *The Making of Energy and Tele Communication Policy,* Praeager, London, 1995.

Grey, Elizabeth : *The Story of Journalism*, Longmans Young Books, London, 1968.

Hernandez, Ramos, P.F. and Schramm, W. : *Development Communication—History and Theories*, in *International Encyclopedia of Communications*, Oxford University Press, New York, 1989.

Hohenberg, John : *The Professional Journalist*, Holt, Rinehort and Winston, New York, 1969.

Holsti, O.R. : *Content Analysis*, Amerind, New Delhi, 1969.

Johnson, Stanley and Julian Harriss : *The Complete Reporter*, The MacMillan Co., New York, 1942.

Joseph, M. K. : *Textbook of Editing & Reporting*, Dominant Books, New Delhi, 2000.

Kichar, R. S. : *Electronic Media and the Library Services*, Discovery Publishing House, New Delhi, 1999.

Klapper, J.T : *The Effects of Mass Communication*, Free Press, Glencoe, Illinois, 1960.

Knightley, Phillip : *The First Casualty : The War Correspondent as Hero, Propa-gandist and Myth Maker*, Harcourt Brace Joronovich, New York and London, 1975.

Kothari, O.S. : *Report of the Indian Education Commission, 1964-66*, Concept, New Delhi, 1966.

Lent, John A. : *The Asian Newspaper's Reluctant Revolution*, The Iowa State University Press, Ames, Iowa, 1977.

Maclagan, Michael : *Clemency Canning*, MacMillan, London, 1962

McClelland, D.C. : *The Achieving Society*, Princeton, New York, 1961.

McCully, C.H. : *The Media—Instrument of Change*, National College Record, Bombay, 2001.

Melkote, S.R. : *Communication for Development in the third World : Theory and Practice,* Sage, New Delhi, 1991.

Menon, Mridula and Prakash Gandhi : *New Information Order,* Kanishka Publishers, New Delhi, 2001.

Mohan, Jag, M.C. : *Selected Editorials and other Writings of M. Chalapathi Rao,* Young Asia Publications, New Delhi, 1976.

Moven, Kiran : *Studies in Educational Broadcasting,* Deep & Deep Publications, New Delhi, 1996.

Narayana, Andal, : *Communication : Theory and Model,* Himalaya Publishing House, Delhi, 1999.

Natrajan, J. : *History of Indian Journalism,* The Publications Division, Government of India, New Delhi, 1999.

Pachori, Sudhis : *Jan Sanchar Madhyaam : Bhasha,* Rohit Publishers, Meerut, 1990.

Paletz, D.L. and Entman, R. : *Media, Power and Politics,* Free Press, New York, 1981.

Parthasarathy, R. : *History of Journalism in India,* Sterling, New Delhi, 1991.

———— : *Journalism in India from the Earliest Times to the Present Day,* Sterling, New Delhi, 1999.

Righter, R. : *Whose News? Politics, Press and the Third World,* Times Books, New York, 1979.

Shartle, Carrol, L. : *Occupational Information,* Prentice Hall, New York, 1961.

Shaw, David : *Journalism Today,* Harper's College Press, New York and London, 1977.

Smith, Anthony : *The Newspaper—An International History,* Thames and Hudson, London, 1979.

Srivastava, K. M. : *News Reporting and Editing,* Sterling, New Delhi, 1997.

Tahmankar, D.V. : *Lokmanya Tilak,* John Murray, London, 1956.

Verma, Adarsh Kumar : *Management Mantaras of Journalism,* Kanishka Publishers, New Delhi, 2001.

Waldrop, A. Gayle : *Editor and Editorial Writer,* Rinehart & Co., New York, 1955.

Zachariah, Aruna : *Media Power : People, Politics and Public Interest,* Kanishka Publishers, New Delhi. 2001.

Index

A

Administration, 68, 170, 241, 242, 247, 291.
Apathy of the Teachers, 213.
Archival Information, 130.
Art of Making Headline, 17.

B

Brief History of the use of Audio-visual Aids, 203.
Broadcast Programmes Benefit Schools, 65.
Broadcasting, 12, 67, 68, 69, 199.

C

Class Control and Discipline, 52.
Closed Circuit Television, 73.
Command, Planning and Organisation, 51.
Communication, 51, 61, 63, 64, 67, 77, 84, 85, 86, 88, 89, 90, 91, 92, 93, 94, 95, 96, 97, 98, 99, 100, 101, 102, 103, 105, 106, 145, 183, 186, 188, 198, 200, 201, 203, 216, 222, 229, 230, 247, 255, 256, 257, 258, 259, 261, 262, 264, 265, 266, 267, 268, 269, 270.
Communication Satellites, 199.
Components in the Learning Process, 57.
Components of the Teaching Process, 57.
Concise Dictionary of Education, 107.
Constitution, 8, 93, 168, 169, 170, 190, 248.
Contrived Experience, 216.

D

Developing of Social, Moral and Spiritual Values, 249.
Development of Higher Faculties, 209.

Development of Models, 89.
Development of Study Habits, 79.
Distribution Maps, 227.
Dramatic Lighting, 230.
Dramatic Participation, 217.
Dramatic Sound Effects, 230.
Dramatic Utilization, 230.

E

Editing Symbols, 26.
Editor, 3, 5, 6, 7, 8, 9, 11, 12, 13, 14, 16, 19, 20, 21, 22, 23, 24, 25, 26, 27, 40, 41, 43, 125, 126, 127, 128, 129, 131, 134, 135, 136, 137, 138, 139, 140, 141, 142, 143, 146, 148, 149, 150, 151, 153, 154, 155, 156, 157, 282, 290.
Education, 5, 54, 61, 63, 64, 65, 66, 68, 69, 70, 82, 87, 105, 106, 107, 109, 110, 111, 113, 117, 165, 179, 188, 195, 203, 204, 205, 209, 228, 235, 239, 240, 243, 245, 246, 248, 250, 251, 252, 253, 254, 262, 273.
Education Commission, 228, 239, 240, 241, 243, 249, 252, 253.
Educational and Cultural, 66.
Educational Authorities, 243.
Educational Bodies, 240.
Educational Centres, 229.
Educational Change, 62.
Educational Circles, 210.
Educational Conferences, 239.
Educational Endeavour, 58.
Educational Experiences, 61.
Educational Films, 80, 213, 234.
Educational Innovation, 181.
Educational Institute, 51.
Educational Institutions, 62, 183, 237, 246.
Educational Institutions, 241, 242.
Educational Instrument, 66.
Educational Level, 43.
Educational Materials, 162.
Educational Objectives, 53, 63.
Educational officers of the Central and State Gove, 242.
Educational Organisations, 239.
Educational Pattern, 239.
Educational Planners, 241.
Educational Planning, 241.
Educational Point, 228.
Educational Policy, 243.
Educational Problems, 251.
Educational Process, 53, 62.
Educational Programmes, 63, 245.

Educational Purposes, 236.
Educational Research and Technology, 182.
Educational Revolution, 206.
Educational Standards, 43, 251.
Educational System, 58, 217, 243.
Educational Technology, 62, 64, 181, 203.
Educational Television, 69.
Educational Topics, 234.
Educational Value, 211.
Effective use of Space, 230.
Electronic Media, 87.
Encouragement to Healthy Classroom Interaction, 208.
ETV in the World, 69.

F

Federal Communications, 12.
Film Society for Children, 81.
Fundamental Rights, 190.

G

Gandhi, 98, 99, 116, 117, 205.
General Principles, 111, 117.
Geographical Maps, 227.
Group Communication, 85.

H

Helpful in Attracting Attention, 207.
Helpful in Fixing up New Learning, 208.
Historical Maps, 227.
History of School Broadcasting, 68.
Human Interest, 4.

I

Illustration of all the Learning Situations, 79.
Improper Selection of Films, 214.
Increased Reading Interests of the Students, 78.
India, 3, 30, 36, 42, 65, 81, 88, 89, 93, 95, 97, 99, 103, 104, 106, 123, 168, 169, 170, 171, 181, 189, 200, 233, 253.
Indian Communication Systems, 97.
Indian Conditions, 181.
Indian Education Service, 242.
Indian Festival, 81.
Indian Independence Act, 170.
Indian Languages, 104, 179, 213, 248, 254.
Indian Media, 93, 98.
Indian National Satellite System, 200.
Indian People, 250.
Indian Prime Minister, 96, 97.

Indian Programme in Educational Planning, 241.
Indian Scene, 106.
Indian Schools, 182.
Indian Society, 241.
Indifference of Students, 213.
Ineffectiveness of the Aids, 213.
Instant Alterations, 43.
Integration and Cultural Promotion, 85.
Interactive Cable Distribution Systems, 199.
Interpersonal Communication, 85.

J

Journalism, 12, 43, 183, 186, 187, 188, 195, 271, 282, 283, 284.
Journalist, 185, 281, 282.

K

Kinds of Educational TV, 73.
Knowhow of Techniques, 30.

L

Lack of Facilities for Training, 213.
Learning Experiences, 55.

M

Media, 62, 63, 64, 65, 68, 70, 85, 86, 87, 88, 93, 94, 95, 96, 97, 98, 99, 100, 101, 102, 103, 104, 105, 106, 183, 184, 185, 187, 188, 195, 198, 203, 205, 215, 226, 229, 259.
Methodology, 10.

N

National Policy on Education, 64.
Nehru, 97, 99, 101, 253.
Newspapers, 1, 3, 5, 6, 8, 10, 13, 28, 30, 36, 37, 38, 40, 41, 44, 45, 46, 48, 64, 82, 87, 88, 105, 125, 184, 185, 186, 187, 188, 190, 191, 192, 193, 195, 200, 270, 276, 277, 278, 280, 281, 284, 285, 287, 288, 290, 291, 292.

O

Objectives of Social and National Integration, 246.
Open Circuit Television, 73.
Opportunities To Handle and Manipulate, 207.

P

Part Played by Teacher, 74.
Planning and Preparation of TV Programmes, 75.

Political Activities of the Community, 193.
Political and Cultural Imperialism, 93.
Political and Economic Affairs, 276.
Political and Economic Life, 267.
Political and Moral Instruction, 279.
Political and Scientific Advancement of a Country, 71.
Political Bias, 292.
Political Centres, 277.
Political Connections, 284.
Political Development of the Country, 89.
Political Event, 274.
Political Evolution, 104.
Political History, 270.
Political Journals, 275.
Political Line, 291.
Political or Religious Faiths, 268.
Political Organs, 286.
Political Parties, 290.
Political Phrase, 292.
Political Politics, 286.
Political Press, 277, 284.
Political Revolution, 263.
Political Section, 288.
Political Section of the Population, 287.
Political Sense, 284.
Political Significance, 274, 282.
Political Sphere, 287.
Political Study, 280.
Political System, 93.
Political Tendencies, 287.
Political Terminology, 289.
Political Viewpoint, 97.
Positive Environment for Creative Discipline, 209.
Preparation of Physical Control, 212.
Principle of Active Responding, 165, 166.
Principle of Association, 115.
Principle of Correlation, 116, 117.
Principle of Creativity, 116.
Principle of Effective Strategies, 118.
Principle of Exercise or Repetition, 115.
Principle of Goal Setting, 114.
Principle of Group Dynamics, 116.
Principle of Individual Differences, 114.
Principle of Linking with Life, 117.
Principle of Motivation, 112.
Principle of Playway, 112.
Principle of Proper Presentation, 212.
Principle of Readiness, 115.
Principle of Remedial Teaching, 118.
Principle of Selection, 211.
Principle of Self Education, 113.

Principle of Self-pacing, 166.
Principle of Small Steps, 165.
Principle of Stimulation, 115.
Proceed from Easy to Difficult, 120.
Proceed from Empirical to Relational, 121.
Proceed from Indefinite to Definite, 121.
Proceed from Particular to General, 121.
Proceed from Simple to Complex, 120.
Proceed from Whole to Parts, 122.
Promotion of Scientific Temper, 209.
Psychology of Learners, 52.
Punctuation Marks, 24.

Q

Questions to Solve, 13.
Quickness of Movement, 78.

R

Rapid Publication, 127.
Real Learning Situations, 78.

S

Selected Learning Situation, 78.
Significance of Educational Television, 70.
Specific Classroom Objectives, 54.
Spread of Education on a Mass Scale, 208.
Supporting Items, 24.

T

Teacher in the Evaluation of TV Programme, 76.
Teacher in the Presentation of TV Programme, 75.
Teacher in the Production of Tv Programme, 75.
Teaching Instruction, 178.
Teaching Objectives, 54.
Timebound Programme, 152.
Traditional Aspects, 133.

U

Using Record Player, 233.
Utilisation of TV Programme and the Teacher, 75.

V

Video Cassettes' Use, 235.
Video Tapes Played Through TV, 234.
Vocationalising of Higher Secondary Education, 240.

□□□